La Catastrophe

La Catastrophe

The Eruption of Mount Pelee, the Worst Volcanic Eruption of the Twentieth Century

Alwyn Scarth

OXFORD
UNIVERSITY PRESS
2002

OXFORD
UNIVERSITY PRESS

Oxford   New York
Auckland   Bangkok   Buenos Aires
Cape Town   Chennai   Dar es Salaam   Delhi   Hong Kong   Istanbul
Karachi   Kolkata   Kuala Lumpur   Madrid   Melbourne   Mexico City   Mumbai
Nairobi   São Paulo   Shanghai   Singapore   Taipei   Tokyo   Toronto

and an associated company in

Berlin

First published by Terra Publishing, 2002
PO Box 315, Harpenden, Hertfordshire, AL5 2ZD, England
www.terrapublishing.net

Published in the United States of America by Oxford University Press, 2002
198 Madison Avenue, New York, NY 10016
www.oup.com

Oxford is a registered trademark of Oxford University Press

Library of Congress Cataloging-in-Publication Data is available:
0-19-521839-6

9 8 7 6 5 4 3 2 1
Printed in the United Kingdom

Contents

CONTENTS

Preface

I would have stayed in Saint-Pierre on the morning of 8 May 1902 to enjoy the Ascension Day holiday. I would have kept cool and accepted the arguments of the experts. Mount Pelée could bring us no greater harm than a shower of dust and ash. How could I have imagined what even the best scientists in the world could not conceive? Then, at exactly 8.02 a.m., I would meet a sudden and horrible death. And no-one would ever identify my body.

The greatest volcanic catastrophe of the twentieth century was a true tragedy. Fate toyed with the citizens of Saint-Pierre for two weeks. The volcano roared on the horizon; ash rained down on its flanks; the ground shook; submarine cables were cut; waves swept onto the shore; and a huge flood raced down the mountain – nature had gone mad. Who could guess what else might threaten the city? Cool rational analysis was needed. But the victims could not recognize the logic of the eruption, and it was a tragic irony that those who panicked saved their lives.

A century after the destruction of Saint-Pierre, the eruption of Mount Pelée remains one of the most fascinating ever recorded because its interwoven human and environmental themes have retained all their vitality. But this is not just a story of a combat between human beings and the forces of nature. The volcanic crisis heightened over 50 years of economic, social, political, racial and even religious tensions. When Mount Pelée annihilated the city and its people, the survivors consoled themselves with strange notions about the disaster, and constructed nostalgic and mythical illusions about what life had been like in old Saint-Pierre. And innuendoes, misconceptions, half-truths and outright lies have plagued accounts of the catastrophe ever since. Perhaps this book will set the record straight at last.

Alwyn Scarth, Paris, February 2002

Acknowledgements

The author and publishers would like to thank the following for granting permission to make use of material in this book.

The Laboratoire de Minéralogie du Muséum National d'Histoire Naturelle in Paris for permission to reproduce on the following pages 15 photographs from the archives of Professor Alfred Lacroix, and especially to Claire Letort for her help in investigating and reproducing these archives: 15, 25, 34, 76, 86, 107, 121, 122, 125, 128, 167, 170, 181, 204, 205, 206.

Lloyd's Register of Shipping, 71 Fenchurch Street, London EC3M 4BS, England: for the material incorporated on p. 138.

The Service Historique de la Marine, Château de Vincennes, France, for permission to reproduce material on the following pages: 77, 79, 152, 154, 172, 199.

All the translations from French are my own; those from Danish are the work of Shirley Larsen.

For assistance in locating images from the works of Angelo Heilprin, thanks are due to Christopher Kilburn of University College London.

These acknowledgements would be woefully inadequate without a special expression of my gratitude for the help of three friends whom I have known ever since student days in France: Shirley and Knud Larsen, of Åarhus, who researched Danish documents about the catastrophe and translated them into English; and Jean-Louis Renaud, of Paris, who undertook the even more daunting task of reading the text and indicated many invaluable improvements. Any errors are, alas, my own.

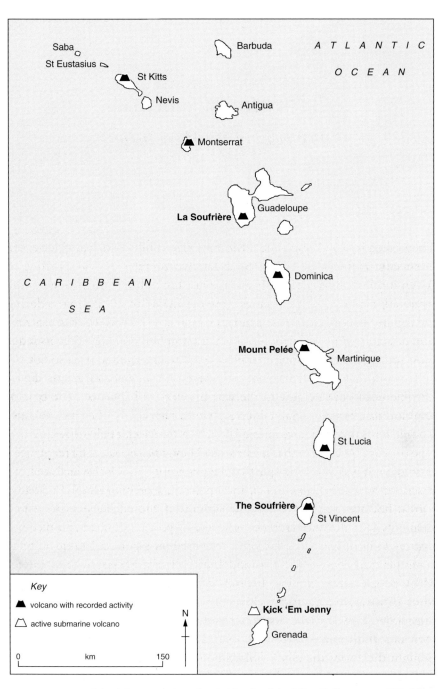

Saba
St Eustasius

ATLANTIC

Barbuda

OCEAN

St Kitts

Nevis

Antigua

Montserrat

La Soufrière Guadeloupe

C A R I B B E A N

S E A

Dominica

Mount Pelée Martinique

St Lucia

The Soufrière St Vincent

Key

▲ volcano with recorded activity

△ active submarine volcano

N

0   km   150

Kick 'Em Jenny

Grenada

Martinique and the volcanic islands of the West Indies.

1

Introduction
"The pearl of the West Indies"

They called it "La Catastrophe". Mount Pelée annihilated Saint-Pierre, the finest city in the West Indies, in about two minutes on the morning of Ascension Day, 8 May 1902. It was the greatest volcanic catastrophe of the twentieth century. So many cities were devastated in so many wars during the century that it is hard to imagine the huge impact that the total destruction of a city and its population really had a hundred years ago. But even our most sophisticated weapons of war have rarely managed to do it so fast.

This is a tragic story. It is not only because thousands of people died a horrible death, but because of the way in which it happened. The type of eruption that destroyed Saint-Pierre played a vital role in the city's tragedy. The citizens could not have guessed their fate, for Mount Pelée threw a lethal type of eruption at them that scientists had never previously fully recognized or studied. It was in Martinique that the phenomenon was first analyzed and described as a nuée ardente – an incandescent, scorching cloud. Suddenly, a great hot blast seemed to tear the summit of Mount Pelée apart. A few moments later, the nuée ardente – gas, steam, glowing dust, ash, pumice and shattered bits of volcano – cascaded down the mountain at 500 km an hour at temperatures between 200°C and 450°C. It shot straight to Saint-Pierre. Many people saw it coming. It reached the city at 8.02 a.m. At 8.05 a.m., Saint-Pierre lay in ruins and its citizens had been despatched to oblivion. This nuée ardente became the first to win international fame and it achieved its own notorious immortality with over 28,000 deaths. Most of those who thought they were the elite of Martinique society died a horrible death.

This is a tragic story, too, because the helpless citizens of Saint-Pierre were caught in a sequence of events they could not understand and could certainly not control. They died also because they tried to behave rationally, and not

1

because they were foolhardy, incompetent, negligent or stupid. Ironically, those who were not brave, who panicked and fled for no logical reason, saved their lives. The aggressor acted with majestic impartiality. Atheists and communicants, mistresses and maids, teachers and tradesmen, intellectuals and ignorant, priests and prostitutes, and black, white and coloured – all perished in a few minutes of agony so awful that death must have come as a merciful relief. Most of their bodies were lost forever. Few of the corpses recovered could be recognized before the soldiers put them on funeral pyres in the rubble that had been their city.

★ ★ ★

When the first French settlers landed on Martinique in the summer of 1635, they found a beautiful island, the very image of a tropical paradise. The rolling hills of the south of the island gave way in the centre to the steep Pitons du Carbet and the bulky mass of Morne Jacob, and went on to reach the northern peninsula where Mount Pelée formed the aesthetic climax to the whole island. Every slope of its 1080 km² was clad in the luxuriant vegetation that makes the tropics seem so rich. Every slope, that is, save those at the crest of Mount Pelée – the "bald", or "peeled" mountain, which was an exception waiting to explain itself.

The settlers chose a shimmering sheltered bay of cobalt blue some 7 km due south of the mountain. Captain Pierre de Bélain d'Esnambuc and about a hundred of his men first built a small fort at the mouth of the Rivière Roxelane in July 1635 and established Saint-Pierre. The settlers quickly proved their colonial credentials by exterminating the indigenous Carib population. Unfortunately for the settlers' descendants, they never asked the poor Caribs about the mountain that graced the northern horizon of Saint-Pierre.

Saint-Pierre flourished along the idyllic bay. Hills hugged the southern parts of the city in a protective embrace, but farther north they stood back and opened out in wider vistas with splendid views of the slopes that led up to the crest of the mountain forming the majestic backcloth to Saint-Pierre.

And Saint-Pierre formed the backcloth to the bay, where the vessels of the world anchored at large mooring buoys. There was no harbour. The hills sheltered the placid waters of the bay from the trade winds that blew so persistently from the east, year in year out, and they even gave it some protection from the occasional hurricanes that are the bane of the West Indies.

Other settlements soon followed. Le Prêcheur, on the western flanks of Mount Pelée, was one of the first. From 1645 to 1647, it had the honour of being the home of young Françoise d'Aubigné, who later became Marquise

Martinique.

de Maintenon, the secret second wife of Louis XIV. Over 250 years later, this village was also the home of Louis-Auguste Sylbaris, who was the most famous circus exhibit ever to leave the island. Fort Royal was founded a little after Le Prêcheur on a wide bay with a safe anchorage that fostered French naval activity in the West Indies. It became the capital of the colony in 1692 and eventually adopted the more suitably republican name of Fort-de-France. Across the bay in 1763 Marie-Josèphe-Rose Tascher de la Pagerie was born, who became Napoléon's Empress Joséphine.

The Bay of Saint-Pierre, with Mount Pelée forming the northern horizon.

Martinique had a healthier and more pleasant climate than most French Colonies. The almost constant warmth and sunshine more than compensated for the frequent tropical downpours. The volcanic soil was fertile. Plants and crops grew quickly and flourished. Huge mangoes and breadfruit trees vied with coconut palms, and, between them, grew cocoa and coffee bushes and fields of tobacco, while spectacular hibiscus, and bougainvillea added their startling colours to the settlements.

During the eighteenth century, sugar cane became the staple crop of the island, and Martinique became one of the world's major sources of sugar and its by-product, rum. Together, they made the fortune of Martinique for over a hundred years. Vast numbers of West African slaves were imported to do the backbreaking work on the plantations that the sugar-cane harvesting demanded. They soon outnumbered the white planters, who led privileged lives on their estates when they were not gathered in their townhouses in Saint-Pierre. Many of the white rulers were very wealthy, but most of the ruled lived in abject poverty, barely educated, illiterate, powerless, and black. Less than a quarter of their children ever went to school for any length of time. Martinique looked opulent, but, as in many tropical islands, such opulence was precarious and fragile. The stresses latent in such a situation eventually burst out into the open during the nineteenth century.

Like many colonial people, the white ruling class spent much time maintaining the traditions of the nation and the church. As the nineteenth century progressed, they felt more and more that political changes, new pernicious notions of democracy, and an economic crisis, had all conspired against them. The black slaves were finally freed in Martinique in 1848, but, for the white population, they still represented an underclass that did not belong to society as they understood it. The blacks were still fodder for the sugar-cane plantations and often for the master's desires, living in shacks and paid shamefully low wages. And, slaves or not, they were still expected to give way to any whites as they walked on the pavements of Saint-Pierre. Colour was all important because it was a short-hand representation of any individual's place in society. Theirs was an unquestionable and unquestioning racist world.

No sooner had the slaves been emancipated than the Third French Republic gave men the vote in 1871. It was a sign of the times, too, that the first non-military governor of the colony was appointed in 1881. The Third Republic was anathema to the colonial whites. They were strongly Catholic; the republic was verging on atheist. The colonial whites were in favour of white supremacy; the republic supported emerging ideas of racial and social

Sturdy stone-built houses bordering the clear waters of the Rivière Roxelane in the northern part of Saint-Pierre. Compare this attractive view with that of the same place after the eruption, shown on page 170.

equality and education for all. The lower orders now had to be bribed and cajoled, whereas the sight of a whip would formerly have sufficed. Indeed, the whites disdainfully boycotted the elections for almost 25 years and started to take an interest in politics only after an encyclical from Pope Leo XIII in 1892 recognized that republics were as legitimate a form of government as any other.

The education policy of the Third Republic gave the black and coloured population knowledge and technical skills, and, with them, power. Thus, in July 1881, the Lycée was established in Saint-Pierre, where education had previously been in the hands of religious bodies at the College–Seminary. This was another visible sign that power was slipping inexorably from white hands. The pupils from the Lycée became the new middle class who were playing an increasing role in the affairs of the colony. Of course, it did not win them social acceptance in the exclusive white clubs of Saint-Pierre. But, in 1902, when the whites judged that the new governor, Louis Mouttet, was on friendly terms with the radical Senator Knight, it was bound to provoke a hostile reaction from them, which was to extend beyond the grave.

During the last decade of the nineteenth century, radical and even socialist ideas and unrest also took root in the non-white population. The sugar-cane labourers went on strike. Events reached a bloody climax at Le François in February 1900, when ten strikers were shot dead and a further twelve were seriously injured. Political passions were running high as the new century dawned, and political antagonisms were often firmly glued to the old racial antipathy. Corruption and bribery bought votes and power. Duels were fought and actions for libel and defamation were frequent. And it should have come as no surprise after the catastrophe that there were wild allegations about the conduct of the governor or of some survivors. However, all of this turmoil affected a very limited group who were seeking political power, and the press that reported their every indiscretion. The silent majority was both very large and very silent. Over 50 per cent of the voters abstained from every general election. Most of those who abstained were black.

The egalitarian changes were compounded by the economic crisis that darkened the last 25 years of the century. In 1902, Martinique still depended heavily on sugar and rum and had 20 large sugar-processing factories and 113 rum distilleries. There were at least 16 distilleries situated in Saint-Pierre, and one of the most important factories, belonging to Monsieur Guérin, lay within sight of the city at the mouth of the Rivière Blanche. These establishments were run by a handful of interrelated wealthy families.

But prosperity depended on colonial protectionist policies and the variable revenues obtained from sugar and rum, especially in the face of new and intense competition from sugar beet and rival spirits. The revenues from sugar exports fell by a quarter between 1880 and 1900. The price obtained for rum almost halved between 1898 and 1901. Many manufacturers were thus feeling the pinch. Times were hard. Loans had to be negotiated. Appearances had to be kept up. And nowhere more so than in Saint-Pierre, where the factory owners and distillers had their townhouses.

★ ★ ★

The enormity of the catastrophe that befell Saint-Pierre and its citizens probably encouraged the survivors to exaggerate its graces, and to try and relive its enchantments in a surge of unbridled nostalgia. There could be no doubt that, for those with money, position and power, Saint-Pierre was a charming city. The views of the rest of its citizens were not canvassed.

Saint-Pierre was the "pearl of the West Indies" and also the "soul of Martinique". At the census taken in July 1901, the colony had a total population of 203,781. Saint-Pierre, with 26,011 people, was its largest city and by far its most important intellectual, religious, social, industrial and commercial centre. Most of the citizens of Saint-Pierre were of Afro-Caribbean descent, although there was also a small minority of Asian-Indians. A quarter of the population was under 14 years of age, and 47 per cent of the citizens could neither read nor write. But Saint-Pierre was really the home of white supremacy and it was reputed to have the greatest concentration of whites in any city in the West Indies. Estimates of their numbers in 1902 varied from 4,000 to as many as 8,000 – about a quarter of the total population of the city. They were proud of their French origin, and jealous of their caste, which did not prevent the white men from fathering innumerable mulatto children. The white men were proud of their offspring, who both proved their fathers' virility and enhanced their prestige. The fathers fostered the interests of their mulatto children and saw that they made their way in the world. The more able became successful businessmen, and their acumen enabled them to grasp new opportunities and often to form the developing middle class. Thus, economic power was also slipping from the hands of the whites.

Saint-Pierre enjoyed a kind of rivalry with Fort-de-France, 22 km away, where long ago the seat of colonial rule had been transferred to a more central location on the island. A regular boat service, run by the Girard Company, linked Fort-de-France to Saint-Pierre. The trip took about an hour and offered by far the best means of transport on the island. The roads were very bad; even the one that twisted across the hills between Fort-de-France and Saint-Pierre was poorly maintained. Thus, the most comfortable journey between the cities was undoubtedly by sea.

Fort-de-France had a population of 22,164 in 1901. Its excellent harbour made it an ideal naval base, although in most respects it remained an ordinary, rather unattractive, small town that could bear little comparison with Saint-Pierre. Indeed, to many people in Martinique, Fort-de-France seemed a dangerous place to live. An earthquake had wrecked half the city in 1839, fire had destroyed much of it once again in 1890, and it had suffered badly from a hurricane the very next year. Moreover, Fort-de-France was built on low-lying, marshy ground that made it easy prey to any passing tidal wave, such as that which had drowned thousands at Galveston, Texas, in 1900. Saint-Pierre had none of these defects and suffered from none of these dangers. There was no doubt about it. Saint-Pierre was the place to live in Martinique.

In French, "pierre" means both "stone" and "Peter", and Saint-Pierre was a city built of stone on solid rock, rock believed worthy of Saint Peter, the rock of the church. It was a 250-year-old monument to French colonial power, religion, and civilization. The plan of the city, and many of the buildings dated from the later part of the seventeenth century, which had bestowed a certain elegance upon many of its façades. It reminded American visitors, in particular, of the French Quarter in New Orleans. The city was paved with volcanic rocks. The walls of the two- and three-storey buildings were 1 m thick, but they were not so solid as they looked, for they were made of volcanic rubble and ash, which made them weaker than if they had been built in dressed rectangular stone. But they had been faced with cement and painted a cheerful pale yellow, contrasting attractively with the red of the rooftops, which sparkled after the rain. The windows had wooden blinds rather than glass, so that the cool morning air could circulate; and thick shutters to keep out the heat of the afternoon. The townhouses of the rich planters, distillers and shippers had more opulent interiors than their façades would suggest, and other large houses graced the airy northern suburbs of Fonds-Coré and Trois Ponts. A horse-drawn tram plied to and fro between the city centre and Fonds-Coré. Saint-Pierre had swift mosquito-free streams and pure piped water, public fountains, telephones, and tree-lined squares. Its imposing public buildings included a theatre, first built in 1786, which was a smaller-scale copy of that in Bordeaux, a fine cathedral, a military hospital, and the impressive Intendance, which had been the seat of government. The hub of Saint-Pierre was the Mouillage, or "landing" district, where the passengers embarked and the cargoes were loaded and unloaded. This was the poorest, hottest and most densely populated area of the city, where the hills crowded over it almost to the shore. The Mouillage opened out northwards towards the Place Bertin, the main square, which was decorated with a fine lighthouse and a gushing fountain. Here, hundreds of casks of rum, mixed with the odour of sugar and garlic, gave the Place Bertin an unforgettable aroma. Just inland, the Rue Victor-Hugo and the Rue de Longchamp, the two main streets of the city, had high pavements to protect pedestrians from the rainwaters that surged along after every storm. They ran almost north–south, parallel to each other and to the shore,

Casks of rum stored along the southern shore of Saint-Pierre, with a row of typical trading ships moored in the anchorage, and smaller craft often used to transport goods and passengers to and from them.

and each offered glimpses of the undulating crest of Mount Pelée, some 7 km away on the northern horizon.

It was often claimed that Saint-Pierre was the "Paris of the West Indies", but this seems to have been at least poetic licence and pure nostalgia, if not simple exaggeration. Country walks and the occasional musical soirée were the main entertainments. Apart from those, "life in Saint-Pierre was either all monotony or all toil" as one citizen remarked. A famous carnival, which reached its climax on *Mardi Gras* (Shrove Tuesday), provided no compensation for a general lack of public social life in the evenings. Even the theatre had been forced to close its doors for artistic performances in May 1901, and the botanical gardens, founded in 1803, had been allowed to run wild.

On Sundays and feast days, people dressed up to take communion at the first mass and then visited their friends, or went out for a trip into the country, sometimes exploring as far as the crest of Mount Pelée. But no photograph of Saint-Pierre, and no account of life within the city, could justify valid comparisons with the *fin de siècle* glamour of Paris during the *Belle Epoque*. Saint-Pierre looked – and seems to have behaved – like a small town in the provinces of France.

For decades after the catastrophe, it was commonly believed that God must have punished the citizens for their misdemeanours. Before the year was out, a children's book was produced that used the fate of Saint-Pierre to illustrate the wages of sin. Sodom and Gomorrah were predictably invoked, although no hint, let alone hard evidence, of orgies was ever presented. Perhaps it was in a deliberate reaction to such accusations that so many letters were published afterwards, written by victims who had bravely stood their ground and done their duty right up to the fatal hour.

Mount Pelée erupted during a general election for the parliament of metropolitan France. The passions it aroused caused all sorts of calumnies to be propagated about the role of the governor in particular, whom many claimed had prevented the evacuation of Saint-Pierre so that the elections would take place "as normal" on the dates prescribed. Thus, many surviving whites (and foreigners influenced by them) held him responsible for thousands of deaths. The social stresses and strains brought about by the decades of class conflict also explain why some people refused to help in the emergency after the eruption. These same social antipathies also explain why the white people were so mortified when so many of their number perished in what seemed a random and unjust natural cataclysm.

There was no radio, newsreels, cine-cameras, or television to record and distribute the dramatic images of the catastrophe and the events that led up to it. The word was all, and of course it was not enough. The eruption provoked anguish, not poetic transports. The eye-witness accounts of the eruption are hardly outstanding works of literature, but even a great stylist might well have been bamboozled by the volcanic pyrotechnics displayed during the two weeks of the crisis. Moreover, many accounts were written as letters to friends and relatives as the events unfolded, and were never intended for publication at all. Five accounts are the most complete and reliable: one by a young planter's wife, Emilie Dujon; a second by her sister-in-law, Elodie Jourdain, who was only 11 years old at the time; a third by Abbé Parel, the Vicar General of Martinique; a fourth by Emile Berté, doctor on a local cable-repair ship; and the fifth, and perhaps the most impartial, by Pierre Le Bris, the commander of the French cruiser, *Suchet*, in his report to the French Navy Ministry. Apart from occasional asides, no accounts seem to have come to light of the views and experiences of the poor, and mainly illiterate, black population, whose terror must have been multiplied because they were largely ignored. As in all similarly turbulent events, some accounts are too flawed to be of any value, but they have unfortunately made their unhappy contributions to the myths and lies that have stuck so tenaciously to the tragedy and its sequels.

The best volcanological and human study of the eruption is a masterpiece. *La montagne Pelée et ses éruptions*, by the great French geologist, Alfred Lacroix, has become one of the great classics of volcanology. More recently, Simone Chrétien and Robert Brousse have analyzed the build-up to the catastrophe in *La montagne Pelée se réveille*, and Léo Ursulet has described the aftermath of the eruption in *Le désastre de 1902 à la Martinique*.

Mount Pelée rose on the northern horizon of the Bay of Saint-Pierre, some 7 km from the city. It looked benign: a pale green pyramid with a rather ill defined hummocky summit that reached about 1351 m above sea level at the Morne Lacroix. At the crest nestled a deep, circular and almost inaccessible hollow, known as the Etang Sec ("dry tarn") because it so rarely contained water. The heavy rains that fell on the summit must always have drained away underground by a network of fissures. It was an old crater, with a steep surrounding rim. However, in the south, the headwaters of the Rivière Blanche had formed a distinct notch or cleft in its outline where they had almost eroded this rim away. This notch was clearly visible from Saint-Pierre. A pessimist might have compared it to a gun barrel that would shoot any large eruptive blast straight towards the city.

2

Prelude

Mount Pelée had signalled several warnings of its bad behaviour since the French had first settled in Martinique in 1635. It had erupted twice. Not very violently. Not for very long. There had been a very small eruption in 1792, which had been almost totally forgotten. And there had been an eruption as recently as 1851. Fifty years later, vague and inaccurate recollections of this episode lingered on in the minds of the older inhabitants of the island. Both volcanic events had been the subject of official reports, but they had vanished long ago into obscure administrative cupboards. These puny eruptions did very little damage and, even then, only near the top of the mountain. As warnings, they were decidedly misleading. They gave the impression that Mount Pelée was a benign old volcano, nearing the end of its life. They induced a false sense of security in the minds of the people of Martinique, who therefore drew entirely wrong conclusions about Mount Pelée's character. Mount Pelée had, in fact, been masking its hand. This was a major factor in the tragedy of 1902.

The early French settlers would have been well advised to ask themselves why the local Caribs had called Mount Pelée the Fire Mountain. But, of course, these indigenous peoples had been exterminated long before they could pass on any volcanological insights to the colonists. Nevertheless, the implication of such a name should have been only too clear. The Caribs were not exaggerating. This was a dangerous volcano.

It seems that the Caribs themselves must have witnessed at least two eruptions before the French settlers claimed their land and then their lives. Around AD 1300, Mount Pelée had exploded much more violently than in 1902. This eruption probably formed the large crater on the summit of the mountain called the Etang Sec, the "dry tarn" that was to play a leading role in the events in 1902. The AD 1300 eruption gave off many nuées ardentes, scorching hot clouds of ash and fumes, as well as towering columns of ash, fumes and pumice into the stratosphere, which devastated a much larger area than in 1902. The ash destroyed and buried Carib villages throughout northern Martinique, including a coastal settlement at Anse Belleville, due west of Mount Pelée. But, at that time, of course, there was no Saint-Pierre to be annihilated. Nor was any survivor able to record this event for posterity; and it is impossible to say how much of this disaster had been stored in the folk memories of the Carib people. But the story of these events contained a lesson waiting to be discovered.

A rather less powerful eruption took place around AD 1600. It devastated the vegetation on the crest of the volcano and gave Mount Pelée its name. The early settlers did not link the baldness of Mount Pelée to what the Caribs called "the Fire Mountain" and they therefore failed to attribute this apparently strange and inappropriate Carib name to a recent volcanic eruption. The settlers could, perhaps, be forgiven. For many decades after the settlement, the thick, impenetrable woods on Pelée's lower slopes discouraged all but the most intrepid of visitors to the crest; and the mountain became more accessible only after its lower slopes had been cleared for sugar plantations. Moreover, knowledge of volcanic activity at that time was very scanty, and

The history of Mount Pelée

At the beginning of the twentieth century, most people in Martinique believed that Mount Pelée was an extinct volcano, if they thought about it at all. No-one knew then about the violent spasms of its volcanic past, and the very few expert volcanologists of the day had no scientific means of predicting – or even guessing – what exactly might happen if ever it erupted again. It was only when volcanic research became much more sophisticated during the twentieth century that the great eruption in 1902 was seen to be part of a series of violent outbursts. The specialists have counted some 25 important eruptions of Mount Pelée during the past 14 000 years. They came in short spasms of great violence. For the rest of the time, Mount Pelée had stayed completely calm, totally masking its violent nature from any potential spectators. But throughout this period, Pelée had not given off a single lava flow. It had produced far more dangerous weapons. Many eruptions had expelled towering columns of ash and fumes, like vast nuclear explosions, that had rained thick ash all over northern Martinique. Other eruptions had unleashed huge blasts that had sent scorching clouds of ash hurtling down the mountainside at hurricane speed. These clouds were the deadly nuées ardentes that were soon to make Mount Pelée world famous.

And, most of these eruptions had been much more vigorous than that in 1902. Thus, in fact, the catastrophe of 1902 could have been even greater than it was.

MORNE ABEL

cathedral towers

Centre

Mouillage

Fort

Fonds-Coré

course of the Rivière Blanche

Saint-Pierre and Mount Pelée around 1900, showing the Fort, Centre and Mouillage districts, the protective arm of Morne Abel, and the course of the Rivière Blanche, notably incised into the upper reaches of the volcano.

the authors of classical antiquity, such as Strabo and Pliny the Elder, were still the main sources of enlightenment on the subject. Little happened on Mount Pelée to disturb this blissful ignorance until 1792.

There are, however, at least two indications that some volcanic hot springs (now called hydrothermal activity) were operating on Mount Pelée during the eighteenth century. In 1763, Thibault de Chanvallon wrote that "Mount Pelée . . . bears all the characteristics of a former volcano, which is also the feeling of the old inhabitants". He did not elaborate, although his statement was soon substantiated. Jean-Baptiste Leblond climbed to the summit most probably in 1767, and certainly between 1767 and 1773. He described steam and hot springs rising from the deep abyss at the very headwaters of the Rivière Blanche, one of the main streams draining the western slopes of the mountain. (Indeed, the very name of the White River suggests that such hot springs had chemically attacked the rocks around the headwaters. The fine fragments formed would be carried along by the river and give it its characteristic whiteness, especially in comparison with the clear waters of its main tributary, the Rivière Claire.)

The eruption in 1792

When Mount Pelée produced a slightly more powerful eruption in the early months of 1792, its eruptive effort was far too modest to divert the limelight from the momentous events in revolutionary Paris, where the whole established order was being overturned. And memories of a mere eruption had no chance whatsoever of competing with the traumas brought upon the colony when the revolutionary government in Paris first decreed on 2 February 1794 that the slaves should be freed.

Citizen Dupuget left the only surviving published account of this eruption. During a military trip to the West Indies in 1784–6, Dupuget had made the first summary of the geology of the region. He noted that "the *soufrières* of Martinique, Saint Lucia, Dominica and Guadeloupe are merely old volcanoes whose activity has diminished through a lack of nourishment". However, he did not publish his study until February 1796, or as the contemporary usage had it, the month of Ventose of the year IV of the French Republic. By that time, he was able to add to his original observations a note about the eruption of Mount Pelée in 1792.

ANNOTATIONS

Sur la soufrière de la Martinique

La soufrière de la Martinique est située dans la montagne Pelée, dont le pic le plus élévé a été mesuré par le citoyen *Dupuget*, qui a trouvé son élévation de 736 toises. Depuis la découverte de l'Amérique, il n'y avait point eu d'éruption dans cet endroit. On y observe cependant, à la hauteur de 500 toises, différents cratères qui attestent l'action des feux souterrains. L'éruption qui se manifesta le 22 Janvier 1792, fut accompagnée d'une assez violente secousse de tremblement de terre. Bientôt une forte odeur de soufre se répandit jusqu'à l'habitation de la citoyenne *Montaval*, qui, avertie par-là de cet événement, eut le courage de se rendre sur le lieu. La terre était criblée de trous par lesquels l'éruption s'était faite. Les arbres avaient subi l'action du feu, dix-neuf manicous (*Didelphis opossum*) et plusieurs oiseaux, surpris dans le cercle de l'explosion, étaient restés morts sur la place.

The beginning of Citizen Dupuget's additional observations on the soufrière *of Martinique.*

The *soufrière* of Martinique is situated on Mount Pelée, [but] . . . there has been no eruption there at all since the discovery of America. However, different craters offering proof of the action of subterranean fires may be observed at a height of 500 toises [975 m, about 400 m below the summit]. The eruption that occurred on 22 January 1792 was accompanied by a fairly violent earthquake shock. Soon, a strong smell of sulphur spread as far as citizen Montaval's plantation. Thus warned, she was brave enough to go up to the spot. The ground was riddled with holes through which the eruption had occurred . . . 19 manicous (opossums: *Didelphis opossum*) and several birds . . . lay dead there.

Five months later, a few local people returned to the area . . . In fact, two months before [probably in late April], citizen Montaval had heard a noise like a cannon shot from that area, and there is reason to suppose that a new explosion had taken place at that time. The trees, and especially the ferns, were copiously powdered with sulphur, and all the rocks were plastered with it. And the little vents that had given off the sulphur could be seen all around. The smoke exhaling from them betrayed the presence of a subterranean fire. Blackish sulphurous water was discharging from a hole 2" [5 cm] in diameter at the foot of a little waterfall and it was so hot that a hand could scarcely be kept in it.

Five or six hundred paces lower down the same stream, there was another sulphurous lair where three small holes also gave off hot sulphurous waters. The explosion of Mount Pelée seemed to have concentrated its efforts on the western side. . . . These details have been taken from the official report drawn up on the spot by the observers. They deposited a copy in a glass jar placed at a man's height on the right-hand side of the ravine, along with an invitation to other enquiring persons who might come to visit this *soufrière* to add their accounts of subsequent events to the story. This report was communicated to citizen Dupuget by one of their number, citizen Aquart.

Thus, in 1792, there were two separate zones of activity at the head of a westward-flowing stream, which gave off fumes or hot springs for at least five months. No account of these eruptions was given in the official correspondence from the colony for 1792. The citizens of Martinique seem to have quickly forgotten these little explosions. Unfortunately, memory did not serve them well. This minor outburst was much more important than it seemed at the time. It meant that the magma – the molten rock and gases that generate volcanic eruptions – was once again rising from the depths towards the surface beneath Mount Pelée. It might halt at depth for many years, or it could rise even higher and cause a devastating eruption in a few years, a few decades, or a few centuries. In a volcano like Mount Pelée, it was only a matter of time. But when would this time come? It is very hard for experts to answer that vital question today. It was impossible in 1902.

After 1792, the magma hesitated for over half a century. But, during this period, no-one ever recorded any volcanic activity. It is true, of course, that the tropical heat, not to mention copious clothing, discouraged all but the most athletic of enthusiasts from making the climb up to the summit. The magma lurking below ground limited its threats to giving off gases that escaped to the surface through any available fissures in the ground. Those who lived around the western flanks of the mountain knew that there was a hot spring, fumes and deposits of sulphur near the source of the Rivière Claire. Indeed, they called the spot the *soufrière* ("sulphurous place"). But few people took the slightest notice of this scientific curiosity.

Except one. In 1838, the pharmacist, Monsieur P. Peyraud, investigated

The chief types of volcanic eruption

Earth scientists have described volcanic eruptions in many different ways and used many different terms to do so. In a simplified form, eruptions can be grouped under four main headings: mild, moderate, vigorous and violent.

Mild eruptions are often termed hydrothermal. They happen where hot magma lies close to the surface and heats the groundwater to boiling point. The heated water rises to the surface and emerges in hot springs, geysers, and mudpots. When fumes emerge as well, the vents are called fumaroles. If they give off sulphurous fumes, they are called by their Italian name of solfataras. These are *soufrières* in the West Indies. Such features are common when a volcano is dormant, between more active episodes. But they also occur when the magma is rising slowly towards the surface, when they can be the harbingers of more serious eruptions. Such eruptions took place on Mount Pelée in the eighteenth and nineteenth centuries, and again from 1900 until the spring of 1902.

Moderate eruptions occur when very hot magma reaches the land surface, usually in the form of fluid lava. If the magma contains little gas, then lava flows are formed. If the magma contains more gas, the gases explode when the pressures on them are reduced as it nears the surface. The explosions shatter the lava into cinders and ash, which build up volcanic cones above the vent or chimney. Such eruptions are the most common on land throughout the world, but Mount Pelée has not produced a single one for at least 14 000 years.

Vigorous eruptions develop when more gas explodes more powerfully and more noisily. They often happen when rising magma heats groundwater and suddenly converts it to steam within the confined space of rock fissures. The resulting explosions form hydrovolcanic eruptions that shatter some of the old, cool, rocks near the vent and scatter their fragments across the land. They often sound like cannon shots. No fragments of glowing hot new magma are expelled, but these eruptions often indicate that magma is nearing the surface.

Violent eruptions occur when viscous, rather cool and rather pasty, magma containing much gas approaches the surface. The gases explode with enormous power, often exceeding that of nuclear explosions. shattering the magma into fine fragments that are blasted far from the vent. They form huge columns that reach the stratosphere and can sometimes distribute volcanic dust all over the globe. These, the most powerful of all eruptions, are called Plinian, after Pliny the Elder, the chief victim of the first such eruption that was ever described at Vesuvius in AD 79. Violent eruptions can also blast sideways, in which case they are called Peléan eruptions, after Mount Pelée itself. Peléan eruptions are generally less powerful than their Plinian counterparts, but they are often more lethal, because they form great clouds of scorching hot fragments, called nuées ardentes, that travel across the land surface, very close to the ground, at 500 km an hour. During the past 14 000 years, Mount Pelée has unleashed about equal numbers of Plinian and Peléan outbursts. Plinian eruptions took place on Mount Pelée around AD 1300 and again around AD 1600. It produced a Peléan eruption in 1902.

the exhalations at the source of the Rivière Claire, about 900 m above sea level, in a position very similar to those described by citizen Dupuget in 1792. He then despatched a short report of his findings to the Minister of the Interior on 20 May 1838. He enclosed a small bottle of the waters, several crystals of pure sulphur, and a specimen of the "yellow stuff" (sulphur?) coating the slopes around the spring, as well as "a piece of wood covered with moss that exuded a pungent smell of brine". He also sent his silver pencil case that the emissions of hydrogen sulphide had tarnished. His letter ended with the regret that nature had placed this spring in such an inconvenient position, where it could not serve as a thermal spa that could have brought economic benefits to the colony.

The eruption in 1851

The next eruption of Mount Pelée began in 1851. Unlike its predecessor in 1792, it had the stage more or less to itself, except that Martinique was suffering from social and economic turmoil when sugar production and prices fell after the slaves had been emancipated for a second time on 27 April 1848. The eruption proved to be a more powerful and more prolonged version of the events of 1792, but it was still a hydrovolcanic outburst, and no molten rock actually reached the surface. The fragments expelled were cool and they consisted entirely of shattered rocks that had solidified after earlier eruptions.

In the early summer of 1851, the people living on the hills above Le Prêcheur, on the western flanks of Mount Pelée, first noticed strong sulphurous smells wafted down the mountain by the trade winds. During July 1851, the smell became a stench of rotten eggs, which indicated emissions of hydrogen sulphide. Several men climbed up to investigate the *soufrière* at the head of the Rivière Claire. They discovered that weak fumes were issuing from a new vent. They also had a surprise: there was now a large lake in the Etang Sec. How long it had been there, no-one could guess. In human memory, even the usual heavy rains on the summit had never accumulated in the dry tarn. The water must have come either from hot springs or from an eruption of steam. But, notwithstanding its new-found wetness, the Etang Sec seems to have stayed inactive throughout the eruption.

On 3 August 1851, the rural policeman, Monsieur Carbonel, visited the site. He collected a dead partridge and saw many other dead birds scattered around the vent. Thus, although the fumes were feeble, they were clearly noxious. It was lucky they had not drifted far away from the summit.

On the evening of 5 August 1851, the full moon was shining from a calm and cloudless sky. It was nearly 11 p.m. when the eruption disturbed this tranquil scene. Monsieur Le Prieur was on his sugar plantation at Fonds Canonville, which lay near the coast about 5 km northwest of Saint-Pierre and 5 km southwest of the summit of the mountain. He awoke, startled, he thought, by thunder, but the rumbling was going on for rather a long time and getting louder. He got up to investigate.

> The terrified local farmers, feared that they would be buried beneath the ruins of their homes, and so they left them and quickly made their way to [safety in] Saint-Pierre. They formed an eerie procession coming down the hillsides, some lighting their way with torches of resin, and others with candles. They were all rushing to escape from a danger that seemed imminent, although they were quite unable to formulate any proper notion about it in the darkness. The explosions echoing around the mountain spread even greater terror, while the ash was carried afar on the winds and rained down upon them, and completed the discomfiture of these unhappy fugitives.

The whole Le Prieur family, household and farmhands spent an anxious and sleepless night, and they all ended up praying at the foot of the Mission Cross that stood at the gates of the plantation. The refugees who passed close to the plantation declared that "the *soufrière* was boiling". Many among them also claimed that they were fleeing to the safety of Saint-Pierre and intended to go to church to beg for divine mercy.

Daylight brought the news that the citizens of Saint-Pierre had been just as afraid as their country cousins. A sinister muffled noise had rumbled in the distance. To some it was like thunder; to others it sounded like a vessel letting off steam; to yet others it was like the noise of a river in flood. As the noise increased, so did the anxiety of the citizens. They made for the confessionals, and it is said that some even decided to marry and regularize their sexual liaisons in the eyes of the Lord. Daylight also brought an extraordinary sight. Every roof, every street and every leaf on every tree was covered with a thin layer of greyish ash. Saint-Pierre looked just like a European town clothed in the hoar frost of an autumn dawn. The ash had enshrouded the whole area between Mount Pelée, Le Prêcheur, Le Morne-Rouge and Le Carbet. The Rivière Blanche, too, was no longer living up to its name, for its white waters were now black with ash and the branches of trees that had been brought down from its tributary, the Rivière Claire. This black ash was clearly of a rather different origin from the white ash decorating the countryside, and suggests that the eruption probably came from two vents.

On that morning of 6 August, when the country folk came down, as usual, from the flanks of the mountain and set up stalls in the Fort market in Saint-Pierre, they spread the disconcerting news that "the *soufrière* had spoken".

Nevertheless, with their characteristic light-heartedness, many islanders even mocked Mount Pelée, because, after so much effort, it had still only managed to give birth to a few fumes. But, as the report of the eruption later confessed, "more serious apprehensions could be detected in every gaze that was fixed upon the long plume billowing from the summit".

On 9 August, several more powerful explosions took place and the discharge of the Rivière Claire continued to increase. Was it this that prompted the governor to act? The governor, Rear-Admiral Vaillant, was not content to rely on hearsay and qualitative assessments of this bizarre situation. He wanted a methodical study of the events. Thus, he duly did what administrators are supposed to do: he set up a committee. On 21 August 1851, he nominated three eminent persons to form an "exploration commission". Monsieur Le Prieur was the chief pharmacist at the hospital in Fort-de-France, but he had won a certain reputation as a man of science after undertaking several expeditions to French Guyana. Dr E. Rufz de Lavisson was a doctor in Saint-Pierre. He seems also to have been the author of a book on the history and statistics of the population of Martinique. Monsieur P. Peyraud had been a pharmacist in the French navy, but had then retired to practise in Saint-Pierre. Monsieur Peyraud had, of course, investigated the exhalations near the source of the Rivière Claire in 1838, perhaps without fully realizing their volcanic origins. But, however conscientious they were, they would still have been most unlikely to produce a valid volcanological assessment of the situation, because they had no real understanding of the phenomena they were studying. But there were no experts at all on the island. In fact, at that time, there were few volcanological experts available anywhere in the world. Oddly enough, volcanology and spectacular volcanic eruptions had largely failed to grip the imaginations of the more eminent geologists of the day. The most talented volcanologists of the time were Alexander von Humboldt in Germany and George Poulett Scrope in the UK, and both were near the end of their careers. In any case it would have taken weeks for visiting advisors to reach the island, by which time the eruption would probably have ended, for better or worse. Therefore, this committee constituted the best the governor could do in the circumstances. Similar problems were to exercise the mind of another governor half a century later.

No sooner had Governor Vaillant set up his commission than the eruption calmed down. Undismayed by this disappointing turn of events, the members of the commission (and their retinue of servants) set off on 28 August 1851 to confront the source of the emissions with their scientific acumen. All told, they made up a party of about 20 people. They spent the night at Monsieur Ruffin's plantation on the flanks of Mount Pelée at about 550 m above sea level. At 7.00 a.m. next morning, 29 August, they started the arduous climb to the summit, alongside the Rivière Claire, the main tributary of the Rivière Blanche. They saw at once that the Rivière Claire no longer merited its name. The clear water was muddy. It was therefore the tributary that had sullied the waters of the Rivière Blanche down stream.

The investigators scrambled up through the tangle of dwarf palms and creepers until they reached slightly more open country around 850 m. Here, dry volcanic mud coated the ground, and many of the bananas, plantains and arums were scorched. Then, the volcanic mud became thicker and they entered a chaos of broken, twisted and uprooted trees thrown down by a "localised whirlwind, as if they had been blasted by an explosion of cannon powder". As they neared the headwaters of the Rivière Claire, "all the horror of the eruption" lay before them. "The trees, leaves and the flowers were enveloped in a greyish shroud", and several landslides scarred the valley sides. No birds sang, and the silent lugubrious air seemed laden with fumes and hydrogen sulphide. Of course, the scene reminded the more cultured members of the party of Virgil's evocation of the underworld in book VI of the *Aeneid*.

Two vents, about 25–30 m apart, were fuming near the head of the valley. They had probably been active in 1792, because they lay at about 966 m above sea level, similar to the height noted by Dupuget. The eruption had devastated the vegetation over an area almost 900 m in diameter. The party gathered in the depths of the muddy ravine to inspect the emissions more closely. Suddenly, a subterranean bubbling and rumbling came from one vent, and a black sulphurous cloud belched from the other. The stream swelled with hot dark-grey liquid.

A general panic seized the onlookers. Most of the party scrambled frantically out of the ravine. Only three intrepid mud-splattered observers stayed behind to do their scientific duty. When the spasm ended a few minutes later, they expected to find their more timid companions sheltering in the nearby woods. They were disappointed. Their companions had fled down hill to Monsieur Ruffin's plantation. And they had absconded with the barometers and the geological hammers, without which every budding geologist feels naked. Fear also seems to have even infected the intrepid trio at this juncture, because they too decided to make a discrete return to base rather than to proceed with a more valorous trip into the crater of the Etang Sec.

Monsieur Le Prieur climbed to the summit once again on 4 September 1851. An area about 1 km by 2 km had been damaged around the headwaters of the Rivière Claire, but the mud had spread much farther afield. Three vents were still operating that day, although another seven had also been active beforehand. They were arranged in a north–south line running – pointing almost – towards Saint-Pierre, some 10 km away. Monsieur Le Prieur also observed that the summit of the mountain, and presumably the Etang Sec, had not suffered from the recent eruptions at all.

This was not quite the end of the story. In late October and early November 1851, activity revived from time to time and seems to have produced the largest of these modest eruptions. Steam hissed from the same vents, loud explosions echoed over the northern parts of the island, and muddy floods again gushed down the valleys draining the mountain. But the explosions soon waned, and ceased altogether in the early weeks of 1852.

The commissioners returned once more to the summit in early February 1852. The vegetation had been devastated. The trees had been overturned or swept away, and gullies and landslides had dissected the ground in some places, while mud and rocks had piled up in others. A small steaming black lake, 100–200 m across, had replaced the highest pair of vents. Hot little fumaroles were dotted about the upper reaches of the Rivière Claire; some were giving off steam, others were giving off hydrogen sulphide, and sulphur crystals abounded. Fifty years later, when these deposits were analyzed, it was discovered that a small proportion might have come from new subterranean magma. This showed that the magma must have been quite close to the surface in 1851. Thus, if the magma had risen only a little more, it would have caused much greater damage altogether.

The commission published its account of the investigation in the *Journal Officiel* on 24 December 1851, and it was reprinted in the *Annuaire 1900 de la Martinique*. Monsieur Le Prieur also published a fuller, more informal account of his observations in 1854. He warned that "although we had got off with being frightened during the first eruption, things might not be the

The Rue Monte-au-Ciel, in one of the older districts of Saint-Pierre, showing flimsy shutters and windows without glass. This district lay at the foot of the Morne Abel, which protected it to some extent from the full fury of the eruption, as is shown in the photograph on p. 204

same a second time". Nevertheless, the eruption was quickly replaced as a topic of conversation by an epidemic of yellow fever.

The reports and warnings remained a dead letter in obscure publications. And not even all the learned were impressed: the eruption of 1851–2 earned no mention, for instance, in Nicolas's *History of Martinique*, published in 1996. All that local folklore remembered was the pleasant little plume of fumes and steam, which had seemed just the sort of picturesque decoration that Mount Pelée needed to give it a touch of majesty. The citizens of Saint-Pierre should have regarded their mountain with rather more suspicion.

Perceived implications of the eruption in 1851

The eruptions of 1792 and 1851 were quite weak. They had produced a few small explosions, several clouds of nasty-smelling fumes, very little ash, and no lava flows at all. Only a limited, remote and inaccessible area near the summit had been affected. These eruptions impressed many of those who saw them at close quarters. They spoke of "horror" and "devastation". Fear was in the eye of the beholder, and observers were still able to reach to within 5 m of the vents. They did not realize that no self-respecting volcano would have allowed them to approach so closely, even during a moderate eruption. But those who viewed events from a much safer distance saw absolutely nothing that could disturb their dreams.

The eruptions in 1851 did not take place in the main crater of the Etang Sec, but at the headwaters of the Rivière Claire draining the southwestern flanks of Mount Pelée. There had been intermittent hydrothermal emissions high on the western flanks of Mount Pelée since at least 1767. However, the clear waters of the Rivière Claire indicated that emissions were relatively infrequent at its source – otherwise its waters would have been discoloured. In contrast, the white mud that gave the Rivière Blanche its name hints that other thermal springs were also in operation in its headwaters, which were not noticed at this time.

The eruptions were short, sharp and sporadic. And they occurred on a few days over a period lasting for several months only. The activity was largely composed of relatively calm hydrothermal emissions with a few hydro-volcanic explosions. Such eruptions either suggest that activity is going to increase as the magma approaches the land surface; or they suggest that the activity is waning as the magma halts or descends again, and the volcano enters an innocuous dormant phase, or indeed becomes extinct altogether. The same symptoms, therefore, can indicate entirely different states and entirely different threats to the surrounding population. In general, however, an increase in activity would indicate a rising magma and a greater chance of a more menacing eruption.

The eruptions in 1851 never progressed to the more violent stages at which magma is expelled. When the eruptions resumed at the beginning of the new century, many therefore assumed that they would follow the same pattern as in 1851. Their early stages resembled the events of 1851 closely enough to make the citizens of Saint-Pierre believe that they faced no danger whatsoever from Mount Pelée. As one survivor commented, "The eruption of 1851 left an impression of absolute security rather than of fear in people's minds. When the first symptoms of the malaise were felt in 1902, people just assumed that there would be only a curious repetition of the volcanic surge of yesteryear."

As the commissioners reported in 1852, "the city of Saint-Pierre, situated more than 10 km from the summit, and the village of Le Prêcheur, 7 km away from it, seem to have nothing to fear from any eruptions that could even be much larger than those that have just taken place . . . The materials erupted . . . only reached the close vicinity of the vents . . . and, they find a natural outflow to the sea down the ravine eroded by the Rivière Blanche . . . The volcano . . . seems only to be yet another curiosity to add to the natural history of our Martinique".

The available evidence indicated that Saint-Pierre was the obvious place of refuge whenever Mount Pelée might erupt again. Indeed, in 1851, the people living higher up on the mountain had fled to the safety of Saint-Pierre as soon as the eruption had threatened them. The volcano thus seemed to present absolutely no threat to the wellbeing of the people living in the towns and villages around its lower flanks and on its coastal fringes. This unforeseeable error made a major contribution to the tragedy of Saint-Pierre, and the tragedy was compounded when the volcano unleashed a weapon that had never been studied by science.

There was little concept at the time that different volcanoes could behave differently. The eruptions of Mount Pelée were not at all like the famous eruptions of Vesuvius, which was regarded – not always correctly – as setting the standard by which all volcanic activity should be judged. Ever since 1631, Vesuvius had often expelled great clouds of ash and many lava flows. People in Martinique feared that Mount Pelée would do the same.

The dangers perceived in Martinique seemed to lie elsewhere. The eruption in 1851 had caused nothing like the devastation of the great hurricane in 1891 that had claimed 700 lives; nothing like the earthquake that had killed 400 people and badly damaged Fort-de-France on 21 January 1839; and nothing like the great tidal wave that had destroyed Galveston in Texas and drowned 5000 people on 8 September 1900. Hurricanes, earthquakes, tidal waves: these seemed to be the clear dangers that threatened Martinique. How could a spluttering old volcano compete with such obvious threats?

Fumes in the Etang Sec

For almost 40 years after the eruption in 1851–2, no volcanic emissions were recorded from any part of Mount Pelée. Father Vanhaecke, a retired teacher at the College–Seminary in Saint-Pierre climbed up to the summit with his manservant "around 1889", but he couldn't remember exactly. The Etang Sec was dry, but he noticed that a small hole, less than 20 cm across, was giving off sulphurous fumes that had scorched the vegetation about 10 m around it. This seemingly innocuous little hole was more important than it looked, because it marked an ominous change in the site of activity on Mount Pelée. The Etang Sec had taken no visible part in the eruptions since the French settlement in 1635. Now activity had returned to the central crater that is believed to have formed in the great eruption about AD 1300.

Father Vanhaecke went too close to the little vent. For a time, he completely lost his voice. His manservant was dumbfounded to see his master struck dumb. He assumed that his unusually mute master had become bewitched. He fled, terrified that he too would become a victim of sorcery. Of course, once Father Vanhaecke emerged from the fumes, he recovered both his voice and his composure, and resumed control of his manservant. At an undetermined time thereafter, the little vent stopped fuming and soon became choked with the fine fragments washed into it from the floor of the Etang Sec. Neither sulphurous fumes nor sorcery then made any further appearances, on the volcano at any rate, for over a decade. Social unrest generated far more heat in Martinique as the century drew to a turbulent close.

3

The eruption begins
4 June 1900 to 25 April 1902

At the turn of the century, the tropical colonial paradise of Martinique during the *Belle Epoque* had a rather tarnished air. Luckily there was Mount Pelée to provide some diverting relaxation.

Warning fumes

Mount Pelée was a symbol of joy and pleasure. A tradition had developed that many groups of people made happy day trips through the floral extravaganza of begonias and balisiers (American reed) to the summit. Not that many black people joined in these jamborees, unless they happened to be taken as servants or guides. Sometimes the trips were organized by local societies, but at other times ad hoc groups of enthusiasts got together and made the climb. Owning neither motor-cars nor mobile phones, they had to walk and talk together and enjoy each other's company. They had a fabulous social outing. Their efforts were rewarded with magnificent views over two thirds of Martinique and by a picnic in the refreshing breeze beside the Lac des Palmistes. The lake lay just below the summit, the Morne Lacroix, which had been apparently so named because a cross had been placed on its crest by Father J. Mary, a great local character who was the priest at Le Morne-Rouge. Nearby, he had also had a chapel built that was dedicated to Notre Dame de l'Etang. Tradition required that the trippers inscribe their impressions of the scene on its walls. Father Mary had somehow broken his arm at the inauguration, and it was said that he had almost fallen into the abyss of the Etang Sec. A discrete veil was drawn over the reason for this incident.

Many of the trips were organized to celebrate the Whitsun holiday. The

29

brothers Roger and Charles Arnoux, for example, took guides and climbed to the summit on Whit Monday 4 June 1900. (Roger was lucky enough to leave Saint-Pierre on the eve of the great eruption and lived to publish his account of events.) When they reached the summit, they saw that two new sulphurous holes had opened up in the crater of the Etang Sec. The vegetation had been destroyed for 30–40 m around the vents. The trees had been thrown down and burnt, and a yellow deposit, which they assumed to be sulphur, carpeted the ground. They recalled that the vegetation had been flourishing when they had visited the self-same spot in 1899.

The change did not worry Roger Arnoux unduly. After all, moribund volcanoes probably did that sort of thing. Indeed, the Arnoux brothers did not make the ascent at all the following year. However, friends who did make the Whitsun trip in 1901 told them that the pair of vents in 1900 had now become five or six. They were belching forth greenish fumes that stank of sulphur, and steam was now also issuing from a new vent in the south-eastern part of the Etang Sec. These developments offered just a slender hint that the dynamics of the molten magma below ground had altered.

The changes on Mount Pelée were slow to take effect, but, once they got under way, they occurred at an increasing pace. In December 1901, there were three or four odd and inexplicable oscillations of sea level in the bay of Saint-Pierre. No-one took much notice, but, in fact, they were probably caused when the molten magma was elbowing its way up through the lower layers of rock and causing earth tremors at the base of Mount Pelée.

During the early months of 1902, the fumes were abundant enough to reach the western shores of the mountain. Duno-Emile Josse, a market gardener at Le Prêcheur, about 8 km north of Saint-Pierre, reported to the newspaper *Les Colonies* that the stinking fumes had been causing disquiet in the village ever since the beginning of the year. At Grand' Case 2 km north of Le Prêcheur, Emilie Dujon had recently married and had gone to live with her husband, Charles, and his parents, on their plantation. She first smelt the fumes one day in February 1902 when she was returning along the coast road after visiting her parents, Monsieur and Madame Décomis, in Saint-Pierre. As she crossed the Rivière Blanche, which drained the western slopes of Mount Pelée, the sulphurous fumes had made her gasp for breath. The Dujon workmen told her that the fumes were coming from the new vents in the Etang Sec. In February, too, the *soufrière*, was again giving off stinking fumes so vigorously that a vegetable plot situated 1 km below it could not be tended for two weeks. Later that month, people living on the coast had

The early signs warning that a volcano might soon erupt

If volcanoes are watched carefully enough, they very rarely erupt entirely without warning, but no-one, except possibly Gaston Landes, was watching Mount Pelée with due care and attention.

A volcano is built up by eruptions occurring at intervals over many decades, centuries or millennia, which take place through a vent, or chimney, that usually extends up to the crater at its summit. Very few volcanoes erupt continually, and most eruptions last for only short periods, separated by much longer intervals when the volcano is dormant and the vent is blocked with the products of the last eruptions. Even today, experts cannot always determine whether a volcano is dormant or extinct. Hence, the uncertainties in 1902 about the exact status of Mount Pelée were quite legitimate.

A volcano erupts when hot molten material, called magma, rises up a vent pierced through the Earth's crust and breaks out onto the land surface as dust, ash, cinders or lava flows. The magma is made up of solids, liquids and gases that are held under great pressure, and at temperatures often well in excess of 700°C. The whole mass has rather the consistency of molten glass, but it has a much more complex composition.

The molten magma makes its way upwards in intermittent surges that push the rocks aside. The sudden displacements send out shock waves that cause earthquakes, which are localized on and around the volcano, and are much less powerful, less widespread and less lethal than their tectonic counterparts caused by movements of the plates composing the Earth's crust. Volcanic earthquakes often give some of the most useful indications that magma is rising under the volcano.

As the magma approaches the Earth's surface, the pressures upon it are reduced. Some of the gases and steam within it can thus separate out and escape upwards through the cracks and fissures in the rocks of the Earth's crust. When sulphur dioxide and hydrogen sulphide start to escape, the magma has risen dangerously close to the point of eruption.

The rising magma also heats up the surrounding rocks in the volcano, which, in turn, heat up the groundwater that circulates through them. The waters can be suddenly transformed into steam. The resulting hydrovolcanic eruptions open the vent and the crater at its summit, and expel cool shattered fragments. These hydrovolcanic explosions often suggest that a more dangerous eruption of red-hot fragments of fresh magma might soon ensue.

Unfortunately, volcanic eruptions rarely behave like clockwork and follow exactly the same pattern. Sometimes, indeed, the preliminary symptoms do not even lead to an eruption, but at least they warn that something sinister might be brewing in the entrails of the volcano. Mount Pelée displayed most of these symptoms, which suggested that the volcano might be about to embark upon an eruption. However, the magma rising into Mount Pelée caused few earthquakes. On the other hand, the eruption reached its terrible crescendo with unusual speed.

started to smell the even stronger fumes of rotten eggs given off by the hydrogen sulphide that had blown westwards on the trade winds.

No-one seemed unduly alarmed. Yet. As some local sages asserted, if Mount Pelée was fuming again, "it was only like an old man snoring. Nothing to bother about. Just his last fling". "After all", they joked, "they had fumes like that all the time in Guadeloupe and people just warmed their coffee on the vents".

"Then," as Emilie Dujon later recounted, "a strange thing rather upset me. Once, after I had been away from Grand' Case for a week, I noticed that all our silver was tarnished with spots like blue steel". This was more serious.

During March 1902, the smells became more and more nauseating throughout the area between Le Prêcheur and Sainte-Philomène, which was only about 5 km north of Saint-Pierre. The horses were distressed. People living on the upper reaches of the mountain, who had always drunk the waters of the Rivière Blanche, complained that they had started to develop colic.

On Palm Sunday 23 March, Louis des Grottes, owner of the Leyritz plantation, climbed up to the summit of the mountain and saw that several vents in the Etang Sec were now expelling fumes. He, too, inscribed his impressions of his visit on the wall of the little chapel of Notre Dame de l'Etang. "Today 23 March", he wrote, "the crater of the Etang Sec is erupting". He could not have realized the drama behind this bald statement.

Throughout the month of April 1902, it was hard to tell exactly what was happening on the summit of Mount Pelée, because clouds so often hid it from view. The fumes seemed to be stronger, more frequent and more abundant, and they were making life increasingly unpleasant in the coastal villages around the western fringe of the mountain. The horses were loath to go forwards on the coast road between Saint-Pierre and Le Prêcheur. On 10 April, for instance, Abbé Duffau, the priest at Sainte-Philomène, complained to some friends: "I don't know what's going to become of us. It's been reeking of sulphur here for some time now. Life is unbearable." About the middle of the month, the ground was rumbling like thunder, and whitish fumes were escaping near the *soufrière*.

The events on the mountain intrigued at least one person in Saint-Pierre. Gaston Landes was a teacher of natural sciences in the Lycée and one of the intellectuals in the city. Indeed, he had written the booklet on Martinique for the great exhibition in Paris in 1900. But in subsequent accounts of the eruption in English, mistranslations of "professeur", the French for "teacher", wrongly designated him as a university professor and thereby unwittingly gave undue weight to his views on the eruption. He was not an expert on volcanic eruptions, but he conscientiously tried to interpret the course of events from his general scientific knowledge of volcanoes. But Gaston Landes did not have to be an expert to be better qualified to analyze the course of events than anyone else on the island. He was also most unfairly blamed later for not correctly forecasting what was likely to happen.

All this was in the future on Sunday 20 April 1902, when Gaston Landes climbed up to the Etang Sec to see for himself what was afoot. His scientific curiosity was rewarded in only a modest fashion. Two additional sulphurous vents had developed on the floor of the crater. He had enough scientific background to realize the implications. He had almost certainly read Monsieur Le Prieur's article about the eruption in 1851, which had recently been reprinted in the *Annuaire 1900 de la Martinique*. On his return to Saint-Pierre, he mentioned to his friend, the magistrate, Monsieur Sainte-Luce, that Mount Pelée might just be about to embark upon another eruption.

At 2.03 p.m. on 22 April, a small earthquake caused a rockslide on the sea floor northwest of Mount Pelée. It cut the telegraph cable between Martinique and Guadeloupe. From 8.00 a.m. on 23 April, three more earthquakes shook the flanks of the mountain. Mrs Clara Prentiss, wife of the American consul in Saint-Pierre, wrote to her sister, Alice Fry in Melrose, Massachusetts (USA): "We heard three distinct shocks. The first report was very loud, but the second and third were so great that dishes were thrown from the shelves and the house was completely rocked."

These were portents that magma was pushing its way to the surface and that an eruption was becoming rather more likely. But in 1902, the re-awakening of volcanoes after a dormant period had hardly ever been studied, and these warnings from Mount Pelée seemed little more than hints that would only fan the fears of paranoiacs. Nowadays, if such features were to develop on Mount Pelée, volcanologists would sprint for the nearest plane for Martinique in order to start their research. But, on such evidence in the spring of 1902, there was scarcely an expert on volcanic eruptions in the world who would have booked his berth on a liner bound for the island.

The eruption begins

At 8.45 p.m. on the evening of 23 April the villagers of Le Prêcheur heard a subterranean explosion, which was also registered by the agent of the

The stone bridge (Pont de Pierre) leading from the Rue Victor-Hugo across the Rivière Roxe-lane to the Fort district. The very image of a French provincial town, old Saint-Pierre seemed rock solid. But the small earthquakes were starting to spread a few doubts.

submarine cable offshore. It could have been either an explosion, or a small earthquake. In any case, it started the second phase of the eruption: hydro-volcanic activity, where the rising magma met waters filtering down through fissures. The confining rocks were shattered. The vent was opened. Billowing columns of dust, ash, and steam hurtled skywards.

For the next two days, a thick cover of cloud often hid events on the summit from observers in Saint-Pierre. There was a short break in the clouds on the evening of Thursday 24 April, and several people walking to Trois Ponts at the northern end of the city had noted masses of dirty white steam surging from the flanks of the mountain. As the newspaper *Les Antilles* reported on 26 April, "this abundant white steam seemed to be coming from a long crater that was probably situated in the valley of the Rivière Blanche".

The explosions continued at intervals throughout the night, although no fragments reached as far as the coastal settlements. But they made enough noise to disturb the sleep of Monsieur Eugène Guérin at his home alongside his factory at the mouth of the Rivière Blanche.

Clear skies on 25 April revealed the crest again. Abbé Parel, Vicar General of Martinique, was among those who admired its "splendid bonnet of white steam" as he took the 6.30 a.m. boat from Saint-Pierre to Fort-de-France.

At about 7.00 a.m. there was a big explosion from the Etang Sec. As *Les Antilles* reported on 30 April, it came "with an enormous splash, noises and explosive crackling, which were accompanied by underground rumblings, several slight earth tremors and the expulsion of considerable projections of ash, steam and enormous spurts of boiling water mixed with rocks and tree trunks". Mount Pelée had already surpassed its finest efforts of 1851.

At 8.00 a.m. that morning, the greatest explosion so far reverberated around Mount Pelée and forced the people of Saint-Pierre to take a little more notice. In Le Prêcheur, it sounded like a cannon shot. The blast threw out a pale-grey dust, which the trade winds carried over the western slopes of Mount Pelée between Le Prêcheur and the mouth of the Rivière Blanche. In Le Prêcheur, it fell thickly but gently for the next two hours. The air was so hot and choked with dust that people 2 m apart could not recognize each other in the streets. The dust reached a maximum thickness of only 1 cm, but it was deep enough to stop work on at least one plantation.

In Le Prêcheur, too, the smell of rotten eggs was becoming more and more repugnant. And old wives tales about the eruption in 1851 began to increase the unease in the village. In fact, there was rather more than unease in certain quarters. Duno-Emile Josse described how: "The people were afraid. They took their children and their most precious goods, and ran hither and thither, as if they had been suddenly blinded. Then they returned

Gaston Landes, teacher of natural sciences at the Lycée, Saint-Pierre.

Amédée Knight, a Radical-Socialist senator and one of the most influential politicians in Martinique.

home, screaming and praying at the same time, and begging help from neighbours, who were so overcome by terror themselves that they remained deaf to all the appeals of their fellow citizens."

Monsieur Josse and five of his friends started out from Le Prêcheur to inspect the source of their troubles. Sometimes the fumes were black, sometimes white, but they were forced into retreat "when the emissions began to resemble the output of several blast furnaces combined together".

The sudden noise and earth tremor frightened Emilie Dujon on her plantation at Grand' Case, 2 km north of Le Prêcheur: "[At 8.00 a.m.], you would have thought that a very heavy object had fallen down in the room above. My mother-in-law and my sister . . . had felt a strange tremor . . . Two hours later, fine ash fell. It was bluish-grey and impalpable, but it was very heavy and had a pronounced smell of sulphur."

At about 9.00 a.m. on 25 April, further explosions came from the crater in the valley of the Rivière Blanche, situated some 400 m lower than the Etang Sec. The columns of steam rose about 600 m into the air. Meanwhile, the hydrovolcanic eruptions from the Etang Sec were now in full spate. A magnificent white plume surged 2–3 km above the crater for most of the day.

The Chamber of Commerce building in the business centre of Saint-Pierre, near Place Bertin. Compare this view with that on p. 167, taken just after the eruption.

The commissioners of 1851 would no doubt have been most impressed.

That Friday, however, the most threatening events could be spied from Saint-Pierre only through telescopes. Mount Pelée was not only expelling ash, but vigorous hydrovolcanic explosions were throwing boulders 400 m into the air. Paul Borde, the president of the Chamber of Commerce, had set up a telescope on the roof of its headquarters in the Place Bertin. Gaston Landes and some of his friends were among those who peered through it to take a close look at the erupting culprit. As *Les Antilles* commented on 26 April, they were not reassured by what they saw:

> White fumes were issuing from the . . . Etang Sec, and could be clearly seen from the town [Saint-Pierre]. These jets . . . succeeded each other at irregular intervals of two or three minutes, and went on throughout the morning of 25 April. In the afternoon . . . the smoke turned black, and issued forth in considerable quantities all the time. Then it disappeared altogether about 4.00 p.m. These emissions seem so benign in appearance, but they have the disturbing capacity of being able to juggle with boulders several cubic [sic] metres in diameter, as could be seen through the telescope at the Chamber of Commerce.

The suspicions of Monsieur Landes were confirmed. A new eruption had started, but it was not yet terrifying. Nevertheless, Mount Pelée had never displayed anything approaching such power since the settlers had first raised their standard over old Fort Saint-Pierre in 1635. And on 25 April as well, two further earthquakes shook yet another warning in Saint-Pierre.

4

An election and other activities
Saturday 26 April to Wednesday 30 April 1902

Like a cat torturing a captive mouse, Mount Pelée then taunted its victims with a pause. The volcano threw out no shattered fragments of any kind for five days. Was it going back to sleep or was it girding up its loins for a greater effort? For the people living around its flanks, hope gradually began to overcome their fears. The respite brought an anxious calm, and even a new assurance, to many citizens in Saint-Pierre. Perhaps the eruption was not going to be much worse than that in 1851 after all? But all was not totally tranquil on the crest of Mount Pelée, where gas and steam were still hissing out unabated. And the smell of sulphur lurked in the streets of Saint-Pierre.

The lighthouse in the Place Bertin, the focus of Saint-Pierre.

On Saturday 26 April, Emilie and Charles Dujon left home, as usual, to spend the weekend with Emilie's parents in Saint-Pierre. Emilie discovered that Monsieur and Madame Décomis "were less preoccupied with their volcanic troubles than with the elections". Nevertheless, sinister parallels were being drawn in the salons of Saint-Pierre. As Emilie later revealed, "It is a remarkable coincidence, but don't they say that Pompeii was buried during an electoral period and that the candidates' policy statements were found inscribed on the walls of the dead city?"

On 26 April, Roger Arnoux examined the source of the Rivière Blanche from Saint-Pierre through his telescope, and saw that the waterfall there was giving off steam as if it were hot. *Les Antilles* on 30 April deduced – probably correctly – that the waterfall, which must have been about 1 m across, was being fed by underground fissures from the Etang Sec.

Not all the citizens of Saint-Pierre were terrified by what they saw. Indeed, the renewed calm of the volcano encouraged several more enterprising people to climb up and take a closer look at the summit. They might have been enterprising, but they were also foolhardy. Mount Pelée could, in fact, have resumed its activity at any moment and bombarded them with ash or even huge rocks torn from its vent. They took a chance and they got away with it – they all escaped unscathed.

Those who made the trip on Saturday 26 April were unlucky because clouds enshrouded the crest for most of the day. Thus, three Fathers of the Holy Spirit from the College–Seminary were neither blessed with a view of the volcanic pit in the Etang Sec, nor consoled with the usual vistas of northern Martinique. They had to make do with the briefest of glimpses when the clouds parted for an indulgent instant. Father Voegtli complained that the strong wind and the sulphurous fumes made it impossible for him to stay at the foot of Morne Lacroix for very long; and all that Father Démaërel could make out was the column of fumes rising to a "prodigious height". However, *Les Antilles* reported on 30 April that five workmen had enjoyed slightly better luck at the summit. Anthony, Daniel, Joseph, Julien and Rémy – the use of forenames suggesting they must have been black – had detected fumes belching from four main vents at the northern end of the Etang Sec.

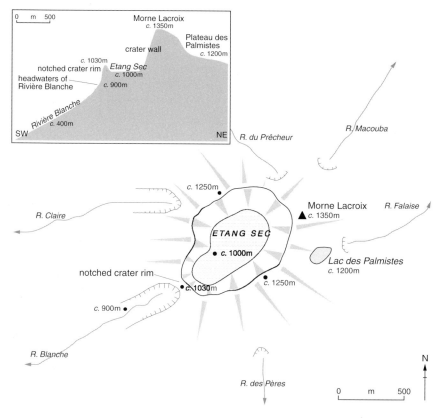

Map of the summit of Mount Pelée on 27 April 1902. Inset: profile of the summit.

Sunday 27 April

Mount Pelée was much calmer on the following day. The volcano seemed to have declared an electoral truce. Sunday 27 April marked the first round of the French general election, by universal male suffrage, of candidates to the Chambre des Députés, the lower house of the French parliament. Any number of candidates could try their luck in the first round. If a candidate obtained more than 50 per cent of the votes, he was duly elected. If no candidate obtained 50 per cent of the votes, then the election proceeded to a second stage that took place two weeks later. Usually, the two leading candidates from the first round fought out this second contest, but, in fact, any candidate who obtained more than 10 per cent of the votes in the first round was eligible to continue. One result of this system was that all sorts of

40

small parties could stand in the first round to advertise their views, even if they had no real chance of success. But the second round gave them some bargaining power because they could urge supporters to vote for one of the remaining candidates. A further result was that the system fostered a multitude of changing political labels and shifting alliances that would have made old Byzantium blush. The politicians played an incessant game of musical chairs to the accompaniment of republican marches. For example, in the parliament elected in May 1898, seven major parties shared most of the 585 seats; and four different governments held power during the next four years. There were more contrasts than similarities between the political traditions of the Third French Republic and those, say, in the English-speaking world, and direct comparisons are often futile. However, the French system also developed a level of political sophistication and debate among the educated that was often absent in similar democracies. Thus, in Martinique, as in metropolitan France, the educated minority often took a passionate interest in politics. But the less-educated majority took no part whatsoever in the proceedings. This is what happened, as usual, in Saint-Pierre in 1902, where, even in the cultural capital of the island, nearly half the population could neither read nor write. Neither did they vote.

At the beginning of the twentieth century, political debate in France was more than usually acrimonious, and opinions had been polarized by the repercussions of the trial of the Jewish Captain Alfred Dreyfus, and his unjust condemnation for spying. Religious, anti-clerical, national and racial feelings ran high and reverberated throughout the political firmament. To add to the confusion of outsiders, new parties were often created, or renamed, for the needs of the hour, or sometimes even to express more permanent principles. Thus, the French Radical-Socialist party was founded in June 1901, and the French Socialist party in March 1902. In Martinique itself, tempers had become particularly frayed when ten men had been shot dead during the strike of the sugar cane workers in 1900.

The governor represented the French state almost as a pro-consul in the colony: administrator and servant of the metropolitan government. He did not take part in these political contests, although he would know the candidates and many of their more prominent supporters. His political views had to remain his own affair — at least in theory. The metropolitan government shifted its colonial governors about with some speed, so that they scarcely had the chance to become too closely implicated in local politics. Thus, Governor Louis Mouttet had arrived in Martinique only in December 1901.

41

In Martinique, the white people were strongly Catholic, anti-republican and often consciously or unconsciously racist. They had treated the democratic institutions of the Third Republic with disdain, and had sulked for 25 years before taking an active part in politics again. Their candidate in North Martinique was Fernand Clerc, a rich and flamboyant white industrialist, who was director of the sugar factory in La Trinité and had been mayor of the town for the previous eight years. He represented the Progressive Party. Fernand Clerc always excited strong political passions and was supported by the newspaper *Les Colonies*. He was opposed by Louis Percin and Joseph Lagrosillière, both of whom were lawyers from the rising middle class of educated mulattos. Louis Percin was Vice-President of the Regional Council of Martinique and was supported by the newspaper *L'Opinion*. He represented the Radical-Socialists and was anti-clerical, ardently pro-republican and favoured the nationalization of the railways and the mines. His more powerful allies included Amédée Knight, a rich mulatto industrialist, who had just been elected to the French senate, and Rodolphe Fouché, who had recently become mayor of Saint-Pierre. The third candidate was young Joseph Lagrosillière, who had returned home from Paris in July 1901. He, too, was an ardent republican who stood for the Socialist Workers Party. It may seem odd to mention the skin colour of the candidates, but colour in that place, at that time, was deemed to represent a great many virtues, or vices, depending upon the prejudices in the eye of the beholder. Both the Progressives and the Radical-Socialists had been in the government coalition, so that the result in North Martinique would have no great importance for the formation of the next government in Paris.

Not surprisingly, political passions were inflamed by the local press. *Les Antilles*, edited by Léon Sully, was the strongly Catholic organ of the whites. *Les Colonies* was edited by Marius Hurard, a flamboyant intelligent mulatto and an ebullient lawyer and journalist, who could raise any rabble at the stroke of a pen. He had been a member of the French parliament and he had also had three duels and several condemnations in the courts, the latest of which had been a fine of 3000 francs on 13 May 1901 for defamation of Victor Sévère, the recently elected mayor of Fort-de-France.

On 27 April, Fernand Clerc topped the poll with 4495 votes, but he was far from obtaining an overall majority of more than 50 per cent. Louis Percin came second with 4167 votes, and Joseph Lagrosillière came third with 753 votes. Consequently, there had to be a second round between the top two candidates, which was scheduled for Sunday 11 May. Louis Percin was expected to gain the votes of Lagrosillière's supporters and win the seat. There had been an abstention rate of 53.6 per cent, which fitted the usual pattern in the constituency, and it was matched exactly in the neighbouring constituency of South Martinique. Thus, the eruption of Mount Pelée had seemingly played a negligible role in the election on 27 April. Many were later to declare that the administration had sacrificed the lives of the citizens of Saint-Pierre by obliging them to stay in the city to vote in the second round. This outrageous claim could be partly explained away by the passions that the contest had aroused among the politically minded class. It was also a claim not borne out by the facts, but a cynic might observe that this would be no handicap to any such political assertion.

After the first round, the outgoing government coalition had already won 243 seats, while the opposition parties had already secured 158 seats. A second round of elections had to take place on 11 May in only 171 seats, and the results were not expected to have any notable influence on the balance of power in the new chamber – and, indeed, they did not. As *Les Antilles* observed on 30 April, the results of the first round of the elections "were coloured with all sorts of nuances . . . but the supporters of the outgoing government coalition remain in the majority". There was thus no logical need whatsoever for any administrator to risk lives in order to coerce people to vote in Saint-Pierre on 11 May.

Other activities

In spite of the elections on Sunday 27 April, Mount Pelée and the weather stayed calm enough to entice several parties of visitors to the summit to see what was going on. One of these groups was composed of Messrs Eugene Berté, Boulin, Waddy, Ange and Decors (or Decord). Eugène Berté published their observations in *Les Colonies* on 7 May. Once they reached the summit, it took them over an hour to scramble down through an almost impenetrable tangle of branches to reach the rarely visited site of the Etang Sec. And all the while, the air was tainted with nauseating gases:

An unexpected spectacle stopped them in their tracks, dumbfounded with admiration . . . [In place of the old Etang Sec there was now] an immense lake and a volcano in activity . . . The trees on the walls of the hollow were plastered with a uniform black coating with a metallic glint. A lake, 200 m in diameter, occupied the bottom of the hollow, and a cone, 10 m high and 15 m across, rose out of the waters right up against the walls on its eastern edge. It was 11.00 a.m. . . . but everything was lit in a strange way. The lake looked like a sea of molten lead or quicksilver, and floating ash was being swept across it by the fierce wind . . . They could hear the tumultuous motion of the boiling liquid. The smoke was flying out in great fluffy batches from the mouth of the volcano, and the water was spurting out, cascading over the edges of the crater, and spreading over the lake . . . The lake waters were grey . . . with impalpable slate-grey dust . . . that resembled manganese dioxide. This water contained a great quantity of gases, among which sulphur and hydrogen sulphide seemed to be predominant. Their silver buttons were blackened . . . [But] the trippers could not approach the crater . . . Here and there in the lake . . . they saw green leaves, and thought they might be able to get a footing, but the guides pointed out that one of these little islets was, in fact, the top of a tree about 20 m high that was just emerging from the water like a bunch of leaves.

All this water, and the cone, had accumulated from the depths since Gaston Landes had visited the same site a week before. Eugène Berté and his friends resolved to return to the summit as soon as conditions permitted. But Mount Pelée was soon to permit no further such conditions.

The old crest of Mount Pelée then received its final visitor. On 10 April, Paul Merwart, artist to the navy, had arrived in Martinique from French Guyana on an assignment. On Monday morning 28 April, he climbed to the summit "to paint the craters that started to smoke about a week ago". Next day, he described his trip in a letter to his brother, the governor of French Guyana. The volcano was clearly disturbed: copious white fumes, smelling strongly of sulphur, were still issuing from the Etang Sec:

Several new little *soufrières* had grown up between the displaced rocks. Some people had apparently seen blocks of rock thrown up in the midst of the smoke, but I wasn't lucky enough to see them myself. The lake . . . is supplied by the abundant waters that are issuing from the most important crater . . . The reddened leaves and the defoliated, apparently burnt, branches amid the constant mist lent an air of a European late autumn or winter to the scene.

44

And it even felt cold. Merwart's two guides were shivering and tried to warm themselves by getting as near to the hot spring as the sulphurous fumes would allow. After the artist's visit, the erupting little cone was never seen again. Neither, for that matter, was the Etang Sec.

Tuesday 29 April and Wednesday 30 April were almost calm. From Saint-Pierre, the columns of fumes could scarcely be distinguished from the clouds. There were other consolations too. On 30 April, *Les Antilles* noted that the owners of several plantations on the slopes of the mountain had remarked that the ash had done their cocoa and coffee bushes the world of good. It had killed the pests that preyed upon them and the sulphurous fumes had brought their flowering forward. "Never in living memory had the blossoms been so early and so abundant." With hindsight, this intermission was seen as ominous silence. Broken only by the press and three earthquakes.

On 30 April, too, Léon Sully, the editor of *Les Antilles*, tempted fate and summed up the volcanic events of the month with flippant delight:

If April has not been comic, it has been doubly tragic. We have seen two volcanic eruptions, one in people's minds and the other at Mount Pelée; one electoral, the other physical; one of speeches, propaganda, rum, money and voting papers, and the other of smoke and ashes. One of them is still not finished, because the electoral volcano is still smoking and will become extinct in only another 12 days. The other is still going on, for our Pelée is still in activity, and will put its fires out we know not when. We do not know what the result will be in either case. Let us hope that it will be nothing bad.

Yes, indeed, April 1902 will stay in our memories, especially because of this physical or volcanic eruption. It will be discussed just as we have discussed 5 August 1851, when the last one occurred. When we heard talk of that one, we felt that we would really have liked to have been there. It seemed such an extraordinary thing; and it was all the more titillating because we had never expected to see an event like it, because we thought our Pelée was extinct. Imagine our surprise, then, when we were told that Mount Pelée was smoking again! At first we took it for an April Fool's joke, and we could believe it only when we actually saw it . . . Even if we live for a hundred years, we will never forget a thing about it. Indeed, we will also keep this mysterious ash that came from the flaming entrails of our globe and was spat several kilometres from the jaws of our volcano . . . we will keep it like a relic. It is fine, light and tiny like cement, but rather more bluish in colour. This ash is like a poem that has already been composed in our imagination. If we ever write it, we'll call it *The ash from the volcano*. And what flames will we make burst out from this ash!

Mount Pelée just saw that the good old customs were dying out, and simply wanted to play an April Fool's trick upon us. Dear old April! But, since you are now going to rest, sleep well! And all hail to thee, May!

The extract gives an inkling of the general mood in Saint-Pierre as the month ended; not to mention a flavour of the current style of the press on the island at the time. But they were all playing with fire. On 30 April, Mount Pelée issued a warning that the danger was far from over. Three small earthquakes occurred at 3.40 p.m., 5.05 p.m. and 6.10 p.m. They were so slight that not everyone felt them, but they showed that the magma was still rising to the surface. The citizens of Saint-Pierre did not know exactly what these small earthquakes implied, but they did serve to increase the now wide-spread, and completely unfounded, fear that a disastrous earthquake could be imminent.

On 30 April, *Les Colonies* carried a notice that must, nevertheless, have filled many citizens of Saint-Pierre with eager anticipation. It announced that, on the following Sunday 4 May, the Gymnastic and Shooting Club was going to organize a great excursion to the summit of Mount Pelée to witness all the spectacle of the eruption at close quarters.

Those who wish to take advantage of this fine opportunity should sign up at once, and get a close-up view of the gaping hole through which those thick fumes have escaped and have not failed to bring terror to the hearts of the people living above Le Prêcheur and Sainte-Philomène. We are given to understand that the number of participants will be large. Messieurs Landes [the teacher] and Saussine [the pharmacist] will be coming along, and it is said that the magistrates will also be among the party. Just so long as the gendarmes don't take it into their heads to arrest the crater! If the weather is fine, the trippers will spend a pleasant day out that they will remember for a long time.

Sad to say, this excursion had to be cancelled. And not because of the weather.

5

Safety in Saint-Pierre
Thursday 1 May to Sunday 4 May 1902

Loud explosions awakened everyone in Le Prêcheur in the early hours of 1 May. Mount Pelée was back in business. Pitch-black fumes belched from the summit. Lightning flashed. Panic swept through the village. Daybreak revealed a shroud of ash stretching all the way from Sainte-Philomène, in the south, to Les Abymes, in the north. All day, the trade winds blew the black ash down the mountain, over Le Prêcheur, and then well out to sea.

The situation around Mount Pelée deteriorated still further on Friday 2 May. Two vents seemed to be active, and they were wider than before. Some believed that both lay within the Etang Sec, others thought that one was at the head of the Rivière Blanche. An ever darkening and ever thickening column of dust, ash, gas and steam soared skywards and enshrouded the hamlets on the lower western slopes of the volcano. Explosions, thunderous rumblings and the lightning flashing through the swirling clouds increased the fears of the farmers and market gardeners remaining on the slopes of Mount Pelée. The trumpeted complaints of their animals convinced some of their masters that it was time to seek refuge elsewhere. Many of the inhabitants gathered up their most treasured possessions, abandoned everything else, left their stock to their own devices, and made their way to what they considered to be the safer havens of Le Prêcheur or Sainte-Philomène. In fact, Le Prêcheur was in the core of the deluge. By 2.00 p.m. on 2 May, the fumes there were so thick that it was as dark as night, and many people had to light their lamps. Some inhabitants were afraid that they were going to suffocate. Monsieur Grelet, the mayor, and Abbé Desprez, the priest, both tried to calm the growing anxiety. They often succeeded, but those who remained unconvinced did not all stay in Le Prêcheur. The exodus began that afternoon. People packed a bag, left their homes, and

Falls of volcanic fragments

The people deluged by volcanic fragments from Mount Pelée always called them *la cendre* ("ash"). They said it had the consistency, and often the colour, of dry cement. If they had used today's volcanic terminology, they would have called it dust. Volcanic dust consists of particles of less than 0.5 mm in diameter, whereas ash is between 0.5 mm and 2.0 mm across. Larger fragments are now closely defined according to their size and are given other technical names such as lapilli (about the size of walnuts), cinders or scoria (composed of rough, irregular lumps like clinker), and blocks and bombs (which can often be over 1 m across).

The heavier, larger fragments soon fall to the ground on the slopes of the volcano. The strength and direction of the wind usually determines the distribution of the finer, lighter fragments, which can often be carried far afield. Really violent explosions can hurl the finest particles and gases into the stratosphere, where the high-altitude winds can carry them around the Earth in about two weeks.

The explosions of Mount Pelée were not of this calibre, and the billowing columns usually rose only 2–3 km above its crest. The trade winds then winnowed out the fragments and distributed them most frequently, and most thickly, over a triangular area on the western flanks of Mount Pelée extending from the summit to Le Prêcheur in the north and to Sainte-Philomène in the south, each of which lay some 6 km from the crater. In contrast, ash and dust rarely fell on villages such as Le Morne-Rouge and Ajoupa-Bouillon, which were situated within 5 km of the crater on the eastern slopes of the volcano. Until the fatal hour, Saint-Pierre itself suffered only when the wind changed and carried the clouds more than 7 km to the southwest. The ash and dust fell over the rest of Martinique, including upon the capital, Fort-de-France, only when an unusually vigorous eruption ejected fragments into the higher zone, where the counter trade winds blew eastwards. Thus, the limited power of most explosions, and the direction of the prevailing winds, determined the areas that suffered during the first two weeks of the eruption. But the climax of the eruption was dominated by entirely different volcanic features – nuées ardentes – whose direction was determined by blast from a weakened part of the rim of the crater.

decamped to Saint-Pierre. The strongest carried the children and the sick. The rest pushed carts through the deepening ash.

This phenomenon was to repeat itself time and again. People always made for the nearest larger settlement, which they assumed would be safer than their own homes. With the poor communications of the day, not to mention the swirling dust, they were in no position to find out whether their destination was really safe until they reached it.

Things were no better on the Dujon plantation at Grand' Case, 2 km north of Le Prêcheur. As Emilie Dujon recalled:

A big black cloud, like those that bring rain, came up from the south, and quickly . . . darkened the sky. Then the ash started to fall, lightly at first, but then so heavily that we could hear it beating down. At the same time, we felt the temperature rise. In an instant, masters and servants gathered in the house. The shutters were closed, as if for a hurricane. But nevertheless, the smell of sulphur followed us throughout the hermetically sealed rooms. Was it fear, imagination or reality that made us think it was getting harder to breathe? An immense human clamour and the cries of animals were rising all around us outside . . . We could hear people weeping and moaning where the women usually grated the manioc. And, one by one, we saw them fleeing from their cabins, sheltering their children's heads with parts of their dresses.

[Even in such exceptional circumstances, it does not seem to have occurred to anyone to invite these fieldworkers to shelter in the house.]

A vision of Herculaneum and Pompeii passed before our eyes. But we did not believe – then – that our premonitions would be realized so quickly and with such horror. Then, after about half an hour, the sky cleared at about 10.30 a.m. or 11.00 a.m.

That afternoon [2 May], my husband suggested a ride down to the Rivière Blanche. I was very much afraid, but I accepted in spite of myself. Our horses were nervous at first, and their hooves were sinking into the ash . . . The branches of the trees were bending under the thick layers. Every now and again, we heard a cracking noise and saw the branch of a coffee tree or a coconut palm break under its weight . . . There was not a bird in the trees. And the silence of death was everywhere . . . Mount Pelée rose beyond Le Prêcheur in all its threatening splendour. Enormous sombre columns were rising without respite into the sky . . . When they reached a certain height, they veered northwards over Le Prêcheur . . . We met my uncle on our way. He urged us to return home as quickly as possible. The result of the trip was that I was terrified – especially since I learned on returning home that, in Le Prêcheur, they had heard the mountain rumbling with a noise that five or six horses would make when they galloped over a [wooden] suspension bridge.

Meanwhile, for some unknown but no doubt ominous reason, the Rivière Blanche had practically dried up. Then, late in the evening of 2 May, the river suddenly began to flood.

The first ash and dust fall on Saint-Pierre

Abbé G. Parel, the Vicar General of Martinique, was staying the night in the College–Seminary in Saint-Pierre, although he was normally based in the capital, Fort-de-France. In fact, he had had to take charge of the diocese because the government had strongly suggested to Bishop de Cormont that his openly reactionary presence on the island would disturb the election campaign. The Bishop was therefore on leave in metropolitan France.

As Abbé Parel later wrote to the bishop:

At 6.00 p.m. [on 2 May], I received a telegram from Abbé Desprez, the priest in Le Prêcheur saying: "Considerable volcanic eruption. We have been under the ash since this morning. Are asking for your prayers."

About [11.30 p.m.] that evening, Saint-Pierre was awakened by a salvo of terrifying explosions. The city could then contemplate one of the great scenes in nature: a volcano in full eruption, spitting out an enormous column of blackish smoke that was riddled with lightning and accompanied by tremendous noises as it rose skywards. A few moments later, ash began to rain down on the city [of Saint-Pierre], and in smaller quantities upon Fort-de-France and over the whole island.

This was the first ash to fall on Saint-Pierre since 1851. But the eruption did not warrant the panic-stricken reactions in the coastal villages – so far.

Abbé Parel was wrong about one thing: Mount Pelée was by no means "in full eruption". As violent eruptions go, this was, in fact, quite minor, and the volcano had yet to expel any molten rock. The dust and ash so far ejected came only from cold rock shattered from the body of the mountain. However, the fine dust swirled into and around every building in Saint-Pierre. It got everywhere – into every room, nook, and cranny, into beds, books, lungs and eyes. It disturbed the horses in their stables. It muffled all the sounds of passers-by and horses in the streets like a thick industrial fog. It stank of sulphur and rotten eggs. It gave everyone nausea. It made everyone hot and breathless, and some soon developed bronchitis and conjunctivitis. And it soon lay 3 cm deep in the deserted streets of Saint-Pierre. The priests opened the churches. The faithful were praying, confessing, taking communion, and listening to the exhortations of their anxious pastors. And the ground rumbled with growls of volcanic discontent that threatened further perils.

50

Le Morne-Rouge and the summit of Mount Pelée 5 km away.

But Saint-Pierre had been spared the excesses of the volcanic temper. The villages to the north were in a far worse position. However, although Le Prêcheur had been deluged in ash for several days, Le Morne-Rouge had suffered little, although it was in an altogether more dangerous situation, a mere 5 km southeast of the crater. Then, Mount Pelée suddenly doused its other flanks with a vengeance.

Repentance at Le Morne-Rouge

Edith Duchâteau-Roger was a novice at the Convent of the Délivrande at Le Morne-Rouge. To this young and not very intelligent girl, the eruption was a test of faith, and she wrote an account of events, which strongly emphasized the repentance and religious zeal that the volcanic catastrophe had apparently inspired.

> At 11.00 p.m. [on 2 May] . . . there was an earthquake, followed by formidable bangs like the rumbling of thunder and violent cannon shots, and . . . there was an incessant roaring like a machine or a lion.
> The terrified inhabitants of Le Morne-Rouge rushed out of their homes and saw before them a spectacle of sublime horror . . . The summit of Pelée was lit by hundreds of flashes of lightning bursting from its

crater . . . A strong smell of sulphur filled the air and a strange rain of ash reached them . . .

There was a general panic. Everyone closed their houses and rushed to the church for the last rites. When the last blacks had arrived, the sanctuary was full, and the confessionals were besieged by the crowd of downcast people. There were disputes about who should enter the confessionals first . . . "I'm a bigger sinner than you", cried a big black man, as he pushed his neighbour aside . . . Another shouted to a poor woman going into a confessional: "Get out of here. Let me go first. You've nothing to say." She had to let him take her place. Might was right. Thus, the night passed in pious tumult. The poor blacks, with their ardent faith and anguished souls, cried out in supplication to the Madonna: "Save us, Good Mother, and we promise you that we'll become converted . . ." The whole church resounded to the clamour of the distraught and the prayers of the confident.

[There seems to have been a certain lack of clerical organization in this hour of need, but Father Mary, the priest of Le Morne-Rouge, eventually took a modicum of control.]

Father Mary, who was all alone with Father Leininger, decided to let a priest from Saint-Pierre, who happened to be in Le Morne-Rouge, take confessions. But there were no vacant confessionals left . . . The kindly priest took over the sacristy. He was hard of hearing . . . It was almost a public confession . . . The crowd stayed in front of the altar all night, praying ardently and waiting for death . . . At dawn [3 May], everyone rushed from the church . . . The ash was still falling . . . infiltrating everywhere: into the houses, into the water, into the bread . . . we breathed it and we ate it.

Such sentiments and ministrations were, no doubt, fine for the hereafter, but Le Morne-Rouge was not yet on the brink of destruction. Perhaps more practical steps to protect the villagers would have been rather more in order. But the only sure means of saving them would have been evacuation. And the authorities would almost certainly have chosen to house them in Saint-Pierre. Out of the frying pan, into the fire. But, for the moment, Le Morne-Rouge was absolved and was almost as white as snow beneath its coat of fine pale dust.

The explosions from Mount Pelée became more frequent. The trade winds pushed the cloud of dust westwards far out to sea, where it coated the decks of ships as far away as Puerto Rico. The erupting column sometimes

---

WARNING ONE
The revival and slow increase from the turn of the century in the emissions of sulphurous fumes and small quantities of steam suggested that magma was rising beneath Mount Pelée. The wind was carrying the smell of rotten eggs farther and farther afield, in a triangular area stretching westwards from the summit to the coast from Le Prêcheur to Saint-Philomène, and eventually to Saint-Pierre.

WARNING TWO
Hydrovolcanic eruptions began on 23 April. They strengthened the suggestion that magma was indeed rising under Mount Pelée and had reached a height where it could interact with the groundwater, form steam, explode, and expel fine bluish-grey dust. This dust fell over the triangular area west of the summit.

WARNING THREE
On 3 May, these hydrovolcanic eruptions increased in intensity and frequency. Electrical discharges in the ash cloud generated repeated flashes of lightning. The "flames" noted by observers could also be ascribed to lightning, but it is just possible that they were true flames caused when escaping gases were ignited. The power of the explosions had apparently increased a hundred-fold. The odds were, therefore, then leaning towards the strong indication that the magma had risen still closer towards the summit.

---

towered 5 km or 6 km above the mountain into the counter trade winds that then carried the dust over the whole island. Thus it was that a thin layer covered Fort-de-France by the morning of 3 May. It was the first volcanic dust to fall on the city since the French settlement. The threat had reached the capital. This was a much more serious matter. It cannot have been entirely coincidental that the administration immediately sent the first official notification of the eruption to the government in Paris:

> Fort-de-France 3 May. Last night, the volcanic eruption of Mount Pelée took on major proportions. The city of Saint-Pierre and the surrounding countryside have been covered by a thick layer of greyish ash, many explosions have been heard, and lightning was noticed playing around the summit of the mountain. Then, at about 2.00 a.m., the crater spat forth flames and ejected stones of a fairly large size, some of which fell on the district near Le Prêcheur . . . that lies more than 2 km from the crater.

But there was no request for any expert scientific help. No-one could properly interpret the warnings that Mount Pelée was issuing.

53

The governor visits Saint-Pierre and Le Prêcheur

On 3 May, attitudes to the eruption changed in Saint-Pierre. Mount Pelée was now no longer providing an entertaining firework display, but was becoming a fearsome threat. At 8.00 a.m., Governor Louis Mouttet and his aide-de-camp, Lieutenant Jacques Granier, took the *Rubis,* the Girard company's regular service steamer, from Fort-de-France to Saint-Pierre. They arrived at 9.10 a.m. and were met at the landing stage by Rodolphe Fouché, the mayor of Saint-Pierre. Colonel Dain, commander of the troops, joined the governor and they went straight on to Le Prêcheur, where the distress, damage and darkness were most intense. This was clearly the place where action had to be taken. The villagers were in a frenzy of distress, but the governor did what he could to calm their nerves. *Les Colonies* reported that "Governor Mouttet promised the villagers that, if the need arose, they would be given refuge in the empty infantry barracks in Saint-Pierre. Everything necessary would be done to bring assistance to those unfortunate people who had suffered much from the eruption already". At 4.00 p.m., the governor took the steamer to Fort-de-France (and not 4.00 p.m. the next day, as was sometimes reported).

Abbé Parel also took the *Rubis* on Saturday 3 May. He travelled in response to a further telegram from the priest in Le Prêcheur that was even more alarming than its predecessor of the previous evening. Abbé Parel went to Sainte-Philomène, Le Prêcheur and Le Morne-Rouge under a rain of dust smelling strongly of sulphur:

> The cannonades were doubling in intensity every six hours. Each village was full of people fleeing from the heights towards the coast; the churches were always full; and the priests never stopped baptizing, taking confessions, and boosting the courage of the terrified people. I tried to reassure them all. As I was returning from Le Prêcheur, I was caught in a cloud of ash of such intensity that it was as black as night.

Meanwhile, *Les Colonies* also noted that the families of the great landowners near the volcano were moving to their homes in Saint-Pierre. The paper claimed that the exodus was incessant, but it did not involve many people, even including the many retainers deemed necessary to cater for the landowners' basic needs in the city. Saint-Pierre was the safe haven. Much safer than the accident-prone capital, Fort-de-France.

Not everyone agreed, however. In Saint-Pierre on the morning of 3 May, the magistrate, Monsieur Sainte-Luce, was watching the eruption with increasing alarm:

> The spectacle that I had witnessed [he said later] seemed to be so serious that I went to the telegraph office in Fonds-Coré and sent the following telegram to Monsieur Victor Sévère, the mayor of Fort-de-France: "Mount Pelée in full eruption. The city is being covered in ash. Immense danger. On behalf panic-stricken population ask you means of transport to evacuate city urgently."
>
> However, when I found out that the governor had gone to Saint-Pierre, I telephoned to Sévère to ask him to ignore my telegram because the head of the colony was already visiting the affected area."

Charles and Emilie Dujon flee to safety

On the plantation at Grand' Case, Emilie Dujon awoke on the morning of Saturday 3 May, to find her home enveloped in swirling ash:

> When my husband went to open his window with his candle in his hand, the cloud of ash . . . was so thick that he could see his own shadow projected onto it as if it were a screen. He quickly gave the alarm. In an instant, all the family was up, and it was decided to leave Grand' Case at once. The vehicles were harnessed, and the lanterns were lit because we couldn't see a thing. I was dreading this exodus because the road between Grand' Case and Saint-Pierre is cut into the cliff in places, and edged on one side by the mountain and on the other by a precipice overhanging the sea.
>
> We had everything to fear. We were wearing our indoor clothes, with muslin ribbons over our eyes, and wet handkerchiefs over our mouths . . . The ash rained down throughout our journey into town. My God! What a race! What a trip it was! I was in mortal agony. I prayed with my crucifix in my hand and I expected death at any moment.
>
> Saint-Pierre was lively, but not too uneasy. The house roofs were still grey. The firemen had been ordered to wash down the streets, and passing black women yelled out to them: "Go and put Mount Pelée out instead". I found that my parents were not feeling anxious, but I burst into tears as soon as I had kissed them.

Governor Louis-Guillaume Mouttet

Louis-Guillaume Mouttet was 44 and he had been appointed governor of Martinique in 1901. He was born in Marseille on 10 October 1857. His career began in Sénégal on 10 April 1886, and he was soon promoted to higher administrative posts. From 22 October 1888, he was seconded to the management of the railways in Réunion. On 10 May 1889, he became one of the chief advisors to the governor of Indochina, and was awarded the Légion d'Honneur on 26 October 1890. At about this time he suffered his first attacks of malaria. On 4 May 1892, he became Director of the Interior, first in Guadeloupe, then in Sénégal, and again in Guadeloupe on 3 August 1894. There his health deteriorated again, but he returned to Sénégal and became acting governor from 19 May 1895 to 18 September 1895. On 14 May 1896, he was appointed governor of the Ivory Coast. However, ill health again forced him to take sick leave in August 1898. He was appointed governor of French Guyana on 11 September 1898. He returned to France on 18 January 1901 and was appointed governor of Martinique on 16 July 1901, and on 9 December 1901 embarked for Martinique. He was thus one of the most successful and most experienced young governors in the French Colonial Service. He was married to Hélène Decoppet, daughter of Pastor Decoppet, a member of the governing council of the Reformed (Protestant) Churches in France. They had three young children.

Pastor Decoppet was a leading figure in the liberal, reforming movements at the end of the nineteenth century in France. His son-in-law shared many of his views and was interested in the underprivileged and in the benefits of the new state education system that had developed in France during the previous twenty years. Mouttet was thus rather untypical of his profession, and it is no surprise that such a man should meet with opposition, criticism, and eventually with denigration from the more conservative elements in Martinique society. His function was, of course, to interpret and execute government policy, whatever its political flavour, although he did have discretionary powers to act on his own initiative during an emergency.

These lamentations were not the plaints of a weak little newly wed. Events were to prove that Emilie Dujon was a woman of some resilience.

Odd things continued to happen at sea, too. During the afternoon of 3 May, another submarine cable was severed, this time between Saint-Pierre and Roseau in Dominica.

A volcanic shroud for Saint-Pierre

Many people from the immediate neighbourhood of Mount Pelée were fleeing to the safety of Saint-Pierre. This extraordinary influx was described by the primary-school teacher, Roger Portel, in the last letter that he wrote to one of his brothers in Toulon on 3 May:

> When I awoke at 5.30 a. m . . . Saint-Pierre was dusted with grey snow . . . It is a winter landscape without the cold . . . [Later on, at the northern end of Saint-Pierre] the dust was raining down, blinding me and getting into my nostrils. And, a man could not be made out 30 m away . . . [People] were . . . fleeing to Saint-Pierre. It was a flight of frightened folk: a higgledy-piggledy array of women, barefoot children, peasant women (who didn't realize that their plaits had become powdered as if they were seventeenth century marchionesses), and great black lads bent double under the mattresses needed for the coming night. And all the while, old women at their windows in the city were muttering their interminable prayers.
>
> At 10.00 a.m. there was already 3 cm of ash in the streets of the Fort area. The streets are gloomy and are no longer resounding to the hastening heels of busy people . . .
>
> *Les Colonies* has opened up a fund for the people living on Mount Pelée and in Le Prêcheur. The firemen have used the fire hydrants to flush the streets. In the higher districts and narrower alleys, a policeman and a man ringing a bell are ordering the streets to be washed down. I can't breathe and my nose is burning.

But it is important to keep a sense of proportion about all this. At no stage did roofs collapse in Saint-Pierre under the weight of ash. The fine dust was inconvenient and suffocating, but it was not in itself disastrous. It never put lives in danger, although it was fine enough to cause breathing problems, especially for those with asthma and bronchitis.

Dust and ash fell on Saint-Pierre virtually throughout 3 May. It had some very disconcerting effects. As one wealthy white lady put it, "the blacks have gone white under the ash. They are the butt of jokes, in spite of their predicament, and they themselves are the first to join in." The birds were no longer able to fly. The school children were given a holiday. Many factories, shops and businesses were closed. The churches were open, and as in Le Morne-Rouge, the priests were busy receiving confessions and comforting their flocks. But so many businesses were shut down that many people now had nothing better to do than throng the streets and spread every alarming tale that they had heard or invented.

Young Elodie Jourdain (then Elodie Dujon), reliable in spite of her 11 years, described discussions in the household during the weekend of 3–4 May:

We spent Saturday and Sunday [3 and 4 May] hoping that the eruption would stop, but worried by the further considerable geological symptoms such as the earthquakes and the sudden floods in the rivers rising on Pelée, when, in fact, there had been no rain. The family talked about nothing else: and I suppose it was the same in all the other families in Saint-Pierre. They questioned each other from their balconies: "Are you afraid? Are you leaving?" Some visitors came to the house to find out what we intended to do, and also brought us news of other people: "You know there is a departure planned for Saint Lucia. The ladies from the Plissonneau, MacHugh, de Grandmaison and Ernoult families are leaving. Their husbands are going to take them, but then intend to come back at once. Why not do the same?" "But", we replied, "they have relatives in Saint Lucia, but we don't know anyone there!" "Yes", some people would add, "we are the same, but we are looking for somewhere on the hills above Saint-Pierre, in the Monsieur quarter or in Le Morne-Rouge, because if the sea rises we'll be safer" . . . Hence, the search for refuge on the hills above Saint-Pierre, where all the houses for hire were occupied at once.

Nerves were tense. Emilie Dujon detailed an episode of panic at evening service in the cathedral on 3 May.

One or two men noticed that the sky had darkened and they were afraid that the ash might soon start to rain down again. So, they came to fetch their wives and children. They were noticed leaving in the midst of the

The modern Mouillage district in Saint-Pierre, with the towers of the rebuilt cathedral and the remains of an old jetty, and the hills of Morne Orange behind.

sermon. Other people took fright. A bench was knocked over. Without looking to see where the noise came from, most of the faithful ran to the altar, shouting: "We're going to die!" A young girl fainted. At length, the priests managed to calm the terrified multitude down, but not without some trouble.

The liner *Saint-Germain* left Saint-Pierre at 6.00 p.m. on 3 May for Guadeloupe and France. The officers and crew had been blinded by the ash and had found docking extremely difficult. Ash rained down as the liner departed, and still completely covered the ship when it arrived in Guadeloupe on the following morning. Several of its 175 passengers were bereaved by the time they reached Pauillac, the outport of Bordeaux, on 17 May.

Volcanic zeal

On Sunday 4 May, Mount Pelée rested. Hopes rose again in the city, but only for a time. The wind had also changed direction, carrying any dust erupted over the northern villages, such as Ajoupa-Bouillon, Basse-Pointe, Macouba and Grande Rivière. The fury in Martinique lay elsewhere.

Hellfire and brimstone reverberated from the pulpits of Martinique on Sunday 4 May. The volcano might have forced the Gymnastic Club's excursion to the summit to be cancelled, but there was no cancelling the volcanic zeal of the priests. The wages of sin and the urgent need for repentance were the order of the day. Indeed, the calmer mood of the volcano seemed to be deferring to the mighty exhortations from the pulpits. The sky cleared, as if Mount Pelée was giving a last chance to the sinners to mend their ways. As Edith Duchâteau-Roger enthused in Le Morne-Rouge:

> In a magnificent sermon, Father Mary exhorted his parishioners to repent. "The fire and the lava are here! My brethren, the fire and the lava are here!" he exclaimed . . . "and God is holding them suspended above your heads, ready to pour them over you if you do not convert to the faith and do penance." This saintly priest, devoured by the zeal for souls, used every available means to bring the lost sheep in his flock back to God . . . All the rest of the day was not long enough to hear confessions and baptize the children that were brought to him.

It did not occur to the ingenuous Edith that neither conversion nor repentance prevented the catastrophe.

Emilie Dujon, whose feet were closer to the ground, recounted how her husband, Charles, took more practical steps.

> On Sunday 4 May, my husband went back to Grand' Case with his father. They found the plantation was . . . still covered with its thick grey shroud. Driven on by hunger and their instincts, the oxen and the sheep were snorting on the grass before they ate it, but the poor beasts were dying of thirst. And the trees were threatening to break under the weight of the ash. The morning passed calmly in town, with only the odd shower of ash . . . After mass, we all went up to each other and asked "Are you afraid?" The bravest just laughed.

A weekend for writing letters

The citizens of Saint-Pierre took advantage of the weekend to communicate with their friends and relatives and to describe their feelings on the advent of this most unexpected crisis in their lives. These letters should be read with caution. Some letters published after the catastrophe display a disconcerting ambiguity. It is hard to glean the true thoughts of the writers, always assuming that they themselves knew what their true sentiments were.

Most people just could not decide what to do, because they had no means of guessing what was likely to happen. The conclusion of the letter that Roger Portel wrote to one of his brothers illustrates some of these conflicting views: ". . . What has tomorrow in store for us? A lava flow? A shower of stones? A jet of asphyxiating gas, some cataclysmic submersion? No-one knows. The excursion that we had organized with the Gymnastic Club has been put back to a later date . . . If I have to die, my dear brother, then my last thoughts will be for you. Do not be too disconsolate."

Thus, although he saw that death was possible, Roger Portel cannot have taken the threat very seriously, otherwise he would never have considered fixing a later date for the Gymnastic Club's trip to the summit of Mount Pelée. Thus, it is hard to distinguish which view prevailed in Saint-Pierre, when such varied opinions could be expressed in a single letter.

Many also seemed to write of their prospects of imminent death as if to ward it off, rather like English ladies who always went out with an umbrella "so that it would not rain". For instance, Monsieur de Grandmaison wrote to Monsieur Reynoird in Paris on 3 May: "I telegraphed you this morning: 'Up to now, eruption without danger.' That was just to reassure you, if by mischance the catastrophe had been exaggerated in Paris. I will reply to your letters by the English packet-boat on Thursday next, if we are still alive."

Madame André Blaisemont-Ancelin, wife of one of the leading rum distillers on the island, wrote to her brother in Marseille on 4 May: "These explosions of nature are horrible, and I would really like to be far away from here . . . André laughs at me, but I can see, nonetheless, that he is full of anxiety himself and wants to look brave to cheer me up . . . André says I should leave, but I am too anxious, and I cannot make up my mind to travel alone . . . Madame Guérin assures me that her husband is not at all happy. He claims that the women and children should all leave Saint-Pierre, as if there were an epidemic in the city. But the men could never do the same, especially men like our own, with a position to keep up. That would make everyone panic."

The gloomiest letter from these days of doubts and doomwatch came from Monsieur Degennes, a teacher at the Lycée. He might have consulted his colleague, Gaston Landes, and might have been able to read the volcanic runes better than his fellows, or perhaps he just had a pessimistic turn of mind. He wrote to his family in metropolitan France on 3 May:

The area is in serious danger. We are threatened by being buried or asphyxiated at any moment. Last night . . . Mount Pelée threw out

What the published letters show and do not show

- They were all published, and in many cases received, after the catastrophe.
- They were given to newspapers or to scientists such as Professor Lacroix who were seeking information about the disaster.
- They were selected for publication when the outcome was known. Any letter describing a sense of foreboding, for example, would be much more likely to be favourably received than one claiming that there was nothing to worry about, which would clearly expose the writer to some ridicule. There would thus be an almost automatic selection of some viewpoints as opposed to others.
- The published letters often represent a hidden agenda. They were published under the effects of the shock of the eruption, and often by religious persons or organizations, who were keen to demonstrate the value of faith in the infinite wisdom of the Almighty, even when His ways seemed beyond comprehension. The letters published by Canon Lambolez clearly had this aim.
- They seem to be an extension of the *propaganda fide,* to boost the morale of the faithful after the catastrophe. They provided edifying stories, like the lives of the saints, that would somehow compensate for the terrible annihilation of the upper and middle classes of Saint-Pierre. They told of the martyrdom of the virtuous souls, who loved their families, did their duty, stood firm at their post in the face of adversity, and feared their God.
- These letters and testimonies were all written by the educated literate class. They expressed a mixture of hope and fear and a certain need to keep up appearances. But they also betray a refusal to act logically in the face of what they themselves perceived as the danger. Few seemed to contemplate leaving the city, although some took their families to safety.
- The testimonies of the thoughts and actions of the illiterate non-white class that constituted over half the population were scarcely recorded at all. It was assumed that they had to be looked after. They were neither consulted nor informed. Indeed, the mayor's poster of 6 May urged citizens to show fortitude, for the benefit of the more impressionable people of Saint-Pierre [i.e. the blacks]. On the other hand, they fell easy victim to every passing fear and rumour. They were no doubt often terrified and helpless.

What conclusions could the elite have come to, then, when they discovered that the survivors found in Saint-Pierre itself were not white?

warm [in fact, the ash was cold] heavy ash that looked for all the world like cement . . . Wet sheets are being placed over the venetian blinds at the windows (which have no glass here) to keep the ash from getting into the rooms . . . Ah! I am being sorely tried! When will I again be able to see my native Poitou [the Poitiers area in France] that is so calm and peaceful! Never perhaps. There is talk of leaving this place. But we will never have enough boats to take all the population away? And in any case we are still hoping. We are waiting until the last minute, and

The Rue Victor-Hugo, the main street of Saint-Pierre, before the eruption. Compare this scene with the picture of the same street on p. 156.

then it might be too late when we take the ultimate decision . . .

Everyone is barricaded indoors. The bravest people are dashing about the streets to try and find out what is happening . . . What is going to happen to us? I am on tenterhooks. I'm afraid of a catastrophe and yet I'd like to keep on hoping. Why do we cling to life so much? I thought I was stronger . . . We are starting to hope again. But still, my chest seems as if it were gripped in a vice . . ."

Monsieur Degennes was not alone in feeling that his chest was in a vice (a common symptom of stress). But why did he not leave? The Lycée was closed and he had no reason to wait until the last minute before departing. Edith Duchâteau-Roger, in a rare burst of practical thought, contacted her mother in Saint-Pierre: "I sent an urgent telegram to my mother: 'Take first mail-boat to Saint Lucia, take your little niece . . . send clothes by messenger. I am calm and have given myself up to Divine Providence.'"

Others used their intelligence to assess the situation in Saint-Pierre, not, it must be said, with any more success than those who followed their instincts. One of these was Eugène Berté, who wrote daily letters to his

Broken submarine cables

A succession of small earthquakes caused submarine slides and flows of debris that broke the cables around Martinique before the climax of the eruption. They occurred with increasing frequency and provided another indication of the growing volcanic crisis.

They took place at the following times:
- At 2.03 p.m. on 22 April, Martinique–Guadeloupe.
- During the afternoon of 3 May, Saint-Pierre–Roseau (Dominica).
- At 7.30 a.m. on 5 May, Fort-de-France–Puerto Plata (Dominican Republic).
- At 6.45 p.m. on 6 May, Saint-Pierre–Saint Lucia.
- At 8.02 a.m. on 8 May, Saint-Pierre–Fort-de-France.

brother, Emile, who was the doctor on the cable-repair ship, the *Pouyer Quertier*, then at anchor in Fort-de-France. On 4 May Emile had leave from the ship and went to Saint-Pierre. It was the last time that he saw his family, but the *Pouyer Quertier* was to play a leading role after the catastrophe. Eugène wrote early on 6 May:

Before I make my decision [to leave Saint-Pierre] I note the following: the nasty smell coming from the city can be explained because it has hardly rained during the night; the explosions are more frequent, but have not increased in intensity . . . there are neither flames nor ash above the crater . . . All things considered, I do not think the time has come for me to follow my panic-stricken fellow-citizens . . . I am staying here . . . I have not yet lost my sang-froid. I'll know the danger is imminent when I cannot take notes any longer.

But Mount Pelée betrayed him and did not behave according to the apparent rules of logic.

6

The first victims of the eruption
Monday 5 May 1902

Mount Pelée stayed in a tranquil mood throughout most of 4 May and 5 May. No ash fell on Saint-Pierre, apart from a heavy shower in the evening on 5 May, but the volcano continued to rumble, and the colour of its column of steam and fumes changed to bluish grey. The Rivière Blanche was the main source of attraction, and trouble, on Monday 5 May.

The floods of the Rivière Blanche increased during the night of 4–5 May. Major pulsations in its discharge seem to have happened about 2.00 a.m., between 5.00 a.m. and 8.00 a.m., and again about 10.00 a.m. on 5 May. This was no ordinary flood. Black mud carrying enormous blocks rushed down the valley and eventually flowed over the top of the flood defences erected to protect the Guérin factory. Two gendarmes, on their way northwards along the coastal route from Saint-Pierre, had still been able to cross the swollen river at 5.00 a.m., but they had then been unable to get back. They had to be rescued, shamefaced, by the steamer, *Diamant*, the next morning.

As Gaston Landes wrote in *Les Colonies* on 7 May, the explosions had been particularly severe around 5.00 a.m. on that Monday morning, and he had seen "torrents of smoke escaping from . . . the upper part of the mountain". He estimated that the floods were five times the size of the usual floods.

Word of these extraordinary events soon spread through Saint-Pierre. As *Les Antilles* reported on 7 May, about 200 astonished onlookers had gathered by 8.00 a.m. to witness the new spectacle and to assess yet another threat to the city. They were not comforted when they saw Lieutenant Maire try to cross the swollen river with several other mounted gendarmes under his command. Their bravado went unrewarded as their horses sank up to their chests in the mud and they were lucky to be able to struggle back to safety. The waters of the formidable torrent were gushing down in furious surges, carrying boulders several metres across. Where the current was relatively slack, the flow was so dense that blocks of rock, pumice and chunks of earth seemed to float on the surface. Emilie Dujon said: "It wasn't water any more, but thick, black, pasty mud that was not flowing but sliding, and carrying along gigantic rocks resembling foetuses. We soon returned to town because we could not stand the sight of it for very long." This torrent would now be called a mudflow. They are known to be highly destructive.

The destruction of the Guérin factory

The factory at the mouth of the Rivière Blanche was a sugar and rum complex owned by Dr Auguste Guérin, who was born in Case-Pilote, Martinique, on 12 May 1831. He had been a doctor in the navy, and had then run the factory before delegating responsibility to his son, Eugène, who had graduated in engineering from the prestigious Ecole Centrale in Paris.

The factory formed a large complex. Apart from the main factory and its outbuildings, it contained a forge and warehouses, as well as a fine harbour, with a flotilla of barges to transport the goods to and from the ships moored in the bay. The homes and cabins of most of the employees stood nearby. The employers lived in a style befitting their station. Dr Auguste Guérin and his wife owned a splendidly appointed mansion to the north of the factory, while his son, Eugène, and his family had a more modest mansion on the southern side of the factory. The whole area stood in the midst of a large sugar plantation, extending over the lower flanks of Mount Pelée, which provided most of the raw materials that the factory transformed into the primary products for the distilleries. Up the hill stood the smaller Isnard factory and plantation.

In May, the sugar harvesting had been completed for the season and the factory was therefore running at a much reduced rate. The arrival of the ash then brought the remaining active machinery almost to a standstill on Friday 2 May. Eugène Guérin had watched the events of the past week with some anxiety. The problems of the falling ash and dust were compounded by the weird and inexplicable changes in the volume of the Rivière Blanche, whose valley, of course, provided the most direct path from the summit of the volcano down its western shores. Eugène Guérin had sent his children to the safety of their grandparents' home in Fort-de-France, but his wife, Aline, remained with him at the factory. He had stayed on to keep the factory

The strange variations in the discharge of the Rivière Blanche

The variations in flow on the Rivière Blanche were not matched by those of any other river draining the flanks of Mount Pelée. The cause of these odd fluctuations must therefore be sought in the headwaters of the Rivière Blanche itself. Although it had hardly rained, the Rivière Blanche had been behaving very strangely since about 23 April, flooding suddenly at one moment, then almost drying up the next. Its waters were also often warm and smelly. On 26 April, for example, *Les Antilles* reported that, during the previous few days, Monsieur Isnard, who lived on his plantation in the valley of the Rivière Blanche, had witnessed an "absolutely extraordinary increase in the discharge of the river". The river was in flood from 28 April to 1 May. On 2 May, Eugène Guérin telephoned his father, Auguste, to announce that the lower reaches of the river had dried up so completely that only muddy pools remained in its bed. Then the raging torrent returned after the eruption during the night. The Rivière Blanche dried up again on the morning of 4 May, only for the waters to return with such a vengeance by nightfall that the river burst its banks and threatened to flood the Guérin factory at its mouth. These inexplicable variations added to the worries of the citizens of Saint-Pierre.

These variations were very probably a direct result of the ascent of magma within the volcano, which pushed the groundwater upwards until it reached the surface, where it was discharged in bulk into the Rivière Blanche. The continual explosions of steam would also add great volumes of water to the river. Moreover, the earth tremors caused when the magma was rising would have widened the fissures on the floor of the Etang Sec, and thus enabled even more water to drain away into the Rivière Blanche.

ticking over, with the laudable aim of keeping his workmen employed, especially at such a time of crisis when they needed everything they could earn. Nevertheless, on 5 May there were far fewer workmen than would normally have been present at the height of the sugar-cropping season.

On the morning of 5 May, the tumultuous headwaters of the Rivière Blanche were eroding more and more into the volcano, and especially into the wall separating the headwaters of the river from the southern rim of the Etang Sec. Each increase in the volume of the stream would increase its erosive power, enabling it to carry away larger and larger masses of earth and rock, which would themselves act as abrasive tools to accomplish yet more erosion. Such erosion was an accelerating process, and the Rivière Blanche had become an increasingly turbulent, muddy and abrasive torrent. Meanwhile, the explosions had been getting louder and louder for over a week, both in the Etang Sec and around the headwaters of the Rivière Blanche. Between these two explosive zones lay the most vulnerable area of all: the low, thin and fragile wall that was holding back the waters of the Etang Sec.

It could only be a matter of time before the erosion or the explosions would destroy this wall. That time came at about 12.45 p.m. on 5 May.

Dr Auguste Guérin, was at the factory with his son, Eugène, and his son's wife. They had lunch at Eugène's house, but they had taken the precaution of asking the captain to keep the steam up on their yacht, the *Le Carbet*, in the little harbour, in case the floods caused them to leave in a hurry.

The details reported in *Les Colonies* of what happened next are rather conflicting. However, the result was only too clear. The family was just making final arrangements to leave after lunch, when Monsieur Clémencin, the director of the Isnard plantation, rushed into the house shouting "Hurry up! Hurry up, or you've had it! An avalanche is coming down! Get away!" In fact, this must have been a preliminary surge of floodwater and not the main mudflow. He also warned the crowd watching the flood nearby of the imminent danger, and thereby probably saved many lives.

Dr Guérin, his son and daughter-in-law, with their heavily laden servants and their chief foreman, hurried towards the yacht, but Dr Guérin, turned back to the house, either to get his pith helmet, or to leave a message for his chief foreman. That was when the mudflow suddenly charged down the valley, swept past the Isnard factory in a front some 50 m high, and rushed down onto the group hurrying towards the yacht. Auguste Guérin had then almost reached his son's house. He had saved his life.

Then I heard a noise that I can't compare with anything else – an immense noise – like the devil on Earth! A black avalanche, beneath white smoke, an enormous mass, full of huge blocks, more than 10 m high and at least 150 m wide, was coming down the mountain with a great din. It . . . rolled up against the factory like an army of giant rams. I was rooted to the spot. My unfortunate son and his wife ran away from it towards the shore . . . All at once, the mud arrived. It passed 10 m in front of me. I felt its deathly breath. There was a great crashing sound. Everything was crushed, drowned, and submerged. My son, his wife, 30 [in fact, 25] people and huge buildings were all swept away . . . Three of those black waves came down . . . making a noise like thunder, and made the sea retreat. Under the impact of the third wave, a boat moored in the factory harbour was thrown . . . over a factory wall, killing one of my foremen, who was standing next to me . . . The desolation was indescribable. Where a prosperous factory – the work of a lifetime – had stood a moment before, there was now nothing left but an expanse of mud forming a black shroud for my son, his wife and my workmen.

It is impossible to outstrip a mudflow rushing down valley at the speed of a victorious racehorse. The only path to salvation is to scramble sideways up the nearest valley slopes. Unfortunately, Eugène Guérin's party made the fatal error of trying to race the mudflow to their yacht. They had no chance. They were swamped. And so was the yacht. The mudflow swept into the sea, sank the *Le Carbet* and another yacht, the *Le Prêcheur*, which was moored 150 m off shore. The mudflow arrived at the mouth of the Rivière Blanche with such force that it literally pushed the Guérin factory and its outbuildings right into the sea. Auguste Guérin, inadvertently, saved his own life by turning sideways away from the course of the torrent. A second mudflow quickly followed the first. Its edges lapped around Auguste Guérin's legs as he struggled southwards to safety with all the strength that a man of over 70 could muster. A third wave swept down almost at once, but Dr Guérin had reached safe ground, to the south of his son's house. He looked back. The irresistible force had removed everything in its path: soil, ash, dust, rocks, boulders, trees, shrubs, most of the Isnard establishment, his house and its outbuildings, as well as his son, his daughter-in-law and their servants. His factory, too, had vanished – except the top of the giant scales (for weighing sugar cane) and the chimney. The chimney was held up by two of its six cables, and was leaning slightly to one side, as if stupefied by its fate.

Gaston Landes was probably the only person who perceived what had caused the mudflow. The fragile southern rim of the Etang Sec had given way at last. Its waters had surged into the headwaters of the Rivière Blanche.

Deep mud covers the site of the Guérin factory at the mouth of the Rivière Blanche. The wave-eroded front of the accumulation, which is in dark shadow, is at least 50 m thick

Gaston Landes estimated that the mudflow must have hurtled down slope with a front some 30 m high at a speed of about 120 km an hour.

Mount Pelée had taken its first victims. On 6 May, *Les Colonies* listed 23 fatalities. Next day, the newspaper added to the death-toll the names of a sick child and a baby who had been drowned in a boat off shore.

Seven men who were watching events from a rowing boat off shore had a very lucky escape. The front of the mudflow, with its armoury of tree trunks, just reached them and smashed their boat to pieces. They were rescued in the nick of time, as *Les Colonies* put it, by Monsieur Raoul Rénus of Sainte-Philomène (evidently a gentleman, who was congratulated by the paper), and a fisherman, Thomas (evidently not a gentleman, who was not).

When Captain Eucher (not the commander of the yacht) saw the mudflow coming, he and the stoker, Louis Bessarion, jumped aboard the *Le Carbet* and put the pressure up. But the mudflow arrived too quickly, hurled the yacht 300 m out to sea, and sank it. Luckily, it threw the two men into the sea, where they found themselves among the barges. They survived.

The lower 2 km of the valley of the Rivière Blanche was filled with mud at least 20 m thick and 300 m wide. The flow roared into the sea and thrust the waters away from the land. The sea took two minutes to return. By then, the mudflow had formed a black delta, like a ploughed field, swelling, bubbling, puffing and whistling with little white plumes of escaping gases. The force of the muddy invasion had generated a sea wave, or tsunami, which soon rushed across the bay to astonish the inhabitants of Saint-Pierre.

The sea wave, or tsunami

The sudden arrival of masses of mud at the mouth of the Rivière Blanche generated a shock wave in the sea that quickly travelled across the Bay of Saint-Pierre. It damaged the largely abandoned houses in Fonds-Coré, smashed the nets, fishing boats and cabins of the fishermen on the shore, and

---

WARNING FOUR

The devastating mudflow that rushed down the valley of the Rivière Blanche constituted the fourth warning to the population of Saint-Pierre. Over 5 million cubic metres of materials were carried down valley in three successive waves just after mid-day on 5 May. Many other smaller mudflows followed the first lethal trio. On the morning of 6 May, for instance, they arrived every six or seven minutes, but none had the power of those that devastated the Guérin factory. All were caused when the Etang Sec emptied as the magma rose towards the surface.

The victims of the mudflow according to *Les Colonies,* on 6 May
- Monsieur Eugène Guérin, director of the factory.
- Madame Eugène Guérin, née Rollin, daughter of the former president of the General Council of Guadeloupe.
- Monsieur Joseph Du Quesne, who had been married to Mademoiselle Préville for three months.
- Mary, the English maid to Monsieur Guérin the elder.
- Marie and Cécé, maids to Monsieur Eugène Guérin.
- Labrune, sister-in-law of the former yacht owner Captain Coucoute, and her daughter, both attached to the factory.
- Madame Henri Albert Coucoute, sister of the above.
- Roland Dutréneau, captain of the yacht *Le Carbet.*
- Ti-Joseph, one of the sailors on this yacht.
- Mémé Léandre Marius, coachman to Monsieur Guérin.
- Rémy Barbe, who was alone on the yacht, *Le Prêcheur.*
- Georges Hugore, mechanic.
- Antime, apprentice weigher.
- Sarah Bourrouet. She lived in the Rue de Longchamp. Formerly maid to Monsieur Apo. She had gone to see the flood and was eight months pregnant.
- Pauline Fleurisson, a hawker, found dead on the road. Her body has been placed at the mechanical cooperage. [The following day it was reported that her body had not, in fact, been recovered].
- Julie. She had gone to see the flood. She was called the Queen of the coal workers. She usually unloaded coal at Saint-Pierre.
- Pierre Mauléon, a fisherman; Sylvestre, a cooper; Lucien Corinne and Césaire Corinne. When the avalanche arrived, these four and an unidentified person, were passing in front of the factory.

It is interesting to note the way in which the dead were described according to their perceived importance: some with their qualifications, others without even a surname. The newspaper expressed its condolences to the members of the Guérin, Rollin, Du Quesne and Préville families in their bereavement – and only to those families – as if the other victims had no relatives . . . Even in such a crisis, there were the respectable dead and the rest . . .

swept onto the Place Bertin at the hub of Saint-Pierre. The wave probably reached the city about 15 minutes after the third mudflow had completed the devastation of the Guérin factory. But curiously, neither event was timed.

As is common with such waves, the sea first retreated some 30–60 m from the shore in Saint-Pierre, exposing the landing stages, grounding the *Rubis* (the Girard company's steamer) and causing many ships at anchor to hit the bottom. Two minutes or so later, the sea came rushing back in a wave, about 4 m high, that flooded into the Place Bertin and lapped up to the houses in the lower parts of Saint-Pierre. Within the next 15 minutes many similar but smaller waves swept back and forth on the sea front at Saint-Pierre. A few small craft sank and many larger vessels hastened to reach the open sea.

This sea wave caused alarm far in excess of the danger that it ever presented to Saint-Pierre. The wave seemed to confirm some of the citizens' worst fears: that the sea was very likely to come and swamp the city, just as Galveston (Texas) had been inundated in 1900. Many ran as fast as they could to the higher parts of Saint-Pierre. It seems that the people in Saint-Pierre did not link the sea wave with the mudflow. It was seen as yet another source of terror to add to the other apparently random threats menacing the city. The extraordinary events at the Rivière Blanche had just killed 25 people. Now the sea had flooded in. Nature was obviously in turmoil. Where would the next danger spring from? Since people could not make up their minds where the greatest threats lay, they could not decide how to avoid them.

Emilie Dujon had no sooner returned from the fluvial tantrums of the Rivière Blanche than this marine crisis beset her.

We heard shrill screams. "The sea is rising! The sea is rising!" Dishevelled working-class women were fleeing in tears . . . Everyone ran out into the streets. We wondered what to do. "Wait a bit", said the men, "we ought to find out if the news is true first." So they ran to the Esnotz battery [at the north end of the town] where they could see the whole bay. They came back in a minute, with distress written all over their faces. One of them declared: "I don't know exactly what is happening,

The remains of the Esnotz battery and the northern shores of Saint-Pierre.

but there is certainly deep trouble in the sea. The Girard company's [steamer] was twice left high and dry, and twice the water came back". Some people wanted to leave for higher ground, but others said that if the sea really did rise then we would not be safe anywhere. Should we leave or should we stay put? People were running in all directions all the time. One or two coaches went by at full gallop on their way to Le Morne-Rouge . . .

Then, all of a sudden, the news spread like lightning through the city: "The lava [sic] has just swept the Guérin factory away!" So we all ran out to look at the sea. In the distance, where the factory roofs used to be, everything had disappeared . . ."

That the devastation of the Guérin factory was commonly attributed to burning lava did nothing to calm fraught nerves in Saint-Pierre. Indeed, Emilie Dujon herself was so distraught that her account of the rest of the day's events is unusually confused and inaccurate. The following day, 6 May, *Les Colonies* reported the panic in rather more sober, but politically incorrect, tones.

All these people . . . in an extreme state of panic and agitation, ran hither and thither in the streets and along the shore, and the women especially behaved as if they had just escaped from a lunatic asylum. A wave of humanity climbed up from the lower areas of the Mouillage district in the southern part of Saint-Pierre . . . People were fleeing, with all sorts of formless parcels; and mattresses were being carried in all directions . . . They wanted to escape, but they did not know where to go. Saleswomen ran about carrying parcels; one had her corsets under her arm, another was wearing odd boots. They were all wearing ridiculous outfits that would have been laughable if the panic had not broken out at such a sad moment . . ."

Yet, in the midst of this hullabaloo, people were still taking refuge in Saint-Pierre. Edith Duchâteau-Roger's Aunt Lydie, for instance, urged her niece to "hurry up and join us in Saint-Pierre, because you are in much greater danger in Le Morne-Rouge than we are here."

Others had already begun to reflect more calmly on whether they should leave Saint-Pierre. They included those who might have been fired by faith, such as the members of the Congregation of the Holy Spirit, who ran the

College–Seminary in Saint-Pierre, which was normally attended by the children of the white Catholic elite. Its acting head, Father Le Gallo, suggested that they should disperse to parishes in the sheltered south of the island. Although some of the chaplains were rather nervous at the turn of events, they wanted to stay at their posts. But most of the fathers and brothers were loath to miss any part of the increasingly grandiose volcanic spectacle. Father Le Gallo reiterated his misgivings at lunch on 5 May: "Perhaps you are wrong not to leave", he suggested. Some of his companions agreed, but one claimed that they were in no danger; and another argued that it would be "grotesque to believe in any possible wickedness on the part of Mount Pelée". Their general conclusion was that they had nothing to fear. Nevertheless, Father Bruno and Brother Gérard did eventually leave the college for Le Morne-Rouge on 7 May, and thereby lived to describe these discussions.

As soon as the news of the disaster at the Guérin factory reached the College–Seminary, about a dozen priests harnessed the mules to the break and rushed off to help. Most of the victims had been deeply buried, but fathers Bruno, Fuzier and Schott were able to give the last rites to those who had been drowned on the edge of the mudflow. There was little that they could do thereafter but return to Saint-Pierre.

There was panic and a consolation in one household that day, as Elodie Jourdain later described:

After lunch . . . there was a frightening explosion . . . We rushed to the balcony, where we had a very good view of the mountain. The crater was suddenly notched by a mighty avalanche of volcanic materials: stones, hot mud (etc.) that we took for lava at first. We saw an immense trail of white steam follow the valley of the Rivière Blanche and sweep away the Guérin factory like a wisp of straw . . . We were terrified and worried for our friends the Guérins, and for their workers. We all talked at cross purposes – and all at once. Aunt Rosette's lamentations kept popping up in the midst of the babble: "Let's leave . . . Joseph, I beg you, go and find us some shelter! I'll go mad here if this goes on much more!" But my father [Monsieur Dujon] said: "The volcano will calm down now that it has blown out its stopper [like a barrel of rum]. Just as it did in 1851."

The exodus from Fonds-Coré

On 6 May, Marius Hurard in *Les Colonies* described how Fonds-Coré, the elegant northern suburb of Saint-Pierre, had been abandoned:

> The road to Fonds-Coré . . . was covered with ash that sometimes reached 10 cm deep . . . and completely covered the tramlines. A whole legion was bustling about, with whining babies in their arms, amid a crowd that was completely carried away, shouting and begging for the mercy of heaven . . . This district used to be so pretty, but now it had a pitiful air. Most of the villas were already closed up, and people were in a frenzy of furniture removal in the rest. They were transporting their few goods and chattels, piled high and chaotically on hand carts, in a total disorder that betrayed their panic . . . We passed several such carts in this human rout, where a dozen pushing arms could turn the wheels only with the greatest difficulty in the thick layer of ash.
>
> Then we passed two men carrying a hammock suspended from a strong bamboo pole. They had been sent to remove the body of Sarah Bourrouet, one of the victims of yesterday's catastrophe, which had been left in the special police station in Fonds-Coré. A dense crowd had already surrounded the building when we got there. The sea-soaked body was stretched out on a panel on the veranda, and we watched them take it away.

Fonds-Coré had indeed been abandoned. No-one had organized an evacuation. It was every man for himself and his family. The authorities seem to have done nothing to help. Such an attitude was lax. But had *any* administration ever previously *organized* an evacuation of a population in danger from an eruption? People had often fled in terror from eruptions, but the administrators had usually regarded them as a threat to law and order, rather than hapless, helpless victims seeking succour. This was true on Etna in 1669 and in Lanzarote in 1730–36. But, in Martinique the authorities had very little time to formulate a policy, let alone implement it. Mount Pelée had been erupting since 23 April, but the real crisis had developed only since 3 May. And those who were apparently in a position to forecast what might happen next had averred that Saint-Pierre had nothing to fear. Thus, the people of Fonds-Coré naturally sought refuge in Saint-Pierre.

Fonds-Coré, the prosperous northern suburb of Saint-Pierre. Compare this tranquil scene with that depicted on p. 167.

The arrival of the Suchet

The naval cruiser *Suchet* was stationed at Fort-de-France under Commander Pierre Le Bris. However, since 12 April the *Suchet* had been absent from the capital on exercises with two other naval vessels on the nearby French island of Guadeloupe. Commander Le Bris had been notified on 3 May about the eruption of Mount Pelée, but the vessel's return to Martinique was unrelated to the growing volcanic crisis. At that time, there was indeed no reason to believe that the ship would ever be involved in these events. The commander waited in Guadeloupe until the transatlantic liner, the *Saint-Germain*, arrived on 4 May, because he wanted to send seven convalescent members of the crew back to France. Only then did the *Suchet* depart for Fort-de-France, where it arrived at daybreak on 5 May. Most of the actors in the tragedy were now in place. Only a few vessels and a nuée ardente were missing.

Le Bris took the vessel directly into a dock to clean the hull. The *Suchet* had to prepare for departure to Havana on 10 May, where it was scheduled to arrive on 15 May for the celebrations marking the inauguration of the first president of the new Cuban Republic, Tomás Estrada Palma, on 20 May.

At 2.00 p.m. on 5 May, the commander received two successive messages from Governor Mouttet, asking to be taken to Saint-Pierre as soon as possible. Whereupon, Commander Le Bris went to explain that his instructions did not allow him to put himself at the disposition of any governor by a simple requisition: he needed to know the reason.

The governor was keen to act in the face of the new crisis. He described

The 3430 tonne cruiser, Suchet, *was a twin-screw, twin-mast and twin-funel vessel capable of 20 knots, launched in 1893 at Toulon, the base of the French Mediterranean Fleet.*

the recent events to the commander, and said that he was needed in Saint-Pierre, but that he could not reach the city because the Girard company's steamer had been thrown onto the shore by a tidal wave. Governor Mouttet asked the commander to take him and added that the *Suchet* might well prove useful if any people needed to be rescued. Commander Le Bris therefore placed himself entirely at the governor's disposal.

Abbé Parel asked if he could come along too, but was politely refused on the grounds that the sight of a high-ranking priest on the cruiser might have increased the panic, and led people to believe that the end was nigh.

Governor Mouttet's second visit to Saint-Pierre

The *Suchet* left for Saint-Pierre at 5.00 p.m. The ship moored off the city to collect Amédée Knight, the senator for Martinique, and Rodolphe Fouché, the mayor of Saint-Pierre. The commander then continued to Le Prêcheur, where he was distressed to see the villagers in such a parlous state.

> They were almost constantly enveloped in the cloud of ash that was falling in great quantities and depriving them of light. They also felt at serious risk of being buried if a mudflow forced the river to burst its banks, or of being swamped by the sea if there was another tidal wave . . . The villagers needed strong support if they were not to succumb to total panic. They were almost completely deprived of food and

Commander Le Bris of the *Suchet*

Pierre Ange Marie Le Bris was born on 21 May 1856 at Saint-Guen (Côtes-du Nord, Bretagne). He was the great nephew of Admiral Léonard Charner and naturally he took up a naval career, entering the Ecole Navale in October 1876. He became a second lieutenant on 29 January 1879 and saw war service first in Tunisia and then from 1880 to 1882 in Cochin China (present-day Vietnam), where he distinguished himself at Hanoi. In 1884 he was transferred to the Indian Ocean and played a prominent role in the operations in Madagascar. In 1886, he became Chevalier de la Légion d'Honneur. In 1887 he attended the submarine defence school at Toulon and then the torpedo school in Paris. He played several varied roles on the west coast of Africa from 1889 to 1894 and was officially congratulated for his part in the operations against Dahomey. Pierre Le Bris married Jeanne Frédérique Pillat on 12 May 1894. In the same year, he joined the Mediterranean squadron as a torpedo instructor, and was promoted to the rank of Commander on 1 July 1897.

He took command of the *Suchet* in the Atlantic Naval Division in 1900. He most successfully defended French interests during the civil strife in Colombia and Venezuela and was officially congratulated by the foreign minister. On 24 July 1901, Commander Pierre Le Bris was designated as president of a meteorological commission set up to establish a weather station in Fort-de-France. It was while the *Suchet* was based at Martinique that the commander played his most direct humanitarian role after the eruption of the Mount Pelée. He was rewarded with promotion to the rank of Captain on 3 July 1902, and was made an Officier de la Légion d'Honneur on 25 July 1902.

In 1902, Pierre Le Bris was well on the way to a brilliant naval and diplomatic career. He became a rear-admiral in 1908, and a vice-admiral in January 1913. He took a leading part in organizing French naval re-armament and in the negotiations for sharing naval defence with the UK in the face of the increasing German threat. He then successfully directed various administrative operations during the First World War. He retired from active service in February 1919, covered with honours and decorations, and he died in Paris on 14 February 1940.

water, and had been separated from Saint-Pierre by rivers of burning [cool, in fact] mud . . . The governor himself wanted to comfort and sustain this spirited and courageous population and wanted to assure them that he would supply the means to evacuate the village, if they were seriously threatened. He went ashore with the senator and other officials and spent some time with these good people.

In fact, an evacuation from Le Prêcheur would have presented serious problems. The only effective means of escape from the village was by sea, which had just unleashed an inexplicable wave. In Le Prêcheur, intelligent

Pierre Le Bris, Commander of the Suchet. *The photograph was taken later in his distinguished career, when he had become a rear-admiral.*

leadership from the mayor, Monsieur Grelet, and the priest, Abbé Desprez, had just managed to keep the people calm. Governor Mouttet's second visit gave their persuasive talents a much welcome boost.

Monsieur Mouttet then asked to be taken to Saint-Pierre, where he wanted to disembark along with Senator Knight. Soon after the *Suchet* set off, however, a blinding shower of ash enveloped the ship.

79

I warned the governor that . . . I would have to make for Fort-de-France. He insisted quite vigorously that I should do as he wished, but I had to make him understand that I was the sole judge of what could be done on board my ship. However, we left the densest part of the ash cloud after we had passed Saint-Pierre and I could see the lights of the city. I was thus able to go back and tie up where the liners moored and disembark the governor and the senator. I then made for Fort-de-France, not wishing to spend the night needlessly in Saint-Pierre.

Thus, contrary to most reports, the governor undoubtedly passed the night of 5–6 May in Saint-Pierre. Once again, he was taking practical steps to assess what exactly was happening. He was not neglecting his duties, as was to be claimed so often later. In his two altercations with Commander Le Bris on 5 May, it was the governor who insisted on going to Saint-Pierre.

In Saint-Pierre on the evening of 5 May, the talk of the town was the mudflow in the Rivière Blanche and the prospects for other disasters to come. Emilie Dujon confessed that they had watched the night approach with some trepidation. Then the electricity supply failed. The whole city was plunged into darkness: ash and dust had clogged the electrical generators.

7

A message from the mayor
Tuesday 6 May 1902

A turbulent night

The citizens of Saint-Pierre and the refugees from the threatened north were far too worried to enjoy much sleep in the atmosphere of panic and anxiety that reigned during the pitch-dark and turbulent night of 5–6 May.

In the early hours of 6 May, lightning flashed and terrible rumblings issued from the volcano. There was indescribable commotion and a nasty smell of sulphur in every street. People were bustling about with parcels on their heads and shouting: "Save yourselves! The river has burst its banks!" In the Rue Victor-Hugo, people were at every window trying to find out what was happening, and all the Mouillage district thronged with homeless folk. Many people left their homes with torches and rushed out to see what new perils could now be threatening their lives. There was an extraordinary dance of lanterns everywhere, and snippets of half-heard, half-understood shouts and whispers added to the general alarm and bewilderment. Of course, the tales were false alarms or rumours spread by jokers and people with more dubious motives. There was even talk that some citizens had returned home to discover that they had been burgled. The mayor, Rodolphe Fouché, took steps to ensure that there would be no repetition of such events.

Throughout Tuesday, smaller mudflows, again generated by explosions near the Etang Sec, still followed their devastating predecessors down the Rivière Blanche. They offered a diverting and terrifying show to hundreds of spectators, who had come out along the coast road from Saint-Pierre.

Although the governor had advised Abbé Parel not to accompany him on the excursion of the *Suchet* on 5 May, the vicar general consoled himself the following morning with an independent trip with an assistant, Abbé Le

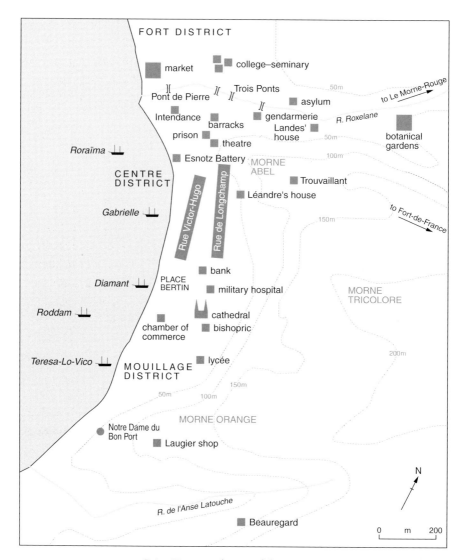

Saint-Pierre on the eve of the eruption.

Breton. The priests took the 8.00 a.m. steamer from Fort-de-France to
Saint-Pierre and made straight for the Rivière Blanche.

> The river was now a raging torrent, crashing and rolling along boulders,
> tree-trunks and steaming mud. With its plume of steam, it could have
> been taken for a locomotive rushing into the sea at full speed. I caught
> a glimpse of the sides of the crater . . . Two pitons on either side formed
> a deep valley . . . from which the muddy waves zig-zagged out.

Abbé Parel had observed the new gash in the rim of the Etang Sec, which had formed the previous day. It led from the Etang Sec directly to the headwaters of the Rivière Blanche, and was pointing straight at Saint-Pierre. Even more menacingly, the steam now rising from the Rivière Blanche showed that its waters were much warmer than before. The hot magma could not now be far beneath the crater.

Eugène Berté described the spectacle to his brother, Emile, in a letter written at 11.00 a.m. on 6 May:

> I went up to Monsieur Isnard's [plantation] and saw the mud coming down. You heard an explosion in the mountain, then a trail of white fumes ran out at lightning speed . . . You lost sight of it for a while, then, suddenly the smoking mud surged in front of you and sped on into the sea . . . Both the valley and the gorge of the Rivière Blanche have been filled up . . . The sea of mud is a hideous thing . . . You come back from these desolate places . . . preoccupied. The phenomenon is beautiful and sublime, because it is so grand, but it is so sad as well.

A change in activity

During the late morning of 6 May, the nature of Mount Pelée's activity changed. Much more ash blackened the billowing columns, which were no longer rising so high into the sky. Eugène Berté observed that the columns:

> . . . were clearly lit up by the fire inside . . . The effect is arresting and captures your imagination in spite of yourself. If I had no children, I would have gone up on a mule with a few friends to witness the marvellous spectacle that must be going on at the bottom of that furnace. Unfortunately, I can only watch it from afar. The population is panic stricken, the women especially . . .

Almost as an aside, Eugène Berté had described the most menacing event of the eruption so far: "The fumes were clearly lit up by the fire inside." The glow betrayed the awesome truth. The magma had reached the crater. Mount Pelée had issued its most explicit threat and was erupting molten rock for the first time since 1600. The warning passed almost unnoticed and no-one realized its implications. A more violent eruptive spasm was now inevitable.

At the time, Gaston Landes and Monsieur Sainte-Luce were observing the eruption through the telescope at the Chamber of Commerce. They saw Mount Pelée throwing huge blocks from the crater. That evening, the blocks glowed in graceful curves against the night sky as they soared from the crater and fell back onto the flanks of the volcano.

The incandescent lava and the denser columns of ash showed that the eruption had moved into a more powerful register. But many observers believed that exactly the opposite had happened. As Roger Arnoux later commented, "when the column of fumes became smaller, many assumed that the eruption was waning".

In Saint-Pierre, political and anti-religious feelings added to the turmoil. The ladies were horrified to hear louts parading in the streets, shouting such heresies as "Send the Virgin back to the stable", and other more controversial slogans that ladies should not hear. The only consolation for right-thinking people was that these vandals could not have been natives of Saint-Pierre. They must be homeless refugees, tainted by republicanism, from the wilder slopes of the volcano. No doubt they were supporters of Lagrosillière . . .

WARNING FIVE

The magma reached the surface on the morning of 6 May. The waters and the mud surging down the Rivière Blanche became hot. Then, glowing rocks were thrown from the crater, which could be seen from Saint-Pierre. The erupting column became denser and blacker. That night, the base of the column glowed.

Governor Mouttet returns again to Le Prêcheur

On the morning of 6 May, Governor Mouttet took the *Topaze* from Saint-Pierre and returned to the focus of his worries, the village of Le Prêcheur. Acting upon his previous concerns, he had already sent some 6000 kg of beans, salted cod and meat to sustain the people, which had been provided at a reduced price by the suppliers in Saint-Pierre. The mayor, Monsieur Grelet, had even issued food coupons to ensure that the rations were fairly distributed. However, when the barge arrived, many villagers tried to help themselves to the food, and it took some time to restore order. Morale was now even lower in the village. The Rivière du Prêcheur had become a roaring torrent and the Rivière Blanche was still cutting the village off from the apparent safety of Saint-Pierre. Above the village, ash, 10 cm or more thick, was blanketing every field within sight. The only way to escape seemed to be by sea. And there, just off shore, was the *Topaze*, which was going to return to Saint-Pierre. When the governor came back on board, so many people piled onto the little steamer to take refuge in Saint-Pierre that it had to make a hurried getaway to avoid being swamped. The hasty departure of the *Topaze* only increased the anxiety and desperation of those left behind in Le Prêcheur, who now faced another night of torment, in complete isolation.

A prophecy

Emilie Dujon was spending the day at her parents' home in Saint-Pierre. It was to be her last. Unlike many of her friends, she did not believe that the danger had been dissipated when the volcano had dispatched its mudflow:

> We could hear the dull explosions from the volcano all the time . . .
> Then something happened that left a strong impression upon me. I was dying of fright, but my young brother . . . laughed at my fears, which he thought were exaggerated. As I was playing, he wrote with his finger on the ash-covered piano the prophetic words from Belshazzar's feast, forecasting the end of the Babylonian empire: "*Mene, mene, tekel, upharsin.*" ["God hath numbered thy kingdom, and finished it; Thou art weighed in the balances, and art found wanting; Thy kingdom is divided and given to the Medes and the Persians." (Daniel 5: 25–8)] . . . He realized that I was unhappy about it, but he said: "You need not be so frightened; it won't make you die!" The poor child did not suspect that he was pronouncing his own death sentence . . .

In Le Morne-Rouge, total panic continued to reign in the Convent of the Délivrande. As Edith Duchâteau-Roger wrote:

> I was in the chapel when I heard shouts of terror and I saw a band of children rushing to me crying "Sister, the sea has flooded into Saint-Pierre; it's all over; we are going to die!". The poor little ones threw themselves onto their knees, begging the divine master to save them.

The convent stood over 400 m above sea level. But who was to say how much more the laws of nature might be perverted? Prayer was deemed as good a solution as any, especially at the convent.

The northern part of Saint-Pierre, with the lighthouse in Place Bertin on the left, the Rue Victor-Hugo running diagonally across the centre and Mount Pelée on the horizon.

A chance to leave Saint-Pierre

As the eruption continued, more and more people started to think about leaving Saint-Pierre. But it was still far from easy to come to a decision. Logic often played a minor role in the process. People left Saint-Pierre for the flimsiest of reasons, if the departures of the Dujon, Décomis, and Marry families were anything to go by. Gut reaction and chance played a greater part than any logical analysis of the situation, but no-one had the facts nor the knowledge to come to a rational decision anyway. After the destruction of the Guérin factory, Elodie Jourdain's Aunt Rosette had begged her brother to find them all shelter. The following day the opportunity arose. By chance, Joseph Marry met Louis Gouyé, the manager of the Beauregard plantation. It turned out that its owners had left, and the place was empty and available. It was a large wooden house, up on the hill, 2.5 km from the southern end of Saint-Pierre. Emilie Dujon's younger brother, Gaston Décomis, stayed behind in Saint-Pierre, but most members of the Dujon, Décomis and Marry families, together with an unknown number of servants, decided to take the

A poster from the Mayor

Dear Fellow Citizens

A new calamity has just stricken our unfortunate land, which has already been sorely tested.

The communes of Saint-Pierre and Le Prêcheur have been most affected by the volcanic eruption of Mount Pelée.

This event has thrown the whole island into consternation.

Those people living near the mountain on the hills above Saint-Pierre, those from the area near the Rivière Blanche and those from Sainte-Philomène are without food and shelter. The invaluable intervention of the governor and the highest authorities has helped the municipal administration to provide initial food supplies wherever possible. Lodgings have been provided for these deserving refugees, these labourers on the land, whose produce has always fed Saint-Pierre, but who have now seen the fruits of all their hard work buried under the ash within a single night.

In these painful circumstances, you have a duty, my dear fellow citizens, to show these victims all the generosity and solicitude that fills your hearts. May you not remain indifferent to their misfortunes, and may your well known feelings of solidarity find yet another opportunity to show themselves here.

The calm and wisdom that you have demonstrated during these past few days of anguish lead us to hope that you will not remain deaf to our appeal.

We are in agreement with His Excellency the Governor, whose devotion to duty is always equal to the occasion, and whom we accompanied yesterday to Sainte-Philomène and Le Prêcheur. We are confident that we can assure you that, in view of the immense valleys that separate us from the craters, no immediate danger is to be feared, and that the lava will not reach the city, and that events will be restricted to those places that have already been afflicted.

Do not, therefore, yield to groundless panic. Do not be discouraged. Please let us urge you to redouble your efforts, as you did in 1890 and 1891. Please resume your normal occupations in order to give the courage and strength necessary to the impressionable people in and around Saint-Pierre in this hour of public calamity,

The mayor, R. Fouché

chance. As Emilie Dujon explained, "they would be safer up there away from the panic and any possible earthquakes in the city". But it was just a little worrying that they could hear the volcano's incessant roaring even more distinctly. "It sounded like an enormous bubbling boiler in ferment".

Removal, they thought, was only a short-term measure. As young Elodie Jourdain wrote, "All we had to do was take everything needed for camping in the house: mattresses, kitchen utensils, and a few plates . . . The adults set up our rudimentary accommodation in the long gallery that they had made into a dormitory." And far from being distracted by the crisis, Elodie soon picked out some trees worth climbing; the older girls were delighted to find some cases full of old clothes that would be marvellous to use for dressing up.

Faced with these irrational departures and the mounting anxiety of the population, Rodolphe Fouché, the Mayor of Saint-Pierre, prepared a poster and had it distributed to calm the fraught nerves of his fellow citizens. He seems to have drafted the poster in haste, for it is awkwardly written and not entirely clear and precise. It was displayed on all the prominent walls in the city during the evening. He probably issued it on his own initiative, perhaps after some discussion with, say, Gaston Landes about the likely development of the eruption. The mayor's poster has sometimes been presented as part of the plot of calculated blandishments to hide the real dangers from the citizens of Saint-Pierre, so that they would remain calm, obey the law, and stay in the city until the second round of the elections. If plot there was, the governor played little direct part in it. He might possibly have known of its contents, although there is no evidence of this. He could scarcely have been involved in drafting the poster, because he spent much of the day in Le Prêcheur before he returned on the *Topaze* to Fort-de-France that evening.

This poster was itself a tragedy. It stressed that safe refuges had been provided in Saint-Pierre for those in danger. No lava flows could reach the city for some time, given the 7 km between it and the volcano; and they would have to be of huge volume to cross two large valleys and swamp Saint-Pierre. On all known scientific grounds, Saint-Pierre was safe from lava flows. But the city was in grave danger from what science did not then know.

Meanwhile, in Fort-de-France, Commander Le Bris was busy preparing for the departure of the *Suchet* for Havana on 10 May. Problems had arisen with the boilers: a condenser was producing salty water, several joints in the steam pipes were leaking, and some munitions of doubtful value were to be removed from the ship on the morning of 8 May. Such banal problems were to have vital consequences.

The night of 6–7 May was fairly calm and gave a little respite for Saint-Pierre. The columns of ash were not rising as high above the crater. By the evening, too, the smoking mudflows in the Rivière Blanche were less powerful and were no longer reaching the sea. But, on the other hand, the change in wind direction had showered still greater amounts of ash over the north and northeast of the island. But, on the whole, prospects looked rather brighter at nightfall than they had seemed at dawn.

Rumours and misconceptions circulating in Saint-Pierre

- The danger of earthquakes has been brushed aside by the eruption.
  - No evidence for this.
- The volcano has burst its stopper with the eruption of the mudflow.
  - The eruption was becoming increasingly powerful.
- The lava flows are a threat but they will not reach Saint-Pierre.
  - Mount Pelée had erupted no lava flows for 14 000 years, but even if they had erupted they would have presented little danger to Saint-Pierre.
- The mudflow in the Rivière Blanche had been a torrent of lava.
  - False, but the rumour increased fears that lava could reach Saint-Pierre and travel as fast as the mudflow.
- Saint-Pierre is built on solid rock and has less to fear from an earthquake than Fort-de-France.
  - Probably basically sound, but a major earthquake was not to be expected in relation to an eruption.
- When the eruptive column did not soar so high on 6 May, many thought that the eruption was waning.
  - The eruption was becoming more dangerous because the magma had reached the surface; the column was denser because more ash was erupting.
- The boa constrictor had escaped from the botanical gardens.
  - If this was correct, the boa had acted wisely.
- All the animals and birds that could escape, such as the cats, the rats, and the snakes, had already done so.
  - There is no evidence to confirm or deny this.
- It was asserted at various times that Fonds-Coré had disappeared; that the Guérin factory had collapsed under a mass of rocks and lava; that the sea had already invaded the Fort area, the Mouillage district and the market.
  - Apart from the disappearance of the Guérin factory, all these tales were not only   false, but could easily be verified by those in Saint-Pierre.
- The sea presented a greater danger than the volcano, especially after the tsunami on 5 May.
  - There was no evidence that the sea would soon threaten Saint-Pierre.

8

"What better place to be . . ."
Wednesday 7 May 1902

Mount Pelée roared like a rampant lion throughout 7 May, punctuating its monotonous background noise with muffled cannonades that hurled huge blocks high into the air. Monsieur Sainte-Luce later told Professor Lacroix that the erupting columns gushing from the crater had turned still darker after 8.00 a.m. Ash rained down as far away as Le Carbet.

Abbé Parel returns to Sainte-Philomène and Le Prêcheur

Abbé Parel did not go home to Fort-de-France on 6 May, but took a room at the College–Seminary in Saint-Pierre so that he could be closer to the areas in need. He was not rewarded with a good night's rest.

> Loud explosions kept me awake . . . from 4.00 a.m. . . . . Two red craters [with molten lava from the magma] were exposed for half an hour, spitting out flames like blast furnaces. I noticed four sorts of noise: first the claps of thunder that came some 20 seconds after the lightning; then, the dull and powerful explosions from the volcano, as if several cannons had been fired at the same time; the third noise was the continuous roar from the crater; and finally, like the bass note of this sinister music, there was the solemn agitation of the surging, rushing waters . . . as some 30 ravines all burst their banks at once.
>
> When the daylight lit up the bay, a cry of stupefaction arose. As far as the eye could see, the water was covered with floating islets, the opulent remains of fields and forests, gigantic tree-trunks, and wrecks of all kinds that the raging torrents had discharged.
>
> I wanted to go to Sainte-Philomène and Le Prêcheur with Father

Ackerman and Father Fuzier on 7 May . . . We had to take a small boat and make our way through all the wreckage, which itself was not without its dangers. The dirty black waters [of the rivers] were as heavy as molten lead where . . . they tumbled into the sea.

I wanted to bring help to both parish priests and encourage the people in their misfortune. I found both men in their churches, exhausted. but still full of energy and courage, and busy preparing their flocks, as if for a great sacrifice. Half the people [in fact, much less] had already taken refuge in Saint-Pierre, where the governor had made the barracks and the schools available to them.

I resisted their pressing invitations to stay with them because I believed it my duty [as the chief ecclesiastical official left in the diocese] to return to Fort-de-France for Ascension Day the following day. I promised to come back the following evening, or on Friday morning at the latest. I disembarked from the little boat that had brought me back from Le Prêcheur just in time to catch the steamer that left Saint-Pierre for Fort-de-France at half past two. It was crowded with people [perhaps as many as 150 people], who were leaving the city . . .

Cable repairs

When the submarine cable between Fort-de-France and Puerto Plata in the Dominican Republic was cut on 5 May, the most direct link between Martinique and metropolitan France had been severed. Obviously, the cable had to be repaired as quickly as possible. The engineers had located the break off Saint-Pierre, and the cable-repair ship, *Pouyer Quertier*, was sent out to grapple on the sea bed for the two broken ends and bring them to the surface to be joined up again. The ship's doctor, Emile Berté, who was to recount the vessel's subsequent unexpected adventures, described his feelings as nature played still more tricks:

We were not very much at ease that day. The coast was invisible behind a thick layer of ash that penetrated everywhere, suffocating everyone, and preventing us from clearly fixing any points on the horizon [to determine their position accurately]. We were standing some 8 [nautical] miles off the coast . . .

At noon . . . the commander eventually determined exactly where the cable was. A buoy was moored there to mark the place . . . but it immediately began to sink . . . [The commander replaced it with the largest buoy on board], but it, too, had hardly been moored when it vanished into a whirlpool. A very strong current was dragging the ship to the north. Such a current was absolutely unknown in these parts, and quite inexplicable.

Governor Mouttet appoints a scientific commission

On his return to Fort-de-France on 6 May, Governor Mouttet was worried more than ever about the course of events. Recalling the precedent set by his predecessor in 1851, he decided to take more expert advice and try to calm the growing anxiety in Saint-Pierre. At 10.00 a.m. on 7 May, he set up a scientific commission to analyze the eruption. He nominated Lieutenant-Colonel Gerbault of the Artillery, who was to be the president, Monsieur Mirville (pharmacist to the colonial troops at the military hospital in Fort-de-France), Monsieur Léonce (a colonial civil engineer), and Monsieur Doze and Monsieur Landes, who were both teachers of natural science at the Lycée in Saint-Pierre, and who had shown an informed interest in the volcanic crisis. None was an expert on volcanoes or volcanic eruptions. As in 1851, no such experts were available on the island, and few, if any, were to be found within a radius of several thousand kilometres. Within 30 hours, four of the five nominees were dead.

An interview with Monsieur Landes

Just as Governor Mouttet appointed his scientific commission, *Les Colonies* published an interview with Monsieur Landes, "the distinguished teacher at the Lycée". It has brought him considerable, and undeserved, opprobrium.

He correctly analyzed the causes of the terrible mudflow that had destroyed the Guérin factory: "The valley of the Rivière Blanche had received the contents of the Etang Sec, when the wall retaining the waters had given way". He was at pains to rectify the rumour common in Saint-Pierre that a lava flow had caused the devastation. It had been caused, he said, "by an avalanche rather than by a muddy lava flow". However, the terms he used were not too clear, and neither do they match those in current usage, where a clear distinction is made between mudflows (which had occurred), avalanches (which had not occurred) and lava flows (which are entirely different). Nevertheless, Gaston Landes could hardly be blamed for trying.

He recommended, in particular, "that people should leave the valley bottoms and go and live on higher ground, and thereby avoid being submerged by muddy lava as Pompeii and Herculaneum had been. Vesuvius had killed relatively few people. Pompeii had been evacuated in time". These erroneous views about muddy lava and evacuation at Pompeii were very widely held in those days, and Monsieur Landes, again, can scarcely be blamed for not knowing better than the contemporary experts.

The real sting of the interview was in its tail. The last three lines of the report read: "Conclusion: Mount Pelée offers no more danger to the inhabitants of Saint-Pierre than Vesuvius does to those of Naples".

Experts, armed with decades of research and hindsight, have pilloried Gaston Landes for expressing this comforting view ever since. He was not an expert, but a conscientious teacher who was doing his best. In any case, it is doubtful if any expert at the time would have come to radically different conclusions. Indeed, beside the interview with Monsieur Landes, *Les Colonies* published an article entitled "Volcanoes", which reflected the theories and speculations current at the time, which the subsequent progress of volcanology has consigned to oblivion.

In fact, it is unlikely that Gaston Landes actually wrote that conclusion, which was most probably added by Marius Hurard, the editor of *Les Colonies*, to bring the interview to a striking end. If that was Monsieur Hurard's aim, he certainly succeeded, for it was perhaps one of the most controversial sentences that he wrote in a controversial career. In the same edition, he described how the Girard company's steamers were always full of people leaving Saint-Pierre. The numbers of passengers to Fort-de-France had risen during the previous three days from about 80 per day to about 300 per day. He feigned not to understand this panic and asked his readers a rhetorical question: "Was there a better place to be than in Saint-Pierre"? In fact, the inhabitants had no means of knowing what was in store for them, and they were not granted much time to reflect and to reply.

An alternative view from the Orsolina

Another ill informed comparison with Vesuvius on 7 May produced a quite different conclusion. The Neapolitan barque, *Orsolina*, was lying at anchor in the bay, loading sugar for Le Havre. When Captain Leboffe saw the eruption, he told the shippers that he had decided to leave the city at once while the going was good, although he had only half the sugar on board.

The shippers stressed that Mount Pelée had erupted ash before without danger to vessels and that, if he left then, he would not get his clearance papers and would thus be liable for arrest when he reached Le Havre. The captain retorted that, if ever he saw Vesuvius looking like Mount Pelée, then he'd get out of Naples at once. He preferred to take his chance with the metropolitan French authorities rather than with the volcano in their colony. Two customs officers boarded the *Orsolina* to stop her leaving, but Captain Leboffe was adamant. In the nick of time, the customs men had to hail a passing boat to return to the quay as the *Orsolina* sailed away.

Events were to prove that the captain was right for the wrong reasons. During the past 1800 years, Vesuvius had never destroyed Naples, nor sunk any boats in the harbour. He was in no position to know that nuées ardentes had probably destroyed shipping in Naples harbour in AD 79; nor was he in a position to guess the role of nuées ardentes at Mount Pelée.

Lieutenant Hébert visits the Fort market

One of the very rare accounts describing the feelings and opinions of the poorer and more ordinary people in Saint-Pierre came from the pen of Lieutenant Georges Hébert, of the *Suchet*. On 7 May, the vessel was moored at Fort-de-France, and he took advantage of some leave to go to Saint-Pierre, pick up the local gossip, and find out how people were reacting.

We . . . had hardly landed in Saint-Pierre when I realized that a great sadness reigned in the city. I at once felt a malaise and anguish; the atmosphere was stifling; and a fine ash was falling and infiltrating everywhere . . . I went straight to the Fort market . . . It was a kind of special women's forum where you could put your finger on the source of all that was being said, thought and discussed – especially if, like me, you knew the Créole language well enough. There were more than a

A local market in Martinique. The Fort market in Saint-Pierre would have been similar but much larger, and was protected by a hurricane-proof iron roof.

thousand women . . . but there was none of the laughter, the joyful banter, nor the gay exuberance of former times. It was almost silent under the immense iron roof of the building. They were serious and anxious. People were afraid, without knowing exactly what they were afraid of . . . A calamity is sure to happen; the volcano is "boiling" more and more; "it is going to kill us all".

I tried to persuade a nice acquaintance from the happy days of the last carnival – I was young at that time – to take refuge at Fort-de-France. But she replied firmly, with a bitter smile: "No, I'm not leaving because I want to die here with my mother" . . . I just caught the last boat of the day for Fort-de-France.

The first nuées ardentes

During the morning, the first nuées ardentes emerged from the Etang Sec and swept half way down the Rivière Blanche. These scorching hot clouds of fragments and steam were small, weak, unheralded, unprepossessing, unrecognized and unacknowledged. Brother Gérard of the Congregation of the Holy Spirit noticed the very first nuée ardente at about 10.30 a.m.: "We saw a big cloud detach itself from the summit and descend towards Fonds-Coré, but it stopped in mid-slope . . . The same thing happened at hourly intervals thereafter, and they always halted at the same spot".

The nuées ardentes also attracted the attention of Monsieur Sainte-Luce:

At 11.45 a.m., I looked up at the volcano as I was coming back from Fonds-Coré. Suddenly the column of ash and steam lowered and disappeared altogether for . . . about 2 or 3 seconds. Then it soared higher than ever, and its base seemed to be yellow where it came out of the volcano. For an instant, a train of white steam set off . . . obliquely down towards Saint-Pierre, but then it suddenly turned down the valley of the Rivière Blanche towards the sea.

Mount Pelée was ejecting the nuées ardentes in a single blast, like a long puff of smoke without a tail. They were over in a couple of minutes. They careered down the valley of the Rivière Blanche at great speed, until they ran out of power and stopped before they reached the sea.

WARNING SIX: THE FIRST NUÉES ARDENTES

The eruption of the weak nuées ardentes was a very serious warning indeed for everyone living less than about 10 km from the volcano. They were much more threatening than lava flows, because they could travel ten times as fast and could cover a much larger area within minutes. Relatively small explosions generated the first nuées, and they had not enough impetus to reach the sea. The southern rim of the Etang Sec had been gashed open on 5 May and had left an open notch facing southwards. This was where the pressures confining the magma were lowest. If more gas exploded from the magma with a greater blast, then the nuées ardentes would not be constrained and turned westwards by the Rivière Blanche valley. They would shoot southwards, straight from the notch, and at a much greater speed. Saint-Pierre lay due south, 7 km away, directly in their path. A really powerful nuée ardente could reach the city. But no scientist had ever studied such things. The first opportunity was not far away.

A rival eruption

At about 2.00 p.m. on 7 May, loud rumblings and a sea wave coming from the south revealed a fantastic complication to the story that few publishers would allow a writer to include in a thriller. Like Emilie Dujon, most people were at a loss to explain the noise:

> It seemed to come from the south, rather than from Mount Pelée. We thought at first that it was an artillery salvo from Fort-de-France. Then, as the source of the noise seemed to change, we imagined that two Venezuelan vessels were fighting a short distance from the shore. Then, after two hours of indecision, we ended up acknowledging that these so-called cannon shots must be coming from the volcano.

Emilie Dujon was mistaken. For once Mount Pelée was not guilty. The Soufrière of Saint Vincent, 120 km to the south, had suddenly erupted at about 2.00 p.m. It had killed 1565 people, far more than Mount Pelée had managed to exterminate so far.

Anguish in Saint-Pierre

The news of this additional peril gradually filtered through Saint-Pierre and it was not the sort of information to reassure the nervous. All manner of natural catastrophes seemed to be surrounding the colony. Tension and anxiety were causing a certain amount of mindless panic. People were dashing hither and thither in a vain quest for news, or for someone – for anyone – to disprove their worst fears.

An article in *Les Colonies* did nothing to allay them when it declared (rightly) that the base of Morne Lacroix, the highest point of Mount Pelée, had been undermined and (wrongly) that it was likely to cause an earthquake when it collapsed. Anguish was heightened further when, after several days of rumours unfulfilled, both the Rivière des Pères and the Rivière de Roxelane finally burst their banks and start flooding into some northern parts of the city. The crisis must really have been reaching a climax when even the rumours were coming true.

Reports – never confirmed and quite probably wrong – suggested that Gaston Landes had telephoned that afternoon to the governor in Fort-de-France, saying that he now believed that the eruption had become more serious than he had previously thought.

At about the same time, the Mayor of Saint-Pierre, Rodolphe Fouché, also telephoned Governor Mouttet describing the situation in the city. The eruptions had become more violent, with many explosions, incessant rumblings, and a tall column of smoke. Terror was increasing and many people had taken refuge in the barracks; nearly all the stores were closed; all commerce had stopped; and people were suffering great hardship. All this, plus the floods, plus the eruption in Saint Vincent had brought Saint-Pierre to the brink of disorder. The police might soon be unable to cope. Hence, the mayor asked the governor for a detachment of 30 colonial infantrymen to help distribute food and to patrol the streets to prevent any increase in the turmoil. Governor Mouttet readily agreed. The troops were to be despatched the following morning.

Governor Mouttet moves to Saint-Pierre

The mayor's request seems to have determined Governor Mouttet's decision to go and spend the night in Saint-Pierre. His aim can only have been to calm the citizens, to show that their terror was unjustified, and to demonstrate his confidence in their future by joining them in their hour of need. But he was making more than a suggestion that Saint-Pierre was safe. He was making a courageous gesture of solidarity. For the first time, the governor delegated his powers to his Secretary General, Georges Lhuerre, who stayed behind in Fort-de-France. Louis Mouttet took with him his wife, Hélène, and the cream of the higher administration of the colony: Lieutenant-Colonel Gerbault, the Director of the Artillery, and president of the new scientific commission, and his wife; Monsieur Husson, the private adviser to the governor; Monsieur Jallabert, the director of the cable company, Monsieur Dubois, the director of the tax office, Monsieur Fouqué, Lieutenant of the Artillery, as well as several other inhabitants of Fort-de-France.

At 4.00 p.m., the official party left Fort-de-France on the Girard company steamer. An hour later, Mount Pelée greeted their arrival in Saint-Pierre with a vigorous salvo, exploding blocks large enough to be seen by the naked eye from the quayside. The governor immediately called a meeting of the scientific commission at the Intendance. One member was absent: Monsieur Mirville had been detained by his official duties in Fort-de-France. The gist of their deliberations was known in Saint-Pierre that evening, although they were not telegraphed to Fort-de-France until after 7.05 a.m. the following morning. As Commander Le Bris observed, its conclusions were found to be most reassuring. But they were badly flawed.

The conclusions of the scientific commission demonstrated that they, and most of their fellow citizens, were fearing the wrong threats. Lava flows were no menace: it would take weeks for them to reach the city, even if Mount Pelée were to change its behaviour radically and start erupting them. Many also assumed – wrongly – that the eruption was only heralding a devastating earthquake, like that which had caused 400 deaths in Fort-de-France on 21 January 1839. Those who knew about Krakatau feared a great tsunami or sea wave. In 1883, the eruption of Krakatau had sent out enormous tsunamis that had crashed onto the coasts of Java and Sumatra, drowning over 30 000 people. Two small sea waves had already warned of that particular danger in Saint-Pierre. But Mount Pelée would not generate any major tsunamis unless it developed new craters near the coast. Even on the basis of the facts

The communiqué of the scientific commission, which met in Saint-Pierre on 7 May	Comments
• There is nothing abnormal about the phenomena that have occurred hitherto; they are identical with those observed in all other volcanoes.	– True, but a statement of the obvious. It offered no assessment of the dangers likely to face Saint-Pierre. It omitted to state that eruptions often caused damage and death.
• Because the craters of the volcano are wide open, the expansion of the gases and muds should continue in the same way as has already happened, and should cause neither earthquakes nor ejection of eruptive (molten?) rocks.	– There was no direct relationship between openness of the craters and likely progress of the eruption. Mud would not be erupted; it was formed when water was added to other materials. Volcanic earthquakes could continue. Magma had already reached the surface.
• The many explosions that have often been heard are caused by steam explosions limited to the volcanic chimney and are quite unrelated to collapses of the ground.	– There had been steam (hydrovolcanic) explosions; they had now been replaced by more dangerous eruptions of magma. The collapses of the ground were mentioned to allay fears of earthquakes, to which, in fact, they had little relationship.
• The flows of water and mud are localised in the valley of the Rivière Blanche.	– This had been true at first, but many other streams draining Mount Pelée were in flood by 7 May.
• It can be affirmed that Saint-Pierre is entirely safe because of the relative positions of the craters and the valleys opening to the sea.	– Correct, provided the materials erupted were guided by the valleys.
• The blackish waters of the Rivières des Pères, Basse-Pointe, du Prêcheur (etc.) have maintained their normal temperatures and they owe their abnormal colour to the ash they are carrying.	– This was true, but no reasons are given for their abnormally high content of mud and rocks, nor for the causes lying behind the floods, which were related to the ascent of the molten rock.
• The commission will continue to follow subsequent events closely and will keep the population informed of the smallest details observed.	– The eruption prevented the commission from making any further reports.

then known, none of these fears was justifiable. Nor did they turn out to be justified by the subsequent course of events. The cause of the catastrophe was quite different.

In fact, the report of the scientific commission did little more than give a vaguely scientific air to the assertions of the mayor's poster. With the possible exception of Gaston Landes, they do not seem to have wanted, or to have been able, to explain what was happening. Instead they apparently sought, above all, to reassure the citizens and perhaps themselves, in order to calm the fears that men of their position and background could not express.

Miraculous repairs

It is clear that the governor intended to take advantage of his stay in Saint-Pierre to use the city as a convenient base to investigate the plight of the people who seemed most under threat in the stricken villages to the north of the city. He had, after all, witnessed the panic of those in Le Prêcheur as he had left on the *Topaze*. Thus, he tried to requisition the *Suchet* once again. Before Governor Mouttet embarked for Saint-Pierre, he told the Secretary General to ask Commander Le Bris if he would bring the *Suchet* to Saint-Pierre at 7.00 a.m. the following morning to "take him to those points of the island that might be threatened by the volcanic eruption".

The commander replied that the repairs and preparations for the voyage of the *Suchet* to Havana meant that he could not comply before 9.00 a.m. at the earliest. These preparations were to have vital repercussions for the *Suchet* and its crew. They saved their lives. The commander was afraid that he would arrive too late in Havana if he were to follow the governor's orders. He cabled to the Navy Minister for instructions. The minister replied that the *Suchet* had to go to Havana and that Commander Le Bris "should refuse all instructions that were incompatible with this service". The government was thus taking the eruption far less seriously than Governor Mouttet was in Martinique. It was only when the situation had radically altered that the Navy Minister telegraphed on 9 May that the *Suchet* should stay in Martinique.

More decisions to leave Saint-Pierre

The intensity of the eruption increased after nightfall on 7 May, and ash and dust rained down all over the western and southern slopes of Mount Pelée and even far out to sea. The dust began to fall so thickly on the *Pouyer Quertier* that the captain decided to stop work for the day. He had planned to spend the night just off Saint-Pierre, but he could hardly make out the lights of the battery for the dust, and made instead for Fort-de-France.

Nearer the volcano, matters seemed to be even more serious. By accident or design, several individuals decided to leave the city. Thus, for example, Monsieur Célestin, the photographer in Saint-Pierre, retreated to Le Carbet and took an afternoon photograph of the scene of the eruption, and Roger Arnoux went to his house in the hills at Le Parnasse. Dr Rémy Néris also decided to withdraw from the front line, but not without difficulty:

> Little by little, everyone began to get more anxious . . . On the evening of 7 May, I decided to wait no longer because . . . the eruption seemed to be becoming more severe. I should mention *en passant* that my dog had howled pitiably all day [and was therefore attributed some powers of divination]. But the [Girard company's] regular boat . . . had already left. So, we hired a yacht along with another family we knew. We embarked at 7.00 p.m., taking with us a few clothes and a little money. That proved to be all we saved.

Thus, even those who came to a rational decision to leave Saint-Pierre did not regard their departure as anything more than a temporary measure, otherwise they would have taken more goods and money with them.

Elodie Jourdain described how her Uncle Raoul and Aunt Amélie and their family came to join their relatives at Beauregard plantation. Aunt Amélie had originally decided to stay in the city with her disabled mother. However, on the afternoon of 7 May, she got a letter from her young cousins. They said that she should have gone to Beauregard, where she would have been much safer than in town.

> As Aunt Amélie read the letter, she was filled with a sudden apprehension, and glanced at Mount Pelée. At that very moment, a monstrous column of fumes rose from the crater . . . She was overwhelmed by a sudden and violent feeling of terror. "Raoul! Raoul!" she cried,

"Quick! Go get a coach! We're going to Beauregard!" Her husband tried to persuade her that her irrational panic was not based on any new facts, and that the unexpected arrival of five or six people would cause some embarrassment at Beauregard. She would not listen. Her mother protested that, at her age, she herself couldn't camp in such primitive conditions. And, she said, she would be an obstacle to our escape, if there proved to be any danger. Aunt Amélie replied in a sad but firm tone: "Mother, you are putting me in a bad position. You are making me choose between my mother and my children." "Your choice is clear, my girl," her mother replied. "Your first duty is to your children. Leave without any further scruples, and we'll meet again here when things return to normal."

They hastily piled the three children and one or two baskets into the vehicle that Uncle Raoul had . . . obtained, and set off for Beauregard . . . [When they arrived], my uncle looked rather sheepish because he had given way to his wife's fright. She was tense because she had been forced to leave her mother behind. But our cousins were delighted to meet us again in our new surroundings. We made room for them on our mattresses on the floor.

7 May in Le Morne-Rouge

In Le Morne-Rouge, the eruption kept Edith Duchâteau-Roger in her usual frenzy: "Two red craters spat out fire like blast furnaces . . . The subterranean rumblings increased, sowing panic throughout the population, who wondered whether Le Morne-Rouge wasn't going to be destroyed by an earthquake . . . The bravest people hesitated and trembled."

At about 11.00 p.m., it began to rain very heavily. At midnight an earthquake shook the building, thunder rumbled, and glowing fragments surged from the crater. "The volcano seemed to be a boiling cauldron that was ready to burst . . . In a trice, everyone went to the chapel . . . we prayed with our arms crossed . . . we recited the rosary as we awaited death."

Edith noticed that one of the nuns was missing and went to look for her. She had fallen asleep and had been dreaming: "We shall be saved, because I have just seen the Lord who showed me His Sacred Heart and said: 'All the houses marked with my Sacred Heart will be spared!'"

These words filled me with joy for I knew that . . . all the houses in Le Morne-Rouge had carried a plaque representing the Sacred Heart on their doors. After his last trip to France, Father Mary had brought back a great many of these plaques and had never stopped trying to persuade his parishioners to decorate their homes with this divine sign . . . This saintly priest had a great devotion for the Heart of Jesus . . . I ran to tell Mother Superior these astonishing words . . . Another sister and I went to look for a priest at the presbytery . . . After taking the confessions, he gave Holy Communion to the nuns, who were all weak with fatigue . . . It was then 4.00 a.m. in the morning. Then nature calmed down, and the Sun rose radiant. Everything seemed to herald a splendid day.

The night of 7–8 May at Trouvaillant

Monsieur Raybaud, managing director of the Saint James Rum Company, sheltered 26 friends in his house at Trouvaillant on the hills to the east of Saint-Pierre. The ladies spent the terrifying night of 7–8 May at prayer in the salon. The men, perhaps, spent the night trembling in their beds.

During the night of 7–8 May . . . we could always hear the continual racket of the volcano. We could make out three distinct sorts of noises: intermittent explosions like shots from a cannon; the heavy continuous rumbling from the chimney of the volcano; and the constant noise of the storm. Fire [molten lava] splayed out from the crater at the foot of Morne Lacroix all night. There were sparks. There were jets of fire, which lasted for over a minute, climbing straight upwards high into the sky, and then fanning out in sprays of fireworks . . . Flashes of lightning formed when they reached the clouds that were being pushed along by the southeast wind . . . At 4.00 a.m. the rumbling from the mountain increased and woke me up.

Moods in Saint-Pierre on the evening of 7 May

It is very hard to assess the general mood in Saint-Pierre as night fell on 7 May, always assuming that a general mood could ever exist in such a varied city. Perhaps the only people who still felt safe in the city were the refugees from the slopes of the volcano. After 3 May, the most widespread emotion in Saint-Pierre was probably anxiety, which was compounded by increasing fear and helpless panic. Everyone spent sleepless nights and frantic bewildered days, listening for every rumble from the volcano and every rumour from their friends. Among the illiterate half of the population, the wildest stories spread, unchecked, in the overcrowded streets. And yet, they stayed put. Unless the authorities took charge of them, the poor had nowhere to go and no means of getting there. Following the apparent logic of scientific opinion, the authorities offered shelter in Saint-Pierre but not in Fort-de-France.

Elodie Jourdain commented that people had always asked: "Weren't people afraid, didn't they realize the danger?" Not surprisingly, opinions varied greatly even in the same family. Individuals reacted according to their temperament. "In general, it could be said that panic, insouciance, curiosity and courage were felt in equal measure, and even succeeded each other". Those who had been most afraid persuaded the others to leave Saint-Pierre and thereby saved lives, but many others suffered from a kind of inertia and seemed resigned to their fate. On the other hand, many better-informed people stayed in their homes because they believed that they were in less danger in Saint-Pierre than anywhere else. The mayor's poster and the report of the scientific commission reflected their views perfectly.

The Dujons, the Marrys and the Décomis were well connected and wealthy. They would have had no trouble in taking refuge in the safe south-ern half of the Martinique, or indeed in a neighbouring colony. The women and children from several wealthier and pessimistic families had already taken boats to Saint Lucia, and Auguste Guérin, for example, who knew at first hand what Mount Pelée could do, had left for southern Martinique.

Between the people who were informed and those who were not was a third group who were thrilled by the superb spectacle that Mount Pelée was providing. Every fascinating turn of the unfolding volcanic plot persuaded them to wait for more. For instance, even though Eugène Berté was a sensible family man, he could not wait to return to the crater to watch the marvellous show at the bottom of the furnace.

On 7 May, it would have been impossible for anyone without expert knowledge, to assess the risk to the population. The citizens of Saint-Pierre were free to go and most of them stayed.

The last letter from Saint-Pierre

Joseph Dumas was a businessman in Saint-Pierre. On 6 May, he took his wife and four young children to Le Saint-Esprit in the south of the island, about 60 km from the volcano. He himself had to stay in Saint-Pierre to look after the business. He could not sleep during the turbulent night of 7–8 May and he wrote a long letter to his wife.

My dear Marie, my good little children,

It is half past three. I haven't slept for two and a half hours, and I am writing to you in the midst of a firework display that I could not possibly describe.

Imagine two storms together. One is volcanic, with pale glows of an indeterminate blue that assume fantastic forms between dull rumblings that have not a second between them. The other is atmospheric, with brilliant zig-zagging flashes of lightning, cutting across the sky amid a strident noise like a canvas being ripped by a tireless hand . . . It makes the houses tremble and shudder . . . It is really beautiful, gripping, and sublime! . . . I am ashamed of being so small, so ignorant, so "insignificant" in the face of all the powerful forces that these elements unleash . . .

This storm will do the city good. It is raining. We need all this water to cleanse the streets and the rooftops from all this tiresome ash . . . Saint-Pierre is facing up to its Goliath courageously . . . Up until now, the city has been in no danger. What we feared were earthquakes, but they have been brushed aside by the eruption.

But, although we are enjoying a bit of calm, it is not the same in poor Fonds-Coré. I wouldn't give a centime for all that wealthy quarter at the moment. Last night, the two rivers alongside it were almost covering it entirely . . . This isn't the work of the volcano. It is more because the floods have been caused by the great rains that have fallen over the mountain. There is no-one left in the villas in the suburbs . . .

I stopped writing at 4.00 a.m., thinking I would take a little nap, but it was impossible. The storm is still going on, but it is not as bad as before.

On the other hand, the mountain is doubling its efforts and it is roaring horrifyingly! Oh Marie, my dear, I am really glad that you have not been here tonight, because you would have suffered too much; and, my God, our poor little ones would have been in such distress.

It is daylight at last. The Angelus bell is ringing. It's Ascension Day. It brings all sorts of sweet thoughts, pleasures and mellowness into my heart . . . The rooftops have got back their bright colours, thanks to the torrential rain. The trees have stopped looking awful. The pavement is shining again just as it did before . . .

Yesterday, life wanted to go on, but businesses are not working at all. Just think: no more foreigners, no more buyers, not a single transaction!

I am forcing myself to keep cool. Although I am not denying the danger, I can't see that it is as close as all that yet.

I am sending you *Les Antilles* and *Les Colonies*. When you look through them, you will see that I am not the only one who says that there is no danger in staying in Saint-Pierre. Set your minds at rest about me, and let's wait and see what happens. I was looking forward to the idea of spending this great Feast of the Ascension with you, my dears. But this is a good time to remember that "Man proposes and God disposes". I love you all so much, and I send you my most tender kisses.

Joseph Dumas was a responsible family man, who did his duty, stayed at his post and did not panic like the mob. But, apart from the need to protect his property, it is hard to see why he did not leave Saint-Pierre and join his family. Business was at a standstill, and Ascension Day was a public holiday. He could have left. Instead, he posted his letter in time for the 6.00 a.m. departure of the *Topaze* for Fort-de-France, and went back home for a nap.

9

Ascension Day dawns
Thursday 8 May 1902

Throughout the night, the thunderstorm and Mount Pelée vied with each other with awesome salvoes. Lightning flashed and glowing rocks spurted from the crater. The ground rocked and trembled. Rain lashed down.

At about 4.00 a.m., the great storm abated. The volcano hesitated. But it was too late for most of the people in Saint-Pierre to get any more sleep. When dawn broke at about 5.00 a.m., the torrents of rain had washed the dust and ash away and rooftops glittered in the morning Sun. The fresh dawn air was cool and limpid. The sky was blue and the sea a mirror of shimmering cobalt. A superb column of glistening steam and fumes billowed straight up from the crater. Some admirers said that it shone like antique silver. The

The last photograph of old Saint-Pierre, taken in the afternoon of 7 May 1902 by the photographer T. Célestin, just before he left Saint-Pierre for Le Carbet. The vessel in the foreground is probably the Teresa Lo Vico.

brilliant tranquillity cheered and even invigorated the citizens of Saint-Pierre, and gave them new hope. The Ascension Day holiday was going to be glorious, perfect for the youngsters to show off their First Communion finery. The cathedral and all the churches would be full.

At 6.00 a.m., the *Topaze* left for Fort-de-France with only 34 passengers on board. They had just won their game of dice with death. About half way to the capital, it passed the *Diamant* on its way to Saint-Pierre. From the deck of the *Diamant*, the controversial young writer, René Bonneville, off to admire the volcanic spectacle – and to die – waved cheerfully to his father, who was fleeing from it on the *Topaze*.

At 6.00 a.m., too, the steamer, *Roraïma*, of the Quebec Line, sailed into the bay. All on board turned uneasy glances northwards to the wreaths of fumes pouring from Mount Pelée. The shipping agents only laughed when the crew confessed that they were worried. "You should have been here three days ago," they boasted, "when the Guérin factory was destroyed". But not everyone shared the agents' confidence. Sixty potential first-class passengers wanted to leave Saint-Pierre as soon as possible. Could not the *Roraïma* go straight to Saint-Lucia, take the passengers, unload the cargo bound for that island, and then come back to Saint-Pierre tomorrow? This would, in fact, gain some time, since no cargo could be unloaded in Saint-Pierre because Ascension Day was a public holiday. Captain Muggah happily complied with this request, but he discovered to his chagrin that the consignments in the hold for Saint-Pierre were blocking those for Saint-Lucia. The *Roraïma* would have to lie idle in Saint-Pierre until Friday morning.

At 6.45 a.m., whilst these parleys were going on, the *Roddam* steamed into the bay from Port Castries in Saint-Lucia. Captain Freeman anchored his vessel opposite the Place Bertin, some 400m away from the *Roraïma*. Mount Pelée welcomed the new arrival with a light shower of very fine dust. By now the volcano was, as Captain Freeman put it, "smoking beautifully . . . like big rolls of wool. . .curling up in the shape of great cauliflowers". The *Roddam* was the last vessel to join the steamers and sailing ships that were aligned in the shimmering waters, with their bows heading to the shore, as if they were paying homage to Saint-Pierre. And all manner of smaller craft were bobbing up and down and clapping the little waves along the quayside.

In the northern reaches of the bay, the British cable-repair steamer, *Grappler*, was already at work, sailing to and fro, as the crew grappled for the broken ends of the cable, just opposite where the Guérin factory had stood.

About 7.00 a.m., the *Diamant* steamed into the bay and tied up at the jetty.

A crowd of holidaymakers from Fort-de-France disembarked, eager to see the volcanic spectacle for themselves. Mount Pelée did not let them down. Its magnificent silvery plume soared in hundreds of swirls, high into the northern sky, like a turbulent thundercloud. The mountain growled menacingly. Its admirers gasped with joy – or was it fear?

Then the master of the *Diamant* took the steamer to tie up to a buoy off shore. In Saint-Pierre, people began hurrying through the streets, as the church bells rang for early mass. Senator Amédée Knight's schooner, *Gabrielle*, was moored just opposite the Senator's firm at the Figuier in the Centre quarter of Saint-Pierre. Georges Marie-Sainte, the first mate, had been up betimes, watching the volcano since dawn. Between 6.30 a.m. and 7.00 a.m., he had seen columns of white smoke twisting out some 220m below the summit, as if they were coming from a new crater. If he was right, this new crater might have further damaged the head of the Rivière Blanche and weakened the south-facing upper flanks of the volcano even more.

At 7.10 a.m., Georges Marie-Sainte saw a skiff set out from Saint-Pierre. It was sailing about 400m from the shore and passed about 50m from the schooner. It seemed to be making for Le Prêcheur. He thought it was carrying Governor Mouttet and Messieurs Doze, Gerbault and Léonce of the scientific commission, although others have since cast doubt on his impression. If the skiff had gone directly to Le Prêcheur, it would have reached its destination before 8.00 a.m., but, in fact, it must have stopped en route, perhaps at the threatened village of Sainte-Philomène. Neither the skiff nor its passengers were ever seen again.

The incessant rumblings of Mount Pelée had now become so commonplace that only the most paranoid among the population were now really listening to their every change of tone. However, the sky had become more menacing than had seemed possible just after the glorious sunrise. Ascension Day was not fulfilling its dawning promise.

Out at sea, the crew of the *Pouyer Quertier* were not happy in their work. The previous night the *Pouyer Quertier* had stood off Fort-de-France, where there was normally little drift. By the following morning, the *Pouyer Quertier* had drifted to the north and was actually lying in the Dominica Channel. The vessel had thus had to return southwards to its grappling position off Saint-Pierre. The rumbling from Mount Pelée was becoming louder, the crew, and the dust was making them cough and splutter. Visibility was so poor that Captain Thirion was afraid that they might be sliced in two by another vessel. He decided to sail farther out to sea until the dust cloud dissipated.

> **WARNING SEVEN**
>
> The last warning signal from Mount Pelée came quickly after the sixth. A dome of viscous molten lava had started to ooze from the vent and into the crater on the evening of 7 May. The magma was now expelling gas which probably reached the surface via a vent alongside this rising dome. On the morning of 8 May, each batch of exploding gas shattered the molten rock into clouds of fine black ash that were blasted chiefly westwards or southwestwards. They shot well over Saint-Pierre before they lost their impetus and rained down over the sea. These explosions were unusually powerful for their type, and they must have much reduced the pressures on the gases in the magma rising within the volcano. Thus, if the rising magma contained any very large masses of gas, the chances were that they would be released with an almighty outburst. Soon.

The volcano was hurling great clouds of dust and ash well beyond Saint-Pierre so that they fell onto the sea over 5 km from the city. From the deck of the *Gabrielle* close inshore, Georges Marie-Sainte saw that "the wind was blowing black whirlwinds to the west and hiding the sky over a vast area". But the wind was not responsible: it was the blasts from Mount Pelée. In Saint-Pierre, the eastern sky was clear and sunny, but the western sky was dark and glowering.

A general anxiety spread throughout the city. People clustered in groups along the shore, speculating about the cause of this new aberration of Nature. Some claimed that the combination of full daylight over the city and twilight over the sea, could best be explained by an eclipse of the Sun forecast in the local almanac. Given that the Sun was over Saint-Pierre to the east, this explanation was manifestly idiotic, but it shows how fear could give credence to any daft hypothesis that was proposed. But, in fact, other people perceived correctly that the sooty-black fumes thrown out by the volcano had caused the darkness in the western part of the sky.

Meanwhile, the white dust was still falling gently and silently down onto the *Roddam*, like fine snow on a windless morning. It soon covered the deck and the uniforms of the crew. It was maybe just after 7.30 a.m. when Joseph Plissonneau, their ship's agent, came out to the *Roddam* in his small boat. Captain Freeman welcomed him from the upper deck. Supercargo Campbell greeted him from the steps of the companion ladder. Monsieur Plissonneau drew alongside, but did not come aboard.

"What do you want here this morning?" he laughed. "Don't you know it's Ascension Day? Everyone's on holiday. You won't get a single stevedore to come out and work for you today. You'd better go for a pleasure cruise and come back another day!"

Then Joseph Plissonneau adopted a more serious tone. He confessed that people in Saint-Pierre were in a gloomy mood. Most of the shops had been closed the previous day because of the falling ash and dust. Several families had left the city and he himself had taken his wife and children to stay in Saint-Lucia until the eruption was over. Captain Freeman asked if there would be any point in going ashore to try and get men to unload their cargo; or would it be better to go to Guadeloupe first . . . It was just the sort of banal conversation that captains have with shipping agents in ports . . .

The swell rocked the small boat for a moment. Joseph Plissonneau took hold of the ship's ladder to steady himself. The volcano thundered out an almighty roar. He turned round to look at Mount Pelée. The Reaper was about to reap.

10

The nuée ardente
8.02 a.m., 8 May 1902

And the second angel sounded, and as it were a great mountain, burning with fire, was cast into the sea; and the third part of the sea became blood, and the third part of the creatures which were in the sea, and had life, died; and the third part of the ships were destroyed.
(Revelation 8: 8–9).

The most horrific volcanic eruption of the twentieth century achieved immortality at 8.02 a.m. on 8 May 1902. It was far from being the most powerful eruption of the century, but it caused its greatest catastrophe.

Telegraphic testimony

The telegraphic times in Martinique were calibrated to the international network, and they established the exact time of the eruption with macabre precision.
- 8.00 a.m.   To start the day's business, the telegraph clerk in Saint-Pierre signalled "go ahead" to his colleague in Fort-de-France.
- 8.01 a.m.   The telegraph clerk in Fort-de-France asked, as usual, for the morning's news and gossip from Saint-Pierre, and waited for the reply.
- 8.02 a.m.   The telegraph clerk in Fort-de-France heard "a very short trill on the line. Then nothing more." The line fell totally silent.

At the very same moment, a businessman in Fort-de-France was telephoning to a friend in Saint-Pierre. "He had just finished his sentence when I heard a dreadful scream, then another much weaker groan, like a stifled death rattle. Then silence."

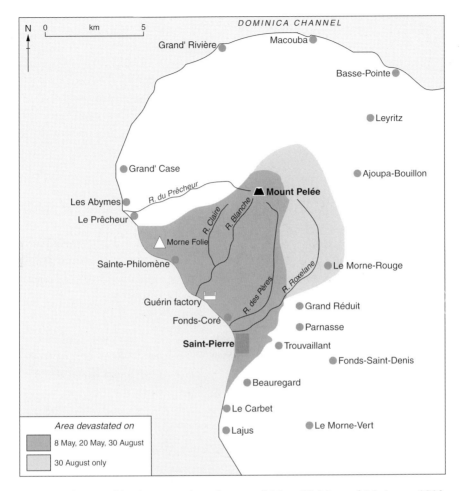

The areas devastated by the great nuées ardentes on 8 May, 20 May and 30 August 1902.

Raoul Lodéon was the clerk at the Fort-de-France telephone exchange. At 7.40 a.m., he spoke to his colleague in Saint-Pierre, Monsieur Thésée, who told him that the city was under a thick dark cloud. About 8.00 a.m. he called Saint-Pierre again. All he heard at first was the ringing sound. "I shouted 'Allo!' three times before Thésée answered, but in a shaky voice, as if he was deeply perturbed . . . Then I heard him cry out in great pain. He gave out a long 'Aaaahhh'. At the same time, I heard a tremendous noise as if an enormous block of iron had fallen onto a sheet metal roof. Then electrical discharges came down the line and I felt a violent shock that threw me from the telephone."

The nuée ardente

There was no warning. Those who had the finest and most terrifying impression of the nuée ardente died almost at once – if they were lucky. The safest vantage points lay on the hills south of Mount Pelée and east of Saint-Pierre, where several eyewitnesses watched the spectacle with amazement that quickly turned to horror and then to mourning. One moment they were admiring the beautiful shining column of fumes billowing 3 km above the crest of Mount Pelée; the next moment they were sure that they were going to die.

Just before 8.00 a.m., Mount Pelée indulged in a minute or two of treacherous calm. Then, the ground started to tremble within the volcano as if a titanic struggle was being fought in its heart. Hundreds of small earthquakes resonated through the mountain, like the bell tolling the knell of old Saint-Pierre. Suddenly, Mount Pelée shuddered. The crater groaned. The air seemed to be heavy, stupefying, dead. This was one of the moments when an instant lasts an hour and when an hour flashes by in an instant.

An explosion blasted out huge boulders in a fog of dark fumes that gushed 100 m into the air and angled down towards the Rivière Blanche and Saint-Pierre. It shattered the dome of lava that had lain in the crater for over a day. It cleared the volcanic throat and released the pressures on all the gases in the magma lurking below. Mount Pelée poised to strike. In a fraction of a second, a stupendous explosion unleashed the blast of hot air. There was a blinding flash and a deafening salvo that was heard in Venezuela. A moment later the nuée ardente fired from the crater in an angry turbulent emulsion of scalding steam, gas, black smoke, scorching ash and dust, glowing cinders, hot rocks and enormous boulders. The nuée ardente shot straight down to Saint-Pierre with unimaginable power. It moved down slope so fast that people thought that the whole flank of the volcano had split open. It could not have been worse if it had. The nuée careered on, bounding and rolling down hill, rampaging across valleys and ridges alike. A thousand billows swirled skywards in a beautiful turbulent cloud of violet and reddish-grey, like a huge agitated tropical thunderstorm. A dense network of flashes of lightning sparked and crackled through it amid the awesome noise. The spectacle of a lifetime, dealing death.

The nuée ardente reached Saint-Pierre in less than two minutes. The turbulent cloud itself would kill almost everything that it touched, but it carried its most destructive and lethal weapons in its denser base. It smashed

Nuées ardentes

It is a pity that Shakespeare never described a nuée ardente. Any other pen is inadequate to evoke their glorious and terrifying beauty and their totally lethal menace. Nuée ardente is a French term often used to describe huge and sometimes glowing clouds of scorching hot gas and volcanic fragments, ranging in size from dust, ash and pumice to large rocks, which are expelled at great speed in a turbulent aerosol-like mass. They are the features of violent volcanic eruptions that commonly produce their greatest catastrophes. Their dense base rushes across the ground at speeds of up to 500 km an hour and at temperatures of between 200°C and 450°C, while their less dense upper parts form soaring clouds of ash, dust and steam. During their inexorable advance, the nuées ardentes devastate everything in their path and even pick up fragments of masonry, trees and vehicles, which they add to their lethal armoury. Few buildings, and even fewer human beings, have ever been known to survive their onslaught.

In 1902 Mount Pelée displayed its true colours for the first time since the French settlement and produced its first Peléan eruption since about 1600. With it emerged the first "nuée ardente" that was ever analyzed in a scientific manner. The penetrating studies of the eruption by the French geologist, Alfred Lacroix, made his book, *La montagne Pelée et ses éruptions*, one of the foundations of modern volcanology. By the same token, nuées ardentes and Peléan eruptions, and the annihilation of Saint-Pierre, became some of the best-known features in the volcanic repertoire.

In fact, the eruption of Mount Pelée in 1902 was not the first time that nuées ardentes had been named, nor was it the first time that they had been witnessed. Small nuées ardentes were first described during an eruption on the Portuguese island of São Jorge in the Azores in 1580. However, the term only came into common volcanological usage when it was revived by Alfred Lacroix. It is likely that he learned the term from his father-in-law. Madame Catherine Lacroix was the daughter of the eminent French volcanologist, Ferdinand Fouqué, who had published accounts of the volcanoes of the Azores in 1867 and 1873.

As the twentieth century brought a great upsurge in volcanological research, it became increasingly clear that nuées ardentes had often played a major role in some of the most celebrated eruptions in the past. Thus, for example, they had rushed down from Vesuvius and killed most of the victims in Pompeii and Herculaneum in AD 79: and, in 1883, they had raced 40 km across the Sunda Straits from Krakatau and burned thousands of people to death in Sumatra. But the nuée ardente that destroyed Saint-Pierre was the first to gain international fame, and nowhere in human experience has a nuée ardente wreaked such a catastrophe in such tragic and dramatic circumstances. When it hurtled down the southern flanks of Mount Pelée, it laid a new foundation stone of volcanology. It also removed most of Saint-Pierre from the face of the Earth. Many people saw it; few survived.

A small nuée ardente erupted on 16 December 1902, which was limited to the valley of the Rivière Blanche. Its dense surging base, which causes most of the damage, can just be distinguished as a small prong jutting out from the front of the main mass. The billowing less dense clouds, rising high into the air, covered the whole sky above Saint-Pierre on 8 May. On 8 May, the frontal prong was much larger and moved much faster.

everything in its path to smithereens – shrubs, trees, huts, plantations, public buildings and private homes, and gathered up the fragments into its immense armoury and swept them onwards to join the assault on Saint-Pierre. The nuée razed Sainte-Philomène and Fonds-Coré from the face of the Earth and then swirled and eddied through Saint-Pierre at speeds of 500 km an hour and at temperatures of 200–450°C. It threw down every building in the Fort district in the north of the city. The pillars of the new Fort market were 30 cm thick and had been built to withstand the mightiest hurricanes. The whole building vanished completely. In the Centre of Saint-Pierre, the nuée scythed down the lighthouse in the Place Bertin, which had masonry 1 m thick at its base, battered the Grand Theatre and the Chamber of Commerce so that only their steps remained, smashed down the Intendance, the bishopric, the bank and the prison. It ripped off the dome of the packed cathedral and flung it into the sea; the nave crashed onto the worshippers; only the tower and part of the facade survived. The terrible surge threw down both the College–Seminary and its rival, the Lycée, where only the entrance arch remained. The walls of the army barracks and the gendarmerie were 70 cm thick; they were razed to the ground. The walls of the military hospital fared little better. They had been 1 m thick, but little more than its facade resisted the onslaught. The nuée blasted the rum distilleries apart and twisted their machinery into surrealistic piles. Mere shops and houses had little chance of resisting such violence. The nuée ardente began to lose a little power as it swept into the southern end of the city. It still knocked down all the walls running from east to west across its path, but a few tottering structures trending from north to south, parallel to the onslaught, managed to stay upright. They, almost alone, betrayed the pattern of what had been a city only two minutes before. Rubble choked some streets, while others had been swept clear, as if by some gigantic broom. The hands on the clock crowning the facade of the military hospital had spun around like a roulette wheel. They halted at 7.50 a.m., bearing false testimony to the time of the cataclysm.

The nuée ardente surged downwards in a single unit, like an enormous puff of heavy fumes. Thus, by the time the head of the nuée ardente had reached the southern fringes of Saint-Pierre, its tail had already left the crater, which was looking clear and perfectly innocent beneath the blue sky.

The return wind

The snout of the nuée ardente seemed about to swallow Le Carbet when, all of a sudden, it halted and started to soar high into the sky, like a huge rearing monster, roaring and flashing. The nuée had caused a shock wave in the air, which had produced a counterblast. A return wind of hurricane power rushed from the south, flattened all the trees and stopped the hurtling nuée in its tracks at the very entrance to Le Carbet. The black sea swirled in all directions, and steep breakers crashed onto the shore. The terrible squall stopped after two or three minutes. The villagers were saved.

The same return wind gusted northwards over the hills above Saint-Pierre and was strong enough to rip the branches from the trees as far north as Le Parnasse. The nuée ardente itself rose higher and higher into the air and blacked out the Sun all over the western and southern flanks of the volcano. Then lumps of lava the size of walnuts rained down in the darkness; then heavy mud, stinking of sulphur, splattered everything and flattened the bushes; then dry ash showered down; then rain fell in torrents; then the Sun started to shine timidly again after about an hour. The summit of Mount

The arch remaining at the entrance to the Lycée of Saint-Pierre.

Pelée stayed clear for a while, giving off only smoke that twisted lazily into the air. But soon a succession of much weaker nuées ardentes began to spew out and rush down the valley of the Rivière Blanche for the rest of the day.

Death in Saint-Pierre

The vision of death hurtled towards its victims in Saint-Pierre with merciful speed. They had no chance. The nuée ardente swept quickly over them, but lingered long enough to make them endure indescribable pain and terror as they died. The sufferings of the victims were extraordinarily unequal. Some were smashed beyond recognition, others remained intact, and some managed to survive the nuée ardente only to succumb to the flames that followed.

Those inside buildings had virtually no warning that they were about to die. They heard the noise of the advancing nuée ardente reach a sudden deafening crescendo. The roofs ripped off, the walls collapsed, then the scalding blast killed them before it could even set their clothes alight. The scorching fumes, ash and gas seared their skin and burned into their throats and lungs as they struggled to flee, or even just to breathe. They had to inhale the hot dust and ash in a desperate effort to stay alive. And they died as their throats and lungs burned out, their tongues swelled up to twice normal size, and blood gushed from their mouths. Then the dust coated their bodies.

In the Rue de Montmirail, a man, woman and child were partly mummified in a cellar. Others were mummified in the asylum, although many wooden cabins there showed no trace of fire. One inmate died strapped to her chair in a straitjacket, released at last. In a house in the Rue Victor-Hugo, a man was sitting at his desk when the nuée ardente arrived. His little girl flung her arms around his neck and his son dashed to his knee, and they all died together in his arms. In another house, a woman died breast-feeding her baby. In the Rue de la Raffinerie, in the Mouillage district, many children and their parents perished together in a chapel, perhaps as they were beginning a service for first communion. Very few bodies were ever recovered from the vast crowd attending the first communion service in the cathedral. The falling masonry battered to death all those who might have survived the scorching blast of ash. Nevertheless, some victims died peacefully. In Monsieur Blausse's home, for instance, the stable lad died lying on his back in bed, just as he was thinking about getting up; a rich white man, a blond white girl with a blue ribbon in her hair, and a black woman and her baby all died in the yard outside. The nuée probably gassed them, for they had not a burn on their bodies, but the dog had been incinerated nearby.

People who were outside in the streets lived a few moments of horror. They saw the terrifying cloud of ash boulders and masonry rushing upon them and started a pitiful race against death. The nuée overtook them in a few strides and they fell face downwards in the street, burnt, bludgeoned, and then often buried in ash or rubble. A wooden beam pierced a woman's thigh; another woman vainly tried to protect her head with her hands; and a man bent double in pain as the ash burnt into his lungs. Others scrambled to find shelter in the nearest building. The nuée ardente caught them before they could get beyond the doorway. They died, clustered together on doorsteps in poignant groups, as if they were clutching their friends, or neighbours, or were just seeking the solace of any other human being in their utter desperation. Not far away, another group of women had tried in vain to push their children into a factory doorway. In the Rue Saint-Jean-de-Dieu, the prostitutes' area, the hapless women died in each other's arms in the street. A group of 18 died together in the Rue de Longchamp. In the same street, the nuée ardente seized Dr Gravier Sainte-Luce as he was leaving his house, and burned his horse, coach and coachman to cinders as they waited at the door.

The nuée ardente stripped many of its victims naked when it trapped them in the streets. Sometimes, though, the soles of their shoes were intact, showing that they had, at least, died on their feet. Their hair was burnt. They had extensive superficial burns, which were mostly like scalding, because the nuée passed over them too quickly to incinerate their skin, or their clothes, more thoroughly. But as they died, and struggled for the unbreathable air, their muscles contracted in spasms so that their limbs assumed grotesque positions. Some looked as if they had been fighting off an assailant; others seemed to be praying or throwing back their heads in agony. Often, too, their faces and heads were swollen, and after a couple of days, their intestines burst from their decaying corpses. Occasionally, the boulders and masonry within the nuée ardente tore off the heads and limbs of its victims as they fled. The ash and dust then covered all of them with a kind of black plaster. The impartial nuée ardente showed no prejudice. Whites could not be distinguished from blacks.

And Governor Mouttet? His body was one of more than 20 000 that were never found or identified. Perhaps he died on the way to Le Prêcheur, or perhaps with his wife in Saint-Pierre, thinking of their three young children.

Within the confines of the city itself, several people lingered on, badly

The skeletons of some of the victims, enshrouded by masonry, rocks, ash and dust from the nuée ardente that killed them.

injured for more than a day, but only two people survived for longer. More might have escaped death had they had the time to take refuge in hermetically sealed rooms, provided, of course, that they had not been bombarded and smashed by boulders or rubble. But the houses in Saint-Pierre had no cellars; and the windows had only flimsy blinds and no glass. When the nuée ardente arrived, the wide open windows gave extra turbulence to the eddying blasts that swept off the rooftops and blew out the walls.

For all this devastation, and excluding the rubble littering the streets, the nuée ardente left less than 1 m of volcanic ash and dust in the north of Saint-Pierre and as little as 30 cm in the far south. By geological standards, it was by no means an imposing eruption. By human standards it was a cataclysm. Fewer than 4500 bodies were ever recovered, and very few indeed could be identified.

At 8.05 a.m., Saint-Pierre was already a graveyard of ruins in a shroud of ash. Most of the citizens, and the refugees who had sought shelter within it, were already dead. Roger Arnoux, at Le Parnasse on the hills above the city, and Emile Berté, on the *Pouyer Quertier* far out to sea, were among those who were weeping for their families.

121

The fires

In Saint-Pierre, the destruction started fires, which soon ignited the countless casks of rum stored about the city. And when the nuée ardente was spent, blazing rum and whirlwinds set Saint-Pierre on fire from end to end. The firestorm began to rage through the city. With temperatures reaching 900°C, the fires were hotter than the nuée ardente itself. They were instantaneous, simultaneous and widespread, but the effects of the firestorm were as irregular as the nuée ardente before it. The temperature of the firestorm could be estimated from the behaviour of the metals that were altered. Brass and zinc objects melted; iron goods rarely melted; pewter, copper and lead remained unchanged; and bronze and silver coins stuck together but did not really melt. The machinery in the distilleries twisted and buckled. The bell at the Centre church was deformed, but 10 m away a wooden altar and its lace altar cloth were found intact beneath a thin coat of ash. Indeed, the ash often proved to be a most efficient insulator, but, even without it, the combined effects of the nuée ardente and the fires were extremely varied within short distances. Glasses, bottles and carafes bulged and twisted, but 8 million francs' worth of notes, gold and silver awaited collection from the vaults of the bank. Butter in boxes in a house in the Rue Victor-Hugo stayed fresh and intact; and a box of live revolver cartridges in a house in the Rue d'Orléans could still be fired when they were found several days later. Electoral posters stuck, barely

Drinking glasses partially melted by the fires that raged in Saint-Pierre after the nuée ardente on 8 May.

scorched, to fragments of walls in the south of the city. Books and notes from lessons, including pages about volcanoes, fluttered around the wreck of the Lycée. Linen and lace, and even candles, survived beside scenes of total devastation.

A few dozen people had the misfortune to live longer than their fellow-citizens. Sailors on the ships moored offshore saw them dashing, and often almost prancing and dancing, in helpless agony for a few minutes around the Place Bertin. In the far south of Saint-Pierre some individuals saw their doom coming, and tried in vain to reach the sea before the scorching cloud enveloped them. On the Morne Orange hill in the far south of the city, many people had just enough time to gather up some possessions. They ran out into the road, but not fast enough. They were thrown down all facing the same way – southwards – striving for salvation.

Unluckiest of all were those citizens who inhaled the scorching concoction near the outermost fringes of the nuée ardente, for they suffered atrociously for several hours. Some people might have lived on for a while in the city. Monsieur Henri Alfred apparently did not die until the morning of 9 May. His maid, who was taken to Fort-de-France, succumbed to her burns later that afternoon.

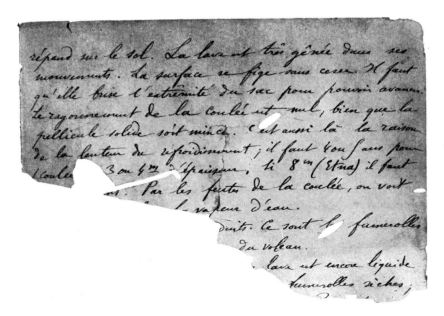

A fragment of notes on volcanoes from the Lycée or the College–Seminary in Saint-Pierre.

The death of Gaston Landes

Monsieur and Madame Montferrier lived in the valley in the northeastern outskirts of Saint-Pierre, much nearer to the volcano than the city itself. The critical boundary of death passed over the Montferriers' home: to the west everyone perished; to the east they lived. Gaston Landes had been preparing to move into a new house, which stood about 50 m to the west of the Montferriers' home.

At 8.00 a.m., Madame Montferrier was in her kitchen, when her husband called her outside:

> I went out, but I had hardly got beyond the doorway when I was horribly burned in the face, and on my arms and legs by a burning vapour. Instinctively, I put my right hand to my face, which saved my eyes, and I rushed back into the house, followed by my husband. It immediately went so completely dark that I could not see my husband when I embraced him. We knelt together under the table, waiting to die. We stayed there for five minutes while the darkness lasted.

When the daylight returned, the Montferriers' first thought was for their children, whom they had sent to church down the valley at Trois Ponts. The couple hurried down to see if they were safe. When they reached the third bridge at Trois Ponts, they "saw a terrifying sight. Saint-Pierre was in flames."

Then, the Montferriers seem to have completely forgotten about the fate of their own children. Was this an effect of shock? They noticed that the house where Monsieur Landes was going to live was still intact. They went into the garden. Madame Montferrier said:

> I found Monsieur Landes in the pool, with his body almost entirely in the water. He got out at once and I noticed that he was wearing a shirt, but his body was red raw. When he saw my husband he exclaimed: "Ah, it's you Montferrier: what on earth has happened?" [Ironically, the keenest student of the eruption had not recognized what it had done]. With Monsieur Landes were young Edouard Thouin, a pupil at the Lycée, the two Desbordes children and two maids. One of the maids was bleeding from her nose and throat. All of them were crying out for water. I got them something to drink, because I was the one who was the least injured, and I wasn't yet in pain. As I was doing so,

The house of Gaston Landes.

young Thouin lay down by the pool. I called out several times to him in vain. He had died.

Monsieur and Madame Montferrier had been tending to the victims for nearly three hours when Samuel and Léon Chantel arrived. They had walked down from Le Morne-Rouge, and had been forced to tie little boards under their feet so that they could bear the heat of the ash. The saw a horrific sight in the garden before them. The Montferriers were both badly burnt. Edouard Thouin was lying dead, with his face in the mud. A young white girl with red hair was leaning, weeping, against a little wall and babbling: "Oh My God, I'm going to die!" (She might have been Thouin's sister, or one of the Desbordes girls; it was never established). The two young black servants were leaning motionless against a wall of the house, with blood and pus oozing from their noses. Gaston Landes had fallen into the garden during his struggles and was rolling about on the ground, groaning and shrieking in great pain below the front steps of the house. He was atrociously burnt and was giving out bloody matter from his nose and mouth. His face was bloated and blistered, and his swollen cheeks completely masked his eyes. The ash had burned and sullied his white jacket, shirt, trousers and shoes. No-one could help him. He died a little before noon, after nearly four hours of agony.

The Montferriers then asked Samuel and Léon Chantel to take them to Le Morne-Rouge. It must have been shock that caused them to abandon all thought of their own children and the three victims lying in their death throes in the garden. As far as Petit-Réduit, half way up to Le Morne-Rouge, burnt corpses littered the roadside. And they passed many people from Le Morne-Rouge going down to Saint-Pierre to inspect the unbelievable destruction for themselves. They reached the village at about 2.00 p.m. The Montferriers were treated at once. Madame Montferrier survived, but her husband had more extensive burns and he died five days later. Their children were never seen again.

About 3.00 p.m., the Chantels returned to the Trois Ponts area of Saint-Pierre. The body of Gaston Landes was lying where he had perished, but the three young people whom they had left dying were nowhere to be seen. No-one knows where they died.

But, by then, as Léon Chantel delicately told Gendarme Lagarde later, "many people were walking about in all directions, and seemed to be looking for things". Pillage had already begun.

Dust, ash and rocks, deposited by the nuées ardentes in the valley of the Rivière Blanche, form the valley floor and constitute all the cliff on the right of the picture, where they are over 20 m thick. The cloud casts a light shadow over the summit dome of Mount Pelée on the horizon.

11

Escape
Thursday 8 May 1902

It seemed altogether impossible to those who saw the devastation caused by the nuée ardente that anyone in Saint-Pierre could have lived through its terrible embrace. They were nearly correct. On the outermost fringes of the cloud and on some vessels in the bay, where its effects were attenuated, life or death depended on a couple of breaths or a couple of metres. A few people had very narrow escapes. Only two men survived in the city itself. All the survivors needed to have had one inestimable quality – luck.

The first survivor

Léon Compère-Léandre was a strong black shoemaker in Saint-Pierre, about 28 years old. He shared a house, sheltered by Morne Abel, in the northeast of Saint-Pierre. Monsieur Delavaud, the clerk of the court, and his wife, son and daughter were among those who also rented rooms in the building. If Léon Compère-Léandre had been at work, he would have been killed, but at 8.00 a.m. on the Ascension Day holiday he was relaxing at his doorstep, gazing at the ships at anchor in the bay.

Suddenly he felt a "violent wind" that started uprooting the trees in the garden. He dashed for cover inside the house. It was only then that he discovered he had been burned on his hands, face and left leg. Then everything went dark. Clouds of dust and ash invaded the room and pelted down onto the metal roof. The terrified shoemaker crawled under a table. At that very moment, the Delavauds struggled into the room – all badly burnt. The little girl died there and then, but the others wandered away again in deep shock. Twenty minutes later, some daylight returned, and the bewildered Léon

The ruins of Saint-Pierre, taken between 8 and 20 May 1902, looking southwards to the Mouillage district. The remains of the cathedral towers rise in the middle distance, and the spur of the Morne-Orange forms the horizon.

went next door. He found Monsieur Delavaud lying dead on his bed. He went out into the courtyard. The corpses of the Delavaud boy and his girl-friend, Flavia, lay entwined on the hot ash. Their clothes were burnt. Léon went back into his room, knowing neither what he was doing nor what to do. The decision was made for him. His woollen waistcoat, hanging on a hook on the wall, suddenly burst into flames and the house started to blaze. He took to the hills. The whole city was on fire. Rubble, hot ash and dust hindered his escape. He saw no other living person as he was running away, but many corpses were strewn across the ground near Trouvaillant. Léon Compère-Léandre took refuge in Fonds-Saint-Denis, and he was taken to Fort-de-France to have his burns treated.

The escape of the Raybaud family

At the critical moment, the Raybaud family and their friends were just going to sit down for breakfast at Trouvaillant on the hills overlooking Saint-Pierre. Suddenly, they heard an appalling noise as if thousands of ships were giving off steam at once. They ran outside to investigate and saw the nuée ardente skimming down below them towards Saint-Pierre:

Cabin homes in the village of Le Carbet.

"Instinctively", said Monsieur Raybaud, "we rushed back into the house. What should we do? We clutched each other tight. We wanted to die together, and we waited for death. My son . . . went outside again, but came back in at once shouting: "Let's get out. We still have time. The sugar-canes are on fire. We can't stay here!"

They needed no persuasion. "The fire gave strength to our legs." They fled under a bombardment of stones and huge chunks of mud to Fonds-Saint-Denis, where Monsieur Raybaud safely installed everyone in the town hall. Then, ignoring the possible dangers, he went back to Trouvaillant. The house had been spared. The sugar plantations on the hills above the house were still intact, but those below it had been destroyed. Their labourers had lived below the house. About 20 had been injured, but 72 had been killed. He arranged for his two coaches and all the carts in the workshops to be harnessed up, and took the survivors to Fort-de-France.

Life and death on the fringes of the nuée ardente

Passioniste Lesage left Saint-Pierre at 7.30 a.m. to walk to Le Carbet. About 2 km from the city and 20 m from the Fonds-Joly plantation, he met a couple of tradeswomen, and they began talking. He had his back to the volcano, which probably saved his life. Suddenly, he heard a tremendous explosion and saw the great cloud fall upon the city. This cloud reached him within two minutes. He tried to take refuge in the plantation, but the blast from the north threw him against a tree, blew off his hat, and thrust him more than 3 m across the ground. At the same time, mud splattered all over him and one pebble was driven into his ankle, while another wounded him painfully in the backside. He could hardly breathe because hot ash and dust had blocked his mouth and nostrils. The blast burned his feet, right elbow, hands and the small of his back (which had been facing the crater), but his trousers and shirt stayed intact. The two women with him, who had been facing the volcano, were killed. At the plantation, he found several people who had not been burned, because they had been able to take shelter just in time. Passioniste Lesage was then able to walk to Le Carbet, and a boat took him to the hospital in Fort-de-France that evening.

Simon Taudilas was chatting with a group of three men and three women near Le Parnasse, when he saw the nuée coming towards them. He ran away with a couple of his friends, but the blast pushed them to the ground, and hot mud splattered over them. All three men recovered well enough to run to Le Parnasse, where one of them, a 20 year-old, died an hour after they arrived. Taudilas and his other friend both felt extremely thirsty and they had to drink the dregs of sugar-cane brandy. They were both transferred to hospital in Fort-de-France three days later. Taudilas survived, but his companion died. The three women took refuge in a nearby plantation building, where they were burned but they survived. It was reported that one of them, Paulémie Germonté, experienced some difficulty in breathing afterwards.

Two miracles

On the Morne Orange hill, at the extreme southeastern end of the area covered by the nuée ardente, two women had the good luck to see the cloud approaching, and had the presence of mind and just enough time to barricade themselves in the Laugier shop. They effectively sealed themselves from the scorching nuée. Luck stayed with them. The shop proved to be air tight and the building resisted the weakening blast. By the time the shop caught fire, the nuée had passed onwards, the air had cleared, and the women could run to safety. It is another measure of the chaos that reigned that the women were neither named nor counted among the survivors.

The second unusual adventure was recounted by Edith Duchâteau Roger.

A young girl had spent the night of 7–8 May at the convent, but she had been so frightened by the eruption that she decided to leave by the morning coach for Saint-Pierre. It had not journeyed very far when the great eruption occurred. She jumped in terror from the vehicle and rushed back towards the village. She was on the brink of exhaustion when she saw a black man fleeing in the same direction. She offered him some money if he would carry her to the church. However, as an astonished Edith declared, "The black man did not let himself be won over by this generous proposition. He sought to ensure his own safety, and let the poor young girl battle on as best she could". The girl reached the church in a pitiful state, but Edith was glad to report that the girl had the consolation of being the first to see the miraculous appearance of the Sacred Heart. She did not record the black man's fate.

The escape of Edouard Lasserre

Edouard Lasserre's youngest daughter, Hélène, was taking her First Communion on Ascension Day, and her parents, older sister and brother were with her in the cathedral. Before the service was due to start, Monsieur Simonet, the manager of their estate near Le Morne-Rouge, came in and announced that some animals had escaped. Edouard Lasserre, left his family in the cathedral and his coachman drove them to the estate. They had gone about 3 km towards Le Morne-Rouge when they saw the nuée ardente erupt.

> We spurred our horses up to the gallop to escape from the danger. We were right at the edge of the area covered by the cloud. Thus, up the hill, 10 m ahead of us, the cloud left no trace of its passage, although two people who were 10 m behind us were killed . . . The clouds caught up with us, our coach was turned upside down, and we found ourselves on the ground, under the vehicle . . . We must have been thrown to the ground with some violence, as our many injuries showed, especially to our heads.
>
> We came round again about three minutes after our terrible jolt . . . It was starting to clear up. We got out from beneath the vehicle. It was then that all three of us discovered that we had been horribly burned. The exposed parts of our bodies, our heads and hands, were particularly burnt, and our legs as far as half way up our thighs. But our feet had been protected by our shoes and were unaffected. The lower part of my

companion's trousers had been burned, but my own clothes showed not the slightest trace of burning . . . The Grand Réduit plantation was about 300 m farther on and we wanted to reach it to get help . . . but . . . stones began to rain down on us and they continued as far as Grand Réduit. These stones were as large as hazel nuts and looked like pumice stone . . . Our vehicle had been overturned at the outermost edge of the clouds . . . There is no doubt that we would have been spared if we had managed to get 10 m farther on.

The trio were more severely burned than at first appeared. As Edith Duchâteau-Roger recounted, they were given first aid by the sisters of the Délivrande in Le Morne-Rouge.

Their appearance was the most horrible imaginable. Their faces were completely disfigured. They were covered with dreadful wounds from head to foot that stopped them from moving their arms and feet. Their bodies were very swollen . . . It took three hours to dress their burns, and the poor patients withstood it always with great courage . . . Three days later, they were taken to the hospital in La Trinité. They were in such a pitiful state that there seemed little hope for them and it seemed inevitable that one of them would lose his legs. They suffered so much that they said that they would rather die than have any more dressings . . . but they recovered in the end.

The eruption experienced from Le Morne-Rouge

The sisters at the Convent of the Délivrande felt the ground shudder, heard a tremendous noise, and dashed to the chapel to die at the altar as the sky went dark. They "implored the clemency of God . . . There was a dreadful smell of sulphur, and thick fumes hid the chapel vault. It burned our throats and chests, our tongues were dried up and it seemed as if we were going to die of asphyxiation, buried under the rocks that were falling with a terrible din onto the roof". It was then that Edith vowed to become a nun.

The sisters spent most of the day at prayer, and Father Mary gave them the last rites in his parish church in Le Morne-Rouge. The church was so crowded that there was hardly room even to stand. Father Bruno and Brother Gérard said the low mass. Father Mary had asked them to come up from Saint-Pierre on 7 May, and had thereby saved their lives. Edith Duchâteau-Roger

The case of the courageous gunners

When the eruption occurred, gunners Tribut and Vaillant were on guard at Colson Camp, near Fonds-Saint-Denis. The soldiers had been forbidden to leave camp, but they could not resist the temptation to go and explore Saint-Pierre as soon as the air cleared. So they absconded. That afternoon, the camp commander himself sent two men on horseback to Saint-Pierre, but the hot ash prevented them from entering the city. As they were coming back, they met Tribut and Vaillant, who were helping a badly burnt sailor, whom they claimed to have found on the beach at Saint-Pierre. He was Raphaël Pons, a stoker from the *Roraïma*, which was ablaze in the bay. They stated that some people must have been still alive in Saint-Pierre, because they had heard shrieks of agony in the ruins. They said that they had even given water to a badly-burnt white family and their servant, and had promised to send them help. "Nonsense," asserted their superior officers, "no-one could survive in such an inferno." Vaillant and Tribut were charged with absconding. But Vaillant stood firm, and was eventually allowed to return by boat to Saint-Pierre on 9 May. He brought a burnt black woman to the vessel, saying that she was the servant that he had seen the previous afternoon. All the family she had served had since died. The servant seemed to agree with Vaillant's story, but she was gravely ill and she died on the way to Fort-de-France. The military authorities refused to believe the gunners' story about Raphaël Pons for two main reasons: superior officers had failed to enter the city from the landward side, and it was argued that Pons could not have escaped from the *Roraïma*. (But in fact other sailors had managed to reach the shore from vessels in the bay.) In spite of the assertions of the authorities, it seems obvious that the gunners must have found Raphaël Pons in Saint-Pierre, and that he had come from the vessel, and therefore survived the nuée ardente. However, it is mysterious that no mention of this incident, nor of the fate of stoker Pons, appears to have survived in the French military records. Alfred Lacroix described the story, but, somewhat surprisingly, was inclined not to believe it. Nevertheless, the ambiguities of the tale most probably illustrate the immense shock caused by the eruption rather than any malicious intent on the part of the military authorities.

described how there had been a "miraculous apparition of the Sacred Heart of Jesus in the monstrance in the church. Several among the congregation saw it, but not always to the same extent. Some saw His whole body; others only saw the Sacred Heart itself. The miracle lasted throughout the mass and the benediction."

The flight from Beauregard

Young Elodie and her cousin, Raymond, were perched in a cherry tree at Beauregard when the nuée ardente erupted. They ran into the house screaming: "The mountain's falling down onto us!" Uncle Joseph alerted everyone and the half-dressed children led the frantic cavalcade away from the great black cloud that was rolling towards Saint-Pierre. After they had run about 100 m, they stopped to see if everyone had escaped from the house. Charles Dujon counted 17 instead of 19 people (not including those who were black). His parents were missing. As the infernal cloud loomed over the plantation, Charles turned to rescue his parents. Emilie clung to him desperately and begged him not to leave her. "Do not follow me!" he ordered, "Do *not* follow me!" She knelt down on the path, moaning in terror, with her arms stretched out as if she was on a cross. "It was a terrible moment", she confessed, as Charles went into the house and the others disappeared along the path through the sugar-cane fields. The noise was deafening.

At last, Charles returned with his mother and his poor blind father. They had been in the bathroom. Old Monsieur Dujon had just climbed out of the bath. He had refused to flee naked, and his wife had refused to abandon him. So, they had dressed and had been resigned to death when Charles arrived.

The four of them fled across the hills as thousands of explosions and fires burst out all around them. "Why bother to run away?" thought Emilie, "We're doomed anyway. Only a miracle can save us. We were tired out. We fell onto our knees to pray before we died."

They had taken the path to the right, but the rest of the family had fled to the left. Each group believed that the other was dead. Suddenly, the fearful return wind blew up from the south. "It pushed back the mountain of death hanging above our heads. We started running again. Then a rain of stones, and tepid, fetid, mud fell upon us. More squalls succeeded the first. We were pale and breathless; our clothes and faces were blackened with the mud and the ash, and our feet were torn to shreds." Charles sent the black boss at Beauregard to find the others.

Meanwhile, the rest of the family had been tormented by the heart-rending shrieks coming from Saint-Pierre just below them. A sinister silence had fallen, as the dark cloud had spread over their heads. Burning mud and glowing stones had rained down and had set fire to the stubble of the sugar cane. The darkness had become even more threatening. They thought they were doomed. In despair, they had sat down beside a flooding torrent and tried to protect their eyes and noses from the ash and mud. Then, the return wind had blown the cloud back over Saint-Pierre and had given them new heart. At that very moment, the black boss at Beauregard had appeared.

They were all reunited at the L'Enfanton plantation, which belonged to Monsieur Pierre-Joseph Fabre, a teacher at the Lycée. It was already full of terrified people. They were given clothing to replace that which the mud had caked into hard plaster. The house stood on a terrace overlooking Saint-Pierre, so that they had a good view of the burning city below – too good. They realized only too well that no-one could have escaped from the furnace in those ruins, even those who were no more than 300 m away, down in the Monsieur quarter of Saint-Pierre. Gaston, Emilie's brother, was one of those who had refused to leave the city. And so had the La Roche family, to whom Raoul Marry and his family owed their salvation. It was a horrifying spectacle. They felt an aching desolation. Some of the women were weeping quietly; the men were gazing into space. Old nanny Rosina fainted. Rosette Marry herself had a screaming fit and then set about reviving nanny.

A pale daylight returned and revealed a lunar landscape covered with white ash. They wondered whether to go back to Beauregard or to make for the coast at Le Carbet and try to escape to Fort-de-France before Mount Pelée unleashed an even larger eruption. They opted for the coast.

But first, the men decided to retrieve a few things from Beauregard. In particular, they went to collect the family jewellery, which they had put into a basket the previous day. They realized that this jewellery had probably already become their only remaining source of revenue. Raoul Marry and Charles Dujon went to fetch the basket and find the horse and coach to carry the weariest members of the party to the coast.

At Beauregard, the house was intact, but all the estate buildings, the stable and the workers' cabins had been badly damaged. They found the basket, and the horse was still alive. Raoul and Charles harnessed it to the vehicle and returned to L'Enfanton.

The convoy set off for Le Carbet, weary, unkempt and mostly barefoot. The oldest women and the children rode in the coach, and a motley array of young ragamuffins and older adults hurried on in front. Blind Monsieur Dujon clung to the coach and held up his wife. Emilie Dujon leaned on her husband, Charles. Joseph Marry had only one trouser leg left because the brambles had ripped off the other as he had fled. Out in front ran Elodie and her cousins. As Elodie confessed later, now that the ash had stopped falling and the Sun was shining, and the dreadful cloud had disappeared, the youngsters felt rather proud to be taking part in such a great adventure.

The brighter mood did not last long. They hurried to the Dariste plantation at the entrance to Le Carbet, only to find it empty. Doubts set in as soon as they saw the sea. A tidal wave seemed to have damaged the shore. The sea might rise again and drown everyone. This was not a safe place at all. They decided to push on to the Lajus plantation. The owners sent a message for them to come and join other refugees up the hill, even farther from the sea. They struggled back up the steep slope under the burning Sun. It was after 2.00 p.m. when they reached a vast mule stable, where about 150 people from Le Carbet had taken refuge. They threw themselves, exhausted, onto the straw. Their throats were on fire, their bruised feet were throbbing in pain, and they had started to tremble with fear again as soon as they relaxed. They had been running from death for nearly seven hours.

The priest from Le Carbet arrived. The crowd begged him to give them absolution. "None of us", wrote Emilie, "knew what fate still had in store for us. Everyone knelt down and the words of the sacrament descended upon our bowed heads." Their tired bodies and anguished minds could take no more. They lay down in a stupor on the straw and tried to rest.

12

The Bay of Saint-Pierre
Thursday 8 May 1902

Some 7–8 km off Saint-Pierre, Emile Berté had finished the medical inspection on the *Pouyer Quertier* and was relaxing on the bridge when two gigantic flashes of lightning suddenly furrowed the air from the crest of Mount Pelée down to the Bay of Saint-Pierre. A dark mass covered the city and it seemed to catch fire.

> I ran to my cabin to get my fieldglasses. I got back to the bridge 30 seconds later – the whole coast was lit up. The mountainside was red, as if it had melted. Something gripped my temples and my throat. There was nothing for it: Saint-Pierre was on fire. I really suffered at that moment. I ran to the bridge to ask the commander to make for the land so that I could go and help my family – Captain Thirion had already started to turn the *Pouyer Quertier* to go and help.

Three minutes later, a thick curtain of ash shrouded the ship in darkness. The *Pouyer Quertier* had to slow down. Suddenly a whirlpool developed to port. It was clearly too dangerous to go on and put in danger the lives of all the 70 men on board, and Captain Thirion turned the vessel back to the safety of the open sea. Bands of terrified porpoises fled ahead of the ship as it made for Fort-de-France and assumed a vital role in the subsequent rescues.

To witnesses in the bay, Mount Pelée seemed to split wide open with a tremendous noise. The nuée ardente blasted down to Saint-Pierre and destroyed all but one of about a dozen larger vessels and scores of smaller craft moored off the city. Most of those on board ship were burned, scalded, suffocated or drowned. Only a fortunate few survived and some of those lived only because their burnt and dying comrades fell on top of them. The nuée

The chief vessels lost in the Bay of Saint-Pierre on 8 May 1902.

Name	Net tonnage	Length (m)	Type (wood/iron)	Built	Registered	Flag	Owner	Captain	Arrived from	Cargo/function
Anna E. J. Morse	651	49.6	schooner (W)	Bath, Maine, USA, 1886	Portland, Maine	US	J. S. Winslow & Co.	Crocker	Philadelphia	coal
Biscaye	159	32.0	brigantine (W)	Bilbao, Spain, 1878	Bayonne, France	French	Vidart & Légasse	Trivily	Saint-Pierre, Miquelon	codfish
L.W. Norton	464	42.4	brigantine (W)	Horton, Nova Scotia, Canada, 1890	Windsor, Nova Scotia	British	G.B. Lockhart	Pardo		
Nord America	558	45.0	barque (W)	Buccari, Italy, 1881	Castellamare	Italian	Pollio Brothers	Cilento		
Sacro Cuore	558	45.6	barque (W)	Venice, Italy, 1877	Naples	Italian	G. Lubrano di Scampamorte	Fasano	Marseille	general
Tamaya	459	49.4	barque (I)	Liverpool, UK, 1862	Nantes, France	French	R. Rozier	Boju	Nantes	general
Teresa Lo Vico	563	44.5	barque (W)	Sestri Ponente, Italy, 1874	Palermo	Italian	A. Lo Vico	Ferrara		sugar for Nantes*
Grappler	498	63.5	steamer (I)	Sunderland, UK, 1880	London	British	West India & Panama Tel. Co	Bonham		cable repair ship
Roraima	1761	103.6	steamer (I)	Glasgow, UK, 1883	Quebec, Canada	British	Quebec Steamship Co.	Muggah	New York	general/passengers

*(According to J.C. Fine, Surveyor, February 1982, the remains of the ship contain piles of building tiles and barrels of cement).

The following vessels were destroyed. They were not mentioned in Lloyd's Register, probably because they were less than 100 net tonnes.

Name	Net tonnage	Length (m)	Type (wood/iron)	Built	Registered	Flag	Owner	Captain	Arrived from	Cargo/function
Gabrielle			schooner			French	A. Knight		Fort-de-France	
Diamant			packet steamer			French	Girard Company		Fort-de-France	passengers

The vessel below escaped from Saint-Pierre and returned to Saint-Lucia.

Name	Net tonnage	Length (m)	Type (wood/iron)	Built	Registered	Flag	Owner	Captain	Arrived from	Cargo/function
Roddam	1794	88.3	steel steamer	West Hartlepool, UK, 1887	London	British	Steel, Young & Co.	Freeman	London	general/passengers

The following French Naval Vessel most active in the events was mentioned in Lloyd's Register.

Name	Net tonnage	Length (m)	Type (wood/iron)	Built	Registered	Flag	Owner	Captain	Arrived from	Cargo/function
Suchet	3430	96.9	steel cruiser	Toulon, 1893		French		Le Bris		

The *Arama* and *Maria Vergine* often cited as lost, were not cited as lost in Lloyd's Register. Their fate is thus uncertain. RMS *Esk* was incorrectly cited as lost in a recent publication.

[Reproduced from the Register of Ships for the years 1902-3 with permission of Lloyd's Register of Shipping, 71, Fenchurch Street, London, EC3M 4BS, UK].

ardente offered no chance whatsoever to vessels near the foot of the volcano. The British cable ship, *Grappler*, for instance, was searching for the broken cable closest to the volcano. With a majestic swipe, the nuée ardente sent the vessel, Captain Bonham and his crew straight to the bottom of the sea. Vessels moored farther away stood a better chance for a moment or two.

The Teresa Lo Vico

The Italian sailing ship, *Teresa Lo Vico*, was moored about 50 m off the southern end of the city, farthest from the volcano. Jean-Louis Prudent was the ship's engineer. About 8.00 a.m., he saw the nuée ardente explode from the crater in an enormous purplish mass and make straight for Saint-Pierre. Then the cloud covered them in darkness and scythed down the masts of the *Teresa Lo Vico*. Most of those on deck died at once. A mast killed Captain Ferrara and removed his face. The ship's boy was below in the engine room and had the presence of mind to plunge his head into a washbasin to protect himself from the blast. Prudent himself was thrown down and some of his comrades fell on top of him. Their bodies – soon to be their corpses – saved his life. He lost consciousness. When he recovered, it was not so dark, and he gazed around him in bewilderment. Saint-Pierre was on fire and the rum distilleries were exploding one after another. First hot mud and then ash rained down on him. The exposed parts of his body seemed to have been scalded, but his beard, hair and shirt were still intact. Mountainous waves swamped the ship when it touched the sea bottom four or five times.

Jean-Louis Prudent was as strong and resourceful as he was brave. He dived into the sea, took control of a small craft that was still intact, and dragged it to the *Teresa Lo Vico*. He managed to pull on board his wife and her maid, Captain Ferrara's widow, and nine badly burnt sailors. The craft drifted southwards to Le Carbet, tossing and turning on the waves, Eventually, Prudent was able to steer their boat towards the relic of a landing stage. They disembarked and waited there like zombies, stupefied with shock and pain, until they were rescued several hours later.

The Diamant

As the time for the *Diamant*'s 8.00 a.m. departure approached, the captain took the steamer from its mooring buoy and went to the quayside to welcome any passengers bound for Fort-de-France. Jean-Baptiste Innocent, the ship's boy on the *Diamant*, was attaching a hawser to the quay when the nuée ardente arrived. He was facing out to sea and never even saw it. All the other members of the crew were killed at once, either by the scorching blast, or when its heat burst the ship's boiler and drenched them in the scalding water. Innocent was extraordinarily lucky. He suddenly found himself in the sea without ever knowing why, bobbing like flotsam on the waves. While the nuée ardente was passing over, Innocent had to dive under water several times to avoid being burned by the falling hot ash. He was soon so exhausted that he had to make for the shore. Suddenly, the sea retreated and he found himself on dry land. Once more, luck was on his side. Before the ash could seriously burn him, a returning wave threw him back into the sea and took him far enough out to protect him, but not far enough out to drown him. He held on to a plank and stayed in the water, bemused and terrified at the destruction all around him, and not daring to go near the blazing shore. He clung to the plank for seven hours before he was rescued.

The Gabrielle

Georges Marie-Sainte was on the deck of the *Gabrielle* off the northern shore of Saint-Pierre when Mount Pelée released the nuée ardente. The captain just had time to have the hawsers loosened and to order the crew to shelter below deck before the nuée struck the schooner. But the port-holes below were still open, so that the scorching cloud burned and killed most of the men. The blast swept off the mast, laid the vessel on its beam ends, scalded Marie-Saintes and four crewmen, and flung them into the sea. They heard a sinister cracking and creaking as the nuée ardente smashed the masts and poops from the other vessels and sank most of them without further ado. It is not clear whether the *Gabrielle* sank at once, or whether it stayed afloat for a while, because the empty casks in its hold gave it a certain buoyancy. At any rate, it offered no refuge for the five survivors from the schooner.

Georges Marie-Saintes managed to get rid of the tackle hampering his movements in the water, and returned to the surface to see Saint-Pierre in ruins and ablaze. The five survivors started swimming about, looking around for any kind of wreck to escape upon. Then the mud and stones whistled down and spattered onto the sea like a fusillade of bullets. As if that were not enough, the desperate swimmers were severely hampered when the turbulent waters of the Rivière Roxelane started sweeping mud, trees, dead animals and human corpses out towards them Eventually, each man found a piece of wreckage that was large enough to keep him afloat.

During a brighter interlude at about 9.00 a.m., they decided to get away from the inferno in Saint-Pierre and make for the open sea. But the change of wind direction that had cleared the air also began to push all the flotsam towards the flaming shore. Marie-Saintes decided to swim out to sea. His companions had neither the strength, nor perhaps the courage, to face the open sea and they decided to keep clinging onto their own pieces of wreckage. Before long, however, the wind changed again and the five met up once more. After a while, they saw a vessel coming towards them, but their desperate signals remained unanswered. They began to lose heart. They had then been in the water for several hours, with a blazing city behind them and no prospect of salvation ahead of them.

At about 2.00 p.m., they saw an empty pirogue canoe floating in the distance. Marie-Saintes swam to get it, but it took them half an hour, bobbing like corks on the huge waves, to empty all the ash from the canoe and make it safe for all five to clamber aboard. By then, they were so exhausted that they could do nothing but sit in it and wait.

The adventures of the Roddam

The *Roddam* carried general cargo between London and the West Indies, and Edward William Freeman had captained the vessel for the previous four years. He was 35, immensely strong, and was British with a strong American accent. The *Roddam* had left London on 11 April and had first called at Trinidad and then at Grenada. In Barbados on 4 May, a man warned them to be careful in Martinique, because Mount Pelée had "wiped out a sugar plantation that had been licked up by the volcano". The crew "began to get a bit nervous" when they heard this wild rumour. The *Roddam* reached Saint Lucia on 6 May and left on the evening of 7 May to sail overnight to Martinique, where the ship entered the Bay of Saint-Pierre at 6.45 a.m. and gave Captain Freeman a grandstand view of the nuée ardente:

141

A contemporary sketch of the Roddam, *the only vessel to escape from the nuée ardente in the Bay of Saint-Pierre.*

There came a sudden roar that shook the earth and the sea . . . I called down to Plissonneau in his boat: "Come up here, you can see better." [Supercargo] Campbell had scrambled on deck, and the agent had just followed, when we saw the city swallowed up.

Then we realized our own danger. There was only one thing to do – make for the nearest shelter . . . I found myself in the chart house. Then the ship was struck as if by a giant hand . . . The *Roddam* heeled far over – had the port-holes of the lower deck been open we should have sunk at once. The hot dust raked us from stem to stern, firing everything that it touched as it drove over us, swirling along in a torrential downpour, filling the ship, penetrating every crevice. Those who were caught on deck, like Campbell and many of the seamen, were swept overboard, to be drowned in a boiling sea; others were caught as they were rushing below decks, and shrieked in agony as the hot stuff scorched their flesh. A blazing blinding shower of dust drove through . . . searing my eyes, my face and hands.

For two minutes I endured the agony – it seemed more like two years. I wondered – will death never come? . . . The worst of it was that the air was so filled with the hot dust that, with every breath you took, you drew it into your mouth [and] into your lungs, so that you were burned inside and out.

I groped my way to the bridge, stumbling over the bodies of my men. The deck was burning, and every step I took scorched my feet, every-thing I touched burned my hands . . . The still waters of the harbour were churned into mountainous waves, and the ship bobbed like a cork, so that I could hardly stand. I heard men rushing about the decks like raving maniacs; now and then someone threw himself overboard, to be drowned in the boiling water.

The first thing to do was to get away . . . I began to shout orders, to call the men together if possible. I gave the engine room the signal, "full speed astern", working the telegraph instrument with my elbows – my hands were too burnt to grasp the handle . . . I caught sight of the first engineer. I told him to go forward and see if the anchor chain held fast. He replied that he could not move, he was so badly hurt; he died about three hours later in awful agony. I was helpless myself and could only give directions . . . I found I had a boatswain and five sailors at my service . . . The engineers went full speed astern . . . and let the anchor chain run out until it snapped. Then we found that the steering gear was jammed on the starboard side [with ash and wreckage]. The ship was uncontrollable. I felt pretty bad then. The waves were tossing us at their mercy . . .

The ship seemed to struggle like some wounded monster, lurching ahead and then lurching astern . . . unable to move in any direction save backwards and forwards. . . . More than once in our wild helpless dashes ahead and astern we nearly collided with the *Roraïma*. Once we drifted to within 150 feet [45 m], and I could see the men on board, and could clearly hear their cries above the turmoil of the waves . . . Her forward decks were crowded with passengers and crew, and I thought I detected cries for help . . . We could only reverse engines and back away from her; to give any help was out of the question, even if we could have brought the *Roddam* alongside.

It was an hour and a half [i.e. 9.30 a.m.] . . . before our steering gear was clear; 90 minutes of drifting that seemed like a voyage of 90 years through an inferno. At last we could . . . make for the open sea . . . It seemed to grow a little lighter . . . But by now the woodwork of the cabins had caught fire and we could prevent the flames from spreading over the ship only by smothering each fire as it burst out.

At first only two dead bodies were found. But 15 wounded men, burnt, and twisted by their contortions beyond all recognition, were brought upon deck, and put in the most sheltered spot – we could do nothing more for them . . . Death came mercifully to eight of the sufferers in the course of the voyage . . . At last we could make out Castries, the port of Saint Lucia. It was now about 5.00 p.m.

When we left, some 18 hours before, the *Roddam* was spick and span in black and white paint with a bright red funnel. Now she was more like a phantom ship than anything else – a ghostly, ghastly apparition.

They soon got the survivors to shore and into hospital. Three died the same evening. Plissonneau, who was badly injured, was sent to his wife and family – to live only a few days. Out of a total of 46 souls on board, 26 were killed by the eruption or died of injuries . . . I lay in hospital for three weeks, my hands and face feeling as though they were being burned in the flames all the time . . .

However, there is one blot on the copybook of this self-confessed hero. Captain Freeman was no good Samaritan. He could surely have made a better attempt to save the injured people assembled on the deck of the *Roraïma* after the *Roddam*'s steering-gear was released at 9.30 a.m. However, the nuée ardente provided a sore test of courage, and most ordinary mortals would have been found wanting.

The Roraïma

Ellery S. Scott, First Mate, of the *Roraïma* was on deck just before 8.00 a.m. and most of the 16 or so passengers were below preparing for breakfast.

"Then an odd thing happened . . . The atmosphere seemed to shudder". The nuée ardente erupted "as if all the dynamite in the universe had blown up the mountain. No train going at full speed could have escaped from it." A few men, including Bensen, the ship's Danish carpenter, ran to the bow to try and raise the anchor, but hot blast drove them back. The blast smashed across the *Roraïma* and swirled mountainous sea-waves over its decks. The vessel hit the bottom and rolled onto her beam ends. Then the scorching cloud and red hot stones hit the ship. The passengers below were burned to

The Roraïma *burning on its side in the Bay of Saint-Pierre in the afternoon of 8 May 1902.*

death by the hot blast, or drowned when the sea rushed in through the starboard scuttles. Everything was razed from the bridge: the iron funnel, the two steel masts, and most of the lifeboats. The hatches were staved in and the ship was listing steeply to starboard. Then the scalding mud splattered all over and dried like plaster casts on everyone's heads. The saloon set alight. The ship seemed doomed. Second Engineer Evans and Fourth Engineer Morris dashed for the shelter of the engine room. Ellery Scott clung to an airshaft with all his strength, only to find that the waves were pushing him into the hole. Two men dragged him below deck. Darkness fell.

From time to time, a burnt sailor, shrieking atrociously, would tumble through the hatch and fall dead on top of him. Ellery Scott was soon buried beneath a pile of bodies. Then someone took him back to the bridge.

Captain Muggah appeared. Scott could recognize him only by his smoking clothes. His face was completely burnt, and his hair and beard had been seared off. Scott never saw the captain after that, but a stevedore said that he had jumped overboard, and taken refuge on an improvised raft. Command of the vessel therefore devolved upon the first mate, Ellery Scott. The new commander first went looking for his eldest son. He never found him.

At about 8.30 a.m. they saw the *Roddam* coming towards them, as if it was going to save them. The able-bodied crew started to collect the passengers at the bows, but to their utter despair the *Roddam* moved away again. As what seemed like their only hope abandoned them, the survivors on the *Roraïma* stood dumbfounded and red raw with burns.

About 8.45 a.m. they distributed life belts to the survivors and laid them down on the bridge. All the survivors were begging for water, but they could not drink it. Their mouths, throats, and stomachs were horribly burnt. Some even had their mouths, noses, eyes and ears completely blocked up. The water suffocated them, and they had to be turned over to help them spit it out again. But they always asked for more. Someone broke open the refrigerator door and gave the victims small pieces of ice, but it made little difference. One woman's jaw had locked. They gave her some ice with a small spoon. She just had enough strength to whisper "thank you" before she died.

By then, the deck was slippery with the hot mud, and the ship was on fire in three places, where the glowing ash had set cushions and carpets alight in the saloons and cabins. They had to control the fires or they were doomed. The most worrying fire was in the port-side wheelhouse, because the holds full of inflammable materials, including timber, were only 4 m away. They began the desperate battle. They had to fill the buckets with sea water, but they had to be careful not to pick up any of the rum that was floating across the water from the burst casks in the distilleries in Saint-Pierre. The passengers who were still alive were huddled forward. Perhaps they were too injured or shocked to lend a hand?

The crew tried to build a raft out of the timber and other pieces of cargo. They did not make much progress, because the fires kept on bursting out again. The pall of smoke in the bay lifted after about 3.00 p.m., but by then the *Roraïma* was ablaze from fore to aft.

Italians saved from the Roraïma

When the eruption occurred, three Italian sailors, Salvador Aiella and Giuseppe Susino, and Francesco d'Angelo, were on the bridge of the *Roraïma*. They rushed down into the battery. One hid under a table; the other two were covered when dying, burnt companions dropped upon them. When the nuée had passed over, they managed to scramble on deck and dive into the sea in the darkness. They took hold of some pieces of wreckage and floated southwards. Eventually they swam to an upturned floating deckhouse. They were astonished and delighted to see that it was manned by three more Italian sailors, who had been in the deckhouse of the *Nord America* when the nuée ardente had swept it bodily into the sea. They had suffered from no more than a buffeting and utter amazement. They also turned out to be the only survivors from that vessel. For the next three or four hours, the deckhouse drifted around the bay on the whim of every changing wind or current.

About mid-day, they saw Captain Muggah clinging to a piece of wreckage. He was practically naked, his beard and hair had been burned off and his face was blistered almost beyond recognition. He could not see them, but when they called out to him, he responded and asked for some water. They helped him aboard their makeshift craft, but they had no water to give him. They were with him when he died shortly afterwards.

The Italian sailors also picked up other survivors who were floating or swimming in the bay, including "a Spaniard and two blacks", but they all soon died from their burns. A little later, the deckhouse drifted towards the Place Bertin, where the fires had almost come to an end. D'Angelo and Susino landed, and Susino quenched his thirst from the cool fresh water that was still gushing from the fountain in the square. Assistant Purser Thompson and a black labourer swam from the *Roraïma* and joined them on the shore, before they all went back to the deckhouse and floated around the bay.

No-one on the *Roraïma* mentioned the departure of Stoker Raphaël Pons, who was apparently picked up by gunners Tribut and Vaillant. His story is tantalizingly brief and incomplete. So, too, is the story of the youngest survivor from the *Roraïma*.

Nine-year-old Margaret Stokes was found safe and sound and petrified on the *Roraïma* in the afternoon. She had been in a cabin with her mother, sister and brother, and her former nanny. The door and the port-hole were both shut. Then, suddenly, there were some strange and muddled jolts and a deep darkness fell. The ceiling of the cabin burst open and the door was smashed to pieces. The terrified child threw herself under her former nanny's skirts, and nanny buried her face in Mrs Stokes' dress. Margaret and nanny woke up from their nightmare to discover that the rest of the family were dead.

The survivors of the *Roraïma*

- Nine members of the crew of the *Roraïma* survived, plus two passengers: Miss Mary Stokes and her unnamed former nanny.
- Two crewmen who were protected in the engine room: Second Engineer Evans and Fourth Engineer Morris.
- Four crewmen who were protected in rooms with firmly sealed doors: First Mate Scott and the ship's Danish carpenter, Bensen, who seem to have been accompanied by Assistant Purser Thompson and "a negro labourer".
- Three Italian crewmen survived because they were protected by the bodies of their comrades, who fell upon them as they lay on the floor of the forecastle: Susino, Aeilla and d'Angelo.
- It is also possible that stoker Raphaël Pons, whom Tribut and Vaillant claimed to have saved from the shore of Saint-Pierre, might also have survived, although the total lack of subsequent news of him suggests that he might well have succumbed soon afterwards.
- In addition to the above, three unnamed, uninjured sailors survived from the *Nord America*.

13

Ruins

Thursday 8 May 1902

Fort-de-France, 8.00 a.m., 8 May

In Fort-de-France, Ascension Day had dawned as gloriously as in Saint-Pierre, and the Girard company steamers had been plying to and fro as usual between the capital and Saint-Pierre. The *Diamant* had left Fort-de-France at 6.00 a.m., and the *Rubis* had left Fort-de-France, in turn, just after 7.00 a.m. Travelling in the other direction, the *Topaze* had left Saint-Pierre at 6.00 a.m. and had docked in Fort-de-France at about 7.00 a.m.

In Fort-de-France, Dr Rémy Néris felt that he had abandoned some of his sick patients in Saint-Pierre when he had brought his family to the capital the previous evening. He therefore decided to spend the day attending to them in Saint-Pierre and he duly took his place on the *Topaze* for its 8.00 a.m departure. In fact, the steamer did not leave on time. "Five minutes before we left we were shaken violently and carried seawards by a sudden surge and almost thrown onto the beach. Within seconds, the sea went wild, the waves broke furiously, and then everything calmed down again".

The steamer set off in spite of these odd events. But the northern horizon quickly darkened.

A minute later, ash came crashing down onto the sea. A little farther on, we were terrified to see that the ash was now mixed with hot stones. Boats were coming towards us, fleeing as fast as they could from the rain of fire [from the north]. Their terrified passengers shouted warnings of the danger. We turned around and made for Fort-de-France, pursued by a hail of red hot pebbles.

Movements of ships on 8 May 1902

Time	Fort-de-France	Saint-Pierre
6.00 a.m.	*Diamant* departs	*Topaze* departs, *Roraïma* arrives
6.45 a.m.		*Roddam* arrives
7.00 a.m.	*Topaze* arrives	*Diamant* arrives, *Pouyer Quertier* off North Martinique
7.00 a.m.+	*Rubis* departs	
7.10 a.m.		Skiff departs for Le Prêcheur
8.02 a.m. NUEE ARDENTE		
8.02–9.30 a.m.		*Roddam* "uncontrollable"
8.10–8.15 a.m.	*Topaze* departs	*Rubis* forced to turn back
8.45 a.m.	*Topaze* meets returning *Rubis*	
9.15 a.m.	*Topaze* and *Rubis* return	
10.00 a.m.	*Rubis* departs	
11.00 a.m.		*Rubis* enters bay
12.00 a.m.		*Roddam* departs for Saint-Lucia
12.40 p.m.	*Suchet* departs	
1.00 p.m.	*Rubis* arrives	
1.30 p.m.		*Suchet* arrives in bay
2.00 p.m.	*Pouyer Quertier* arrives	
2.15 p.m.	*Rubis* departs	
3.15 p.m.		*Rubis* arrives in bay
4.00 p.m.	*Pouyer Quertier, Topaze, Pholade, ?Perle* depart	
5.00 p.m.		*Topaze, Pholade, ?Perle* reach Le Carbet
5.00 p.m. +		*Suchet* leaves bay
5.30 p.m.		*Pouyer Quertier* off Le Carbet
6.00 p.m.	*Suchet* arrives	
9.30 p.m.	*Rubis, Pouyer Quertier, Pholade, Topaze* and *?Perle* arrive	
10.00 p.m.	*Suchet* departs for Guadeloupe	*Pouyer Quertier* well off Saint-Pierre
11.00 p.m.		RMS *Esk* arrives in bay
12.00 p.m.		RMS *Esk* departs

One of the boats was its companion vessel, the *Rubis*, which had been unable to reach Saint-Pierre, and had turned around and dashed back to the safety of Fort-de-France. The steamers returned together to the harbour at about 9.15 a.m. to find the capital in total disarray. The ash that had battered the steamers had spread panic throughout the city.

Just after 8.00 a.m., the sky north of the capital had become as black as ink. Suddenly, ash and hot pellets spattered onto the roofs, and fine dust choked the city. An immense hubbub arose in the town. There was a frightful panic in the church, where mass had just started. The congregation opted to save their bodies rather than their souls. They left the priest alone and fled. It was almost pitch dark. Mount Pelée was thundering in the distance. Three times, the sea receded for several hundreds of metres and swept inland again. Some people stood petrified at their doors, while others went berserk and ran about in all directions. Many made for the hills to escape a possible tidal wave. They were also convinced – quite wrongly – that these same hills would protect them from any earthquakes. As *L'Opinion* put it next day, "there was a fantastic procession of panic-stricken people under the blinding ash, behaving like a herd of sheep . . . surprised by the first gusts of a terrifying storm".

There was no real justification for such panic in Fort-de-France, which resulted more from a collective psychosis than from any logical assessment of the situation. The crew of the *Suchet* continued preparations for their departure to Havana. However, during the eruption, Commander Le Bris noted that the barometer fell sharply by some 3 mm and that the sea had risen and fallen several times by about 1 m. He felt it wise to light the boilers. But, the stones soon stopped falling, the rain of ash and dust was very slight, and Fort-de-France lay 22 km from Mount Pelée. It was an entirely different matter in Saint-Pierre.

Saint-Pierre had been utterly silent since 8.02 a.m. As Abbé Parel recalled, "the most awful anguish gripped our hearts". Anxiety increased a hundred-fold when the *Topaze* and the *Rubis* returned after their aborted attempts to reach Saint-Pierre. Disquiet turned into foreboding. Civilians and soldiers were sent out towards Saint-Pierre, but they all had to turn back some way from the city. What did the silence mean? Why hadn't the *Diamant* returned? Surely, if a disaster had indeed stricken Saint-Pierre, the many survivors would soon start to appear? Was this one the first? A woman appeared on the coast road. But she ignored every question and wanted to embrace everyone in the crowd. She was weeping and only kept on babbling "It was about eight o'clock". She had gone out of her mind. Who she was, and where she had come from, no-one ever knew. She cannot have walked the distance from Saint-Pierre in the time. No-one dared think what could be happening in the city that lay almost at the foot of the volcano. There was only one way to find out.

It was about 11.00 a.m. when the *Rubis* risked setting out again on a reconnaissance. The steamer took Monsieur Labat, a deputy-mayor of Fort-de-France, with an offer to help the mayor of Saint-Pierre with any evacuation that might be needed. The lucky member of the scientific commission, Monsieur Mirville, was also on board, with the troops that the mayor of Saint-Pierre had requested the previous afternoon. As Monsieur Mirville said:

> As we approached the city, the air became warmer and warmer. We could not explain this increase in temperature, but it certainly worried us. Suddenly, we sailed past a small headland and saw a ghastly spectacle that I shall never forget. The whole city of Saint-Pierre was ablaze and formed a colossal inferno, 4 km long. In the bay . . . there was nothing but the shells of burning boats and upturned pirogues. Our little steamer was floating in the midst of the half-charred bodies of the unfortunate sailors from the vessels that had been consumed by the fire.
>
> [In vain, Monsieur Labat scanned the coast through his fieldglasses for any signs of life.] We did not see a living soul. The heat was intolerable. We were in grave danger. There could be another eruption and it seemed more prudent to leave as soon as possible. When I arrived at Fort-de-France, I rushed to the city hall to report the sinister news to the authorities. I had the sad privilege of being the first to announce the destruction of Saint-Pierre to the capital of Martinique.

Monsieur Mirville had been forced to make his way through a large, anxious crowd awaiting news on the quayside. His grim face told all. The horrible truth soon spread through the city. Saint-Pierre was lost. But no-one dared comprehend the likely number of deaths and the extent of the destruction. There must surely be many survivors. Practically everyone in Fort-de-France had friends or relatives in Saint-Pierre. Every hour that they waited increased their utter despair. The administration had stationed troops on the quayside, so as to be prepared for any eventuality. But their presence had multiplied the fears of the crowd, who felt that the authorities must have had news of an even greater cataclysm, but wished to keep it from them.

The role of the Suchet on 8 May

Something of the immense anxiety in Fort-de-France communicated itself to Commander Le Bris on the *Suchet*. He decided to take the cruiser to Saint-Pierre. He had to act entirely on his own initiative, because the administration, now in the hands of Monsieur Lhuerre (the Secretary

151

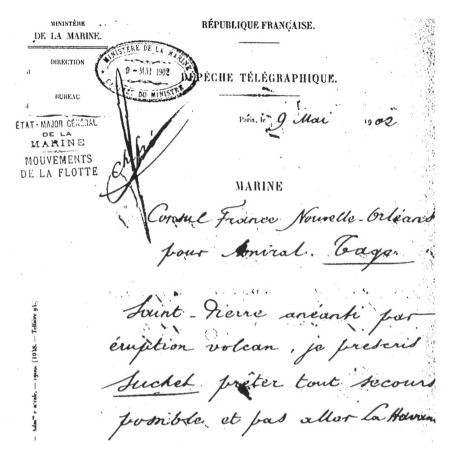

The telegram from the Navy Minister in Paris to Commander Le Bris: "Saint-Pierre having been annihilated by volcanic eruption, I ordain that the Suchet *should give all possible assistance and not go to Havana."*

General), had not yet progressed beyond a few of ad hoc arrangements, perhaps through a combination of inertia, incompetence, ignorance and shock.

The *Suchet* thus left Fort-de-France at 12.40 p.m. for Saint-Pierre. Commander Le Bris first learned the extent of the disaster when the cruiser met the returning *Rubis*. He continued to Saint-Pierre and reached the bay about 1.30 p.m. The commander later confessed that he had assumed at first that a fire must have broken out in Saint-Pierre, or that a ship loaded with petroleum had exploded – something normal. "I was far from expecting the terrifying spectacle that appeared before my eyes when I entered the Bay of Saint-Pierre." Some enormous event had thrown down all the buildings and formed one immense inferno. The *Roraima* was the only vessel still upright in the bay. All the others were wrecked and shattered. "Not knowing whether danger was still lurking in that devastated zone, I proceeded very slowly. Then I paused . . . and inspected the situation with my binoculars."

The commander noticed people making distress signals on the *Roraïma*. Pierre Le Bris was no Captain Freeman and he sent a boat to rescue them at once. Then he learned of other casualties in the bay and sent a steam launch, pulling two other small craft, to collect all the victims who were waiting, stupefied with shock and numb with pain, on fragments of wreckage scattered along the shore. He gave firm instructions that the rescuers should not return until they were absolutely sure there was no one else left to save. Thus, the survivors from the *Gabrielle*, the *Teresa Lo Vico*, the *Nord America* and the *Diamant* were taken aboard the cruiser. Commander Le Bris himself was convinced that no-one could be left alive in the city. He therefore turned back southwards to Le Carbet.

The *Suchet* collected still more casualties from the shore at Le Carbet. They begged to be taken from that God-forsaken spot forthwith. The *Suchet* took many burnt victims on board and about 30 more severely wounded persons, but 9 of those expired as the vessel raced at its full speed of 20 knots to Fort-de-France.

The victims were gathered in the sickbay on the Suchet. Shock affected them differently: some were dumb, some rambling incoherently, some cried out in agony, some were singing. All were burned red raw and suffered from an unquenchable thirst, but many could not drink. The chief medical officer of the *Suchet* noted that those who died first had suffered severe internal burns. They "had swallowed the fire". He deduced that the nuée ardente must have passed over rapidly, because the sailors who dived under water before it arrived had been much less affected.

The *Suchet* arrived at Fort-de-France at about 6.00 p.m. The dead and the injured were put in a lugubrious procession of artillery waggons that made their way like tumbrils through the crowds massed on the Esplanade. Commander Le Bris went ashore as soon as possible. Monsieur Lhuerre (the Secretary General) and the senior administrators were so afraid of receiving more bad news that they could hardly bring themselves to ask him any questions. "When I said that the whole city had been destroyed . . . and that I was convinced that no-one could have escaped, there was total dismay . . . but they abandoned all hope when I gave the details . . . So many of their relatives had died together in this inconceivable disaster. I announced to the Secretary General that it would be hard to imagine a more complete catastrophe".

The telegram sent by Commander Pierre Le Bris to Paris, informing the government of the destruction of Saint-Pierre: "Suchet to Navy Paris: Back from Saint-Pierre, city completely destroyed by mass of fire about 8.00 a.m. Suppose all population annihilated. Have brought back the few survivors, about 30. All ships in bay burnt and lost. Eruption volcano continues. I am leaving for Guadeloupe to get supplies."

At 9.55 p.m. on 8 May, the commander sent a telegram to the Navy Minister in Paris to inform him of the cataclysm.

Saint-Pierre had been the main commercial centre in Martinique, supplying the whole island. All the other towns had only limited resources, which would quickly run out. Monsieur Lhuerre therefore asked the commander go to Guadeloupe for the supplies that would soon be required. The cruiser was hardly suitable for transporting supplies, but it was the largest vessel available. The *Suchet* therefore duly set off for Guadeloupe at 10.00 p.m.

The third trip of the Rubis

Lieutenant Georges Hébert was still on leave in Fort-de-France when the return of the *Rubis* had caused such a sensation and distress in the capital. He hurried to the quay to try and board his ship, but the *Suchet* had already left for Saint-Pierre. On the landing stage, however, he happened to meet the Public Prosecutor, Monsieur Lubin, who was one of the senior officials in the island. Monsieur Lubin said that he had just volunteered to go to Saint-Pierre and that the Mayor of Fort-de-France and the Secretary General had agreed to his request to form an official delegation. Lieutenant Hébert jumped at the chance to join him. Abbé Parel and one of his curates were added to the party, as well as Lieutenant-Colonel Tessier, who was in charge of the 30 infantrymen who had taken part in the abortive attempt to reach Saint-Pierre during the morning. But the police and the gendarmes could hardly control the vast crowds who were eager to get to Saint-Pierre to try and save their relatives and to see what exactly had happened.

Those assembled on the *Rubis* set off at 2.15 p.m. still hoping that events might not turn out to be as bad as they feared. They were soon disillusioned. As soon as the *Rubis* turned into the bay just after 3.00 p.m., the crew and passengers knew the worst. They saw a volcano fuming menacingly on the skyline, a city blazing from end to end, and a bay littered with wreckage and corpses. They saw the little boats from the *Suchet* crossing to and fro over the bay, collecting survivors. Since their main assignment was to enter Saint-Pierre, the *Rubis* slowly picked its way through the wreckage towards the southern end of the city, but the ship had to slow down to avoid smashing its propeller. The steamer hesitated. The master and crew were weeping. They could guess the fate of all their relatives in the city.

As Lieutenant Hébert recalled:

We passed close to a sinking sailing ship. Three or four men on its bows were gesticulating strangely. They seemed to be dancing. But why were they red all over and completely naked? We only understood later. These unfortunate men had been burned all over. Their skin was red raw. They could not lie down. They were probably jumping up and down to reduce their appalling suffering. Then the smoke suddenly hid them from us. When it cleared, there was no longer any sign of either men or boat.

We halted a hundred metres from the shore. In a bright interlude we saw another strange sight. On the remnant of a landing stage, five or six men stood motionless, waiting stoically in this décor of desolation. We signalled to a large rowing-boat from the *Suchet* to come and collect them. They were Italian sailors [from the *Teresa Lo Vico*].

Monsieur Lubin, Lieutenant-Colonel Tessier and Lieutenant Hébert took the dinghy from the *Rubis* and landed on the devastated shore. Less than 24 hours after his last visit, Georges Hébert was back in Saint-Pierre. There was an awesome silence, broken only by the crackling of the fires. They hurried

The ruins of the Rue Victor-Hugo in Saint-Pierre: the view that greeted the first visitors to the city after the nuée ardente on 8 May.

into the first street they saw, but the dust and fumes soon stifled and blinded them. Every building was a smouldering mass of rubble. Now and again, they saw hideously burnt and mutilated corpses, and then more and more as they walked on. Eventually, they realized that the black masses that they had been striding over were corpses too.

There just could not be any survivors amid such destruction. They opted to go and investigate farther north. They landed again but could recognize only the Place Bertin, the main square in the city, from its pool and the remnants of the lighthouse that had snapped off at its base. Yesterday it had been a bustling square; now only the gentle pattering of running water broke the deathly silence. The public fountain was still flowing, and they gratefully washed the smarting dust from their eyes. But the dense smoke made them cough and splutter and thwarted their every attempt to go into the streets nearby. They were afraid of getting lost and being trapped in another eruption. There was the same devastation everywhere: houses thrown down, smoking wreckage and charred bodies. They went back to the fountain. A woman's mutilated body lay entangled in the remains of the smoking trees that had still graced the Place Bertin less than ten hours before. A sea wave had thrown up an enormous dead fish beside her.

"Then our feelings got the better of us. We started sobbing, and tears began to flow." They went back on board the *Rubis* and followed the shore north towards the volcano, but it was to no avail; the farther north the steamer went, the more destruction they witnessed.

> We halted. The two priests [Abbé Parel and his curate] had never stopped praying and trying to ease the distress and sufferings of the crew. Now, for the last time, they recited the prayers for the dead. The sailors knelt down and cried out in their agony the names of all their dear ones who were out there in that appalling inferno. Monsieur Lubin brought this moving scene to a close by reminding us that, as quickly as possible, it was our duty to advise the seat of government about what had happened. It was about 5.00 p.m. He gave the order to make for Le Carbet, where he knew he would find a telephone post.

The telephone had started to work again. Monsieur Lubin told the Secretary General that there could be no hope of finding a living being in Saint-Pierre, but that there were many burnt and injured survivors on the edge of the fire. The *Rubis* was now alone because the *Suchet* had just left for Fort-de-France, and Monsieur Lubin asked for more relief boats to help.

The rescue of the fugitives from Beauregard

Late in the afternoon, the refugees gathered in the mule stable above the Lajus plantation were aroused by the noise of a ship below in the bay. It was the *Suchet*. Without the slightest discussion, the people stood up together and made their way down to the shore as fast as their bruised legs could take them. They stood on the beach at Le Carbet, waving frantically to the *Suchet* like castaways on a desert island. A member of the crew took a loud-hailer and explained that the *Suchet* had to leave because it had already taken many gravely injured survivors on board and needed to hurry to Fort-de-France to get treatment for them. Other boats were on the way.

These boats soon reached Le Carbet. Among them were the *Topaze*, with two barges in tow, (and possibly the *Perle*), from the Girard company, as well as the dredger, *Pholade*, a tug, and a customs surveillance boat.

When they saw the vessels off Le Carbet, other survivors came flocking onto the beach from all the surrounding hills. Like the fugitives from Beauregard, many of them showed signs of shock rather than burns, because they came from areas that had escaped the nuée ardente. However, Georges Hébert recalled that:

157

The blacks employed on the country plantations were transporting their burnt or dying masters on cradles, chairs, or on hammocks hung on bamboos. They, themselves, were nearly all burnt – some of them horribly so. One of them had lost half his foot. When they had deposited their human burden, some of them were at the end of their tether and they dropped down dead.

The steamers took the precaution of mooring well off shore to avoid being swamped by the desperate crowds, and landing craft were sent to collect them from the beach. The captains ordered that not even the smallest parcels could be taken aboard the steamers. Joseph Marry took the basket of jewellery that he had been carrying all day and obediently placed it on the beach. Madame Décomis, Emilie Dujon's mother, was made of sterner stuff. Elodie Jourdain's account of the incident reveals much about the social relationships in Martinique:

[Madame Décomis] called a black man over. "Look here my boy", she declared, "I've had to leave a basket on the beach. You shall have 50 francs [nearly a month's wages for a labourer] if you bring it on board for me". "Very well, Madame", he replied. Half an hour later, Madame Décomis had recovered the basket . . . But only 10 or 20 francs could be collected from all the pockets in the family. However, the black man was satisfied with that. He had never dreamed of opening the basket, which would have seemed like Ali Baba's treasure to him.

What did it matter to them if they had given him only half the reward they

The beach at Le Carbet, from which survivors were rescued on 8 May 1902. Mount Pelée rises on the horizon.

had promised? However, retrieving jewellery was not the only problem on the beach. There was such a frantic rush to the landing craft in the darkness that the white ladies felt that they were certain to be left behind. Luckily, some troops had been sent to keep order and they saw that the ladies secured places. Nevertheless, people rushed into these little boats and they were often half full of water when they were loaded up.

As night fell and the vast red glows from the eruption became more obvious, those survivors who were strong enough to react at all began to panic. Luckily, reinforcements arrived in the shape of three teams of customs officers who brought their pirogue canoes to take the survivors to the ships. They showed remarkable endurance in the darkness, for the sea was high and their canoes capsized several times. By then, most of the 600 or 700 survivors had no strength left and could not even stand up for long.

It was 7.00 p.m. before all the fugitives were safely on board the steamers and the convoy could set off for Fort-de-France. The embarkation had been largely haphazard, and the people from Beauregard found themselves dispersed on three different steamers. For a while, they watched the sinister red glow over Saint-Pierre disappearing from sight, then they settled down on the deck to rest. One ungrateful passenger described the deck as "fairly clean".

The ships arrived in Fort-de-France at about 9.30 p.m. and disembarked their weary passengers. Lieutenant Hébert had to make his way through a jostling crowd to rejoin the *Suchet*. All the people were straining forwards, looking desperately for a friend or relative that they could identify and help. As *L'Opinion* averred, they felt like toys in some sinister nightmare illuminated by the searchlights of the *Suchet*. The onlookers were astonished to see white women in such a pitiful condition. "They seemed green". It was as if they had come from beyond the grave.

The administration had made practically no arrangements to receive and house the refugees. Suddenly a voice called across the crowded quay, "Are there any members of the Dujon and Marry families here?" Dr Auguste Guérin had sent his son-in-law to find them. As Elodie Jourdain recalled, "We gathered around and followed him like chicks around their mother hen. A well stocked table awaited us, and we did justice to the meal because we had not eaten for 24 hours." But the large group had to sleep in different houses. "What a pleasure it was to wash at last. We left real mud in the white marble bath . . . we put on clothes that public charity had provided . . . and went to meet our relatives." They all wanted to leave "this cursed island". Many in the family opted for Trinidad, where they had friends.

But, even in the catastrophe, old tensions died hard and old prejudices loomed large. As Elodie Jourdain described:

As soon as they got to know about the disaster, some Trinidadians hired a vessel and loaded it with everything that the generosity of the businessmen and colonists could assemble: clothes, shoes, fabrics, preserves (etc.). Next day the ship anchored off Fort-de-France. Then, the most typical and grotesque tale of the incompetence of our leaders took place, unless it marked the greatest success of mulatto cunning. When the Trinidadians began unloading their cargo, the customs men arrived shouting "These are English goods. You'll have to pay duty."

"But we're not selling them." protested Messieurs Lange and de Verteuil, the two young leaders of the convoy, who were both of French origin.

"Agreed", said the customs men, "but as the goods are English, we won't allow them in here unless the duty is paid."

The indignant young Trinidadians shouted that it would serve them right if they took the whole cargo back home . . . and without further ado they dumped the contents of the vessel onto the quay. This was clearly what the customs men had intended: a chance of pillage, instead

The customs house and customs officials in Saint-Pierre.

of a correct and fair distribution of the goods. And in the twinkling of an eye, everything was spirited away by the black population.

Emilie Dujon went to Trinidad. "Now, I shall only see the house in my dreams, where I crossed the threshold as a happy young wife, scarcely a year ago." She lost 57 relatives in the catastrophe.

A visit by RMS Esk

Unbeknown to any of those disembarking their human cargo at Fort-de-France, a British Royal Mail ship, the *Esk*, arrived at about 11.00 p.m. in the Bay of Saint-Pierre with an exploration party from Saint Lucia. The captain sent a boat with an officer, Mr Coxwell, to discover if anyone was alive. He said afterwards:

The heat was almost unbearable as we neared the shore. Dust was falling heavily. I put my whistle to my lips and blew several blasts. But no answer came, save the echo of the whistle from the hills. An appalling silence brooded over the city. Except for the savage licking of the flames, not a sound came from the ghastly heap of ruins. We pulled up and down the coast for nearly an hour, without seeing a sign of life and then decided to return to the ship.

As the boat sailed by the wreck of the *Roraïma*, a sudden explosion in her hold hurled wreckage high into the air.

The *Esk* cannot have passed far from the *Pouyer Quertier* off Saint-Pierre. The *Pouyer Quertier* had left Fort-de-France at about 4.00 p.m., had called at Le Carbet, but had found no refugees and anchored for the night about 2 km off Saint-Pierre. Captain Thirion's aim was to continue to search for the broken cable or to take part in any rescue assignments that the authorities deemed necessary. Emile Berté spent the evening in agony, gazing at the ruins of Saint-Pierre and hoping against all logic that his whole family might somehow have escaped the catastrophe.

14

Realization
Friday 9 May to 10 May 1902

Friday 9 May at Saint-Pierre

Friday 9 May was the day when the enormity of the disaster really began to sink into the minds of the administration and the survivors. It was also a day of reflection and hesitation. Much had to be done, but what? The authorities were confronted with an unprecedented situation. There were no ground rules to follow. There was no co-ordinated plan of action, but such plans still had to be developed in 1902. Many top officials were dead; the administration had indeed been decapitated. The remaining civil servants were in a desperate plight. It was unfortunate, too, that the Secretary General, Georges Lhuerre, showed little flair and even less ability in dealing with the emergency. Individual initiatives were always more successful.

On 9 May, an expedition took one of the Girard company's steamers to Saint-Pierre to attend to some basic medical and spiritual necessities. Monsieur Rosé, a military pharmacist in Fort-de-France, went to inspect the state of the corpses and to assess what should be done immediately to incinerate the bodies and to prevent the spread of the diseases as they putrefied. Abbé Parel sent two priests, Abbé Auber and Father Voetgli, to give absolution and spread holy water over the corpses. On Friday 9 May, too, Gunner Vaillant was trying frantically but fruitlessly to persuade his superior officers that some people might still be alive in the ruins of Saint-Pierre.

The ruins of Saint-Pierre viewed from the Morne Orange hill to the south of the city. Contrary to a popular assumption, the figure in the foreground is not that of Louis-Auguste Sylbaris.

Supplies from Guadeloupe

At 7.00 a.m. on 9 May, the *Suchet* arrived at Pointe-à-Pitre, in Guadeloupe, with a delegation led by Monsieur Labat, a Deputy Mayor of Fort-de-France. The authorities and the people in Guadeloupe were eager to do all that they could to help. The administrative council voted 25 000 francs for the disaster and a public subscription was organized at once. The goods supplied were quickly put on board and the *Suchet* left again at 4.30 p.m. with 63 tonnes of goods, including flour, cod, rice, and salt. Commander Le Bris had to stop off en route in the capital, Basse-Terre, to have a quick word with the governor of Guadeloupe, Monsieur Merlin, who had been the Secretary General and acting governor of Martinique during the previous year. He was enquiring, of course, about the fate of his friends in Saint-Pierre. No doubt, he was also fervently thanking his lucky stars that he had left the island. Governor Merlin opened up a public subscription for the three orphaned children of Governor Mouttet and immediately donated 500 francs himself. He also asked that the children should be sent to him to look after until arrangements could be made for them to be returned to France.

The *Suchet* returned to Fort-de-France at 6.00 a.m. on 10 May. The ship's gyrations were far from over, but first the supplies had to be unloaded. This should not have been a difficult task in view of the evident urgency of the situation. Supplies had been short for almost two days; people might be starving. Le Bris enlisted help from the arsenal and from the *Jouffroy*, which was in port, and obtained a duty squad of 50 men from the garrison.

The commander then reported the effects of lethargic administration, as well as the resentment brought about by the social strife of recent years:

> I have to note the lack of enthusiasm or, to put it more clearly, the sheer unwillingness of the population of Fort-de-France when they were asked to help us, both to transport the wounded and to unload supplies, either from the *Suchet* or from other vessels. There was no lack of men strolling in the park near the esplanade, but when they were asked to help they flatly refused. Indeed, the higher administration lacked direction, and nothing had been done to remedy the prevailing disorder. Thus, all the fatigue fell upon the navy and army personnel, all of whom had worked without respite in the heat of the Sun with their usual devotion to duty.

Saturday 10 May at Saint-Pierre

The indefatigable Commander was still very keen to return to Saint-Pierre in spite of all his recent peregrinations. "I wanted to have the city explored, and to be sure that there were no people still waiting to be saved beneath the ruins. That is why I decided to go there that very day." The inauguration of the new Cuban president in Havana seemed very far away. Far away also was any leadership from the Secretary General. Once again, Commander Le Bris decided to return to Saint-Pierre on his own initiative, in spite of all the likely dangers that such a course of action implied. The volcano was still erupting, and no-one could guess if or when it might unleash another terrible nuée ardente. Anyone who went to Saint-Pierre, even with the laudable aim of searching for the injured, was certainly dicing with death.

Rumours circulating after the eruption of 8 May

- Just before the eruption, farm animals and domestic pets had shown many signs of uneasiness, as if they had foreseen the impending danger.

  – There is no evidence for this. Such distress implied no foresight, merely that the ash and dust were stopping them from breathing, drinking and eating.

- Sylbaris was the sole survivor of the eruption on 8 May, or one of two.

  – False: there were at least 64.

- Sylbaris was a murderer awaiting execution in the condemned cell.

  – False.

- The dead in the cathedral were discovered standing upright, holding their prayer-books.

  – They were all crushed when the roof fell in upon them.

- A man was found dead, still holding the match to light the cigar in his mouth.

  – The same rumour circulated about the trenches during the First World War. There is no evidence of this in Saint-Pierre, although several people were found in positions indicating that death took them totally by surprise in the middle of some equally ordinary action.

- A man trying to flee on a mule was almost caught by the nuée ardente. It burned off the mule's tail, but failed to catch him and he escaped completely unscathed.

  – There is no evidence of this. The story is a variant of the climax to Robert Burns' *Tam o' Shanter*, where witches chase Tam and pull off his mare's tail, although he escapes unhurt.

- Shortly before the eruption, people had mocked Christ by crucifying a pig and dragging it through the streets. Hence, Saint-Pierre was destroyed by Divine vengeance.

  – There is no evidence for the original act. Opinions may differ about the degree of Divine intervention.

As Captain Edward Freeman rightly commented, "Hundreds of stories . . . too ridiculous to think about, were circulated. The truth would have been enough." More serious allegations are discussed in the text.

Thus, the *Suchet* left for Saint-Pierre on Saturday morning, 10 May. The metropolitan government had installed Monsieur Lhuerre as the acting governor. Alas, he was promoted above the level of his competence. However, he asked Commander Le Bris to take with him Abbé Parel and two ecclesiastical delegates from Guadeloupe.

The local authorities did not share the commander's humanitarian instincts. They were preoccupied with saving the securities in the bank that had been locked in the vaults. A fatigue duty of gunners was sent to recover them, under the direction of an administrator. Commander Le Bris himself disembarked with four squads of eight sailors, each under the command of an officer or an officer cadet. Each man was given a towel that could be soaked in phenol water to combat the smells that were already strong in the bay. Swarms of flies were beginning to infest the ruins. Pierre Le Bris left firm instructions to his second in command. He must always be ready to leave the bay; he must send agreed signals if a dangerous eruption seemed imminent; and, if the landing craft could not get back in time, he should abandon the craft to its fate, and leave the bay at once to save the *Suchet* and its crew. The volcano was not looking threatening, but that was no guarantee of docility:

> I quickly realized that there could be no hope left of finding any living beings under that pile of smoking ruins . . . There was hardly a trace of the streets in the north, although they could be recognized perfectly in the south, where some of the walls were still upright.
>
> I went around the city guided by a gendarme who knew all the places. I went first to the Intendance, where the governor had stayed. The streets were cluttered with debris from the houses, and the stones we were walking upon were still hot. The fire was still smouldering, and smoke and flames were bursting out in many places. The heat was stifling.

The remains of the entrance to the theatre, with Mount Pelée on the horizon.

166

The ruins of the Chamber of Commerce in Saint-Pierre. The seated officer is probably Pierre Le Bris. Compare this scene with the photo on p. 36, taken before the eruption.

We walked passed bodies in the street. Those lying on the beach showed traces of enormous burns, their clothing had almost completely disappeared, although their bodies were intact. Those in the streets were all burnt to varying degrees. Some had been reduced to a few pieces; others . . . had kept their blackened forms, but their entrails had burst out from gaping holes. An awful smell exuded from all these corpses. It was a mixture of putrefying flesh, and flesh grilled by the fire.

All that remained of Fonds-Coré after the passage of the nuée ardente on 8 May. Compare this scene of utter devastation with that depicted on p. 76.

Eventually we reached the Intendance. Nothing remained. The walls had crumbled . . . everything inside had burned; a little smoke was rising from the ruins. The railings were lying on a pile of rubble, all twisted and deformed. Nearby, a street sign was still attached to an intact piece of wall; it carried the name Rue Victor-Hugo.

Commander Le Bris then went back to the shore. The officers and squads who had searched the north – the market quarter, the fort and the barracks – had not found a single spot where anyone could have taken shelter. They went aboard the *Suchet* and left the soldiers to continue the operation at the bank and return on the *Rubis*. The soldiers were working in very high temperatures, trying to recover the strong boxes of valuables from the ash-covered rubble of the bank. They were stored in old powder kegs for easy transport, but some had to be left overnight on the shore.

"We estimated that there were about a thousand corpses, all of which had been burned to varying degrees. All the rest had been buried beneath the ruins. I had badly wanted to undertake this exploration . . . but there was nothing useful that could now be accomplished in Saint-Pierre." The commander sailed to Le Prêcheur, where the ship arrived at 12.30 p.m.

Meanwhile, Abbé Parel and his party had been prospecting among the ecclesiastical remains of the city. Their discoveries were no more inspiring. They had seen horrible, contorted, twisted and unrecognizable corpses amid the tottering ruins. They could hardly find their way to the cathedral, but they

The remains of the nave and towers of the cathedral in Saint-Pierre.

gained some meagre consolation when they found that the statue of the Virgin lay intact where it had fallen from the facade. But, they could not reach the altar. The presbytery and the bishop's palace had been almost totally razed to the ground, and their occupants buried beneath them. The episcopal safe had burned. The Fort church was nowhere to be seen. The College–Seminary was *tabula rasa*. The cash boxes belonging to the bishopric, the church workshops and the ecclesiastical retirement fund had all vanished.

The dead

The list of the dead made an appalling catalogue. Over 26 000 citizens must have met their doom in Saint-Pierre, not counting those who had flocked to the city seeking refuge. But it made a more personal impact upon the survivors altogether when they named old colleagues, friends and well known businessmen, not to mention their relatives. The administrative, religious, educational, social, industrial and commercial life of the colony had suffered slaughter without precedent in the annals of the French Empire.

Dead, Governor Mouttet and his wife. Dead, most of the top administrators in the colony. Dead, Rodolphe Fouché, the Mayor of Saint-Pierre. Dead, 24 priests and 71 nuns. Dead, teacher Roger Portel and painter Paul Merwart. Dead, Eugène Berté and those who had climbed up with him to the Etang Sec. Dead, Gaston Landes, Monsieur Degennes and most of the teachers in the Lycée. Dead, the staff and children in both orphanages. Dead, all the people in the asylum. Dead, all the prostitutes. Dead, Léon Sully, Marius Hurard and the journalists from the newspapers. Dead, Paul Borde, the president of the Chamber of Commerce. Dead, Joseph Dumas, and nearly all the businessmen who dealt with every branch of commerce and industry.

Saved, an almost unknown shoemaker, Léon Compère-Léandre. Saved, the candidates in the general election. Saved, also, a survivor that no-one yet knew about.

The remains of the iron bridge that crossed the Rivière Roxelane in the north of Saint-Pierre. Compare this scene with that of the same place before the eruption, shown on p. 6.

15

Rescue
Friday 9 May to Sunday 11 May 1902

Once the extent of the catastrophe in Saint-Pierre had been recognized, there seemed to be no hope whatsoever for any of the villages around the flanks of Mount Pelée. Le Prêcheur and its neighbours had borne the brunt of the volcanic attack for over two weeks. They were doomed. They must, therefore, have followed Saint-Pierre into oblivion. All that remained to do was to examine the devastation and incinerate any corpses.

The evacuation of Les Abymes

The *Pouyer Quertier* stayed about 2 km off Saint-Pierre until the first mate came on watch at 4.00 a.m. on 9 May, and he then let the vessel drift north-wards to examine the western flanks of the volcano. At 6.00 a.m. the *Pouyer Quertier* arrived off the hamlet of Grand' Case, near the plantation that Charles and Emilie Dujon had abandoned in such a flurry six days before. To the surprise of the crew, the houses were intact and there were people on the shore. Captain Thirion ordered two signals to be given: no response. The people just stared back impassively. The captain did not insist, matching one strange reaction with another. Instead, he turned southwards to the hamlet of Les Abymes, which was separated from Le Prêcheur by the Rivière du Prêcheur. The houses in the hamlet were intact, but there was not a living soul on the beach. An eerie silence reigned, broken only by the odd growl from the volcano, until the *Pouyer Quertier* sounded its siren. At once, people rushed from their cabins, called for help and made gestures of despair. The captain sent a landing craft for information. Everyone wanted to be taken to Saint-Pierre. They had no idea what had happened to the city.

Le Croiseur "Suchet"

Commandé par Mr Le Bris, Capitaine de frégate

Rapport sur les événements qui se sont produits
à la Martinique à la suite de l'éruption volcanique
de la Montagne Pelée.

Reçu le 11 Mai 1904

112

J'ai l'honneur de transmettre
au Ministre
le présent rapport du
Capne de fte Le Bris, cmt le Suchet.
ce rapport complète
celui du 22 Mars, du même
officier, répond aux questions
posées par le télégramme
ministériel du 20, donne
sur le désastre des détails
du plus poignant intérêt
et démontre une fois de
plus le dévouement sans
bornes dont nos marins
ont fait preuve.

Le C. Amiral Cdt la
1e Division de croiseurs de
la force navale de l'Atlantique

Servan

31 Mai 1902
Fort de France.

La montagne Pelée située au Nord
de la Martinique et sommet le plus élevé de l'île,
qu'une ancienne tradition rapportait avoir été le
siège d'un volcan n'avait donné aucun signe d'acti-
vité depuis l'établissement des Européens dans les
Antilles jusqu'en Août 1851 époque à laquelle
se produisit une éruption.

Cette éruption dont l'intensité
avait été très limitée, n'avait causé aucun dégât important dans l'île. Elle s'était bornée en effet à une
projection de boue aux environs des cratères sur un
espace ne dépassant pas 8 à 900 mètres et à une
pluie de cendres dans la nuit du 4 au 5 Août, phé-
nomène sans gravité qui avait cependant causé une
vive émotion dans la ville de St Pierre.

Les manifestations premières de
cette éruption, qui fut étudiée par une commission
nommée par le Gouverneur et dont le rapport se
trouve

323

The first page of the third report made by Commander Le Bris to the Navy Minister in Paris
on 31 May 1902. Rear-Admiral Servan has added brief comments on the left.

The *Pouyer Quertier* put the cutters to work at once. The sea was rough and the coast rocky. Thus, the local pirogue canoes brought the people out from the land, and the cutters collected them and brought them to the vessel. Boarding the large ship was no easy task. The frightened refugees were not used to the sea and they found it very hard to choose just the right moment to jump from the cutter and clutch the ship's ladder. The crew were tireless. The sailors often had to hang on to the ladder with one hand and scoop up a child or a frightened woman with the other, and then drag them aboard. Each new passenger was then given bread and cheese and some water with a dash of wine. Every child had a bowl of milk.

But all manner of dangers still threatened. There was a nasty moment at 11.00 a.m. The *Pouyer Quertier* suddenly twirled around three times, but luckily its anchor chain did not snap, otherwise the ship would have foundered on the rocky coast, and few among the crew or the refugees would have been able to swim ashore. Other whirlpools developed that reached 25 m across, and floating wreckage swirled around and around.

The *Pouyer Quertier* brought 425 people on board before 2.00 p.m. Captain Thirion knew that such a cargo would be completely unexpected in Fort-de-France. Therefore, he had to reach the capital before nightfall to enable the administration to take steps to help the refugees. He could also break the incredible news that the villagers of Les Abymes were still alive.

The centre of the present-day village of Le Prêcheur, with the summit of Mount Pelée on the horizon.

When the *Pouyer Quertier* arrived in Fort-de-France at 5.00 p.m., Captain Thirion raised the appropriate signals and asked for barges to land the passengers. The signals stayed on the mast for an hour, unseen by the semaphore lookout. Whereupon, an angry captain went ashore to ask the acting governor what he should do with the refugees that he had rescued.

The newly appointed acting governor, Georges Lhuerre, was astonished because no-one had envisaged having to cater for any survivors from that area. Luckily, Victor Sévère, the Mayor of Fort-de-France, was altogether more capable. He organized places of shelter without delay and the refugees were landed within the hour. They disembarked between rows of distressed onlookers on the quay and were quietly led to temporary homes that had been found for them, in both private homes and public buildings.

Saturday 10 May at Le Prêcheur

The acting governor did not stop dithering after his night's rest. The following day the *Pouyer Quertier* and the *Suchet,* which had brought the supplies from Guadeloupe, were both kept idle for most of the morning because "the administration was deliberating". At 10.00 a.m. on 10 May, the *Pouyer Quertier* was ordered to continue reconnecting the direct cable to France, and it set sail accordingly. However, while the vessel was in the Bay of Saint-Pierre, one of the Girard company's steamers signalled that it had just got a message from the administration asking the *Pouyer Quertier*, after all, to continue evacuating the refugees from the north. Captain Thirion wasted no more time; a whole morning had been wasted already.

The *Pouyer Quertier* arrived off Le Prêcheur to find that Senator Knight was already there. He could have been on his own yacht, or he was more probably aboard the *Rubis*, which was of a similar size, which had left Fort-de-France at 10.00 a.m. It was he who had persuaded the administration to requisition the *Pouyer Quertier*. But the Senator had been able to pick up only about 200 of those who most needed help: the sick, the injured and those with small children. The *Suchet* also arrived off Le Prêcheur at about the same time as the *Pouyer Quertier*. Together, the three vessels had the capacity to effect a proper evacuation.

Eleven pirogues plied back and forth across the extremely choppy seas from the shore to the ships. It was no easy task. Two pirogues capsized. In a flash, several sailors from the *Suchet* dived into the water, seized the women and children struggling for their lives in the waves, and brought them to the outboard ladder.

It took 5 long hours for the 40 oarsmen to embark the 1200 remaining women and children, but no men, onto the three vessels. Night was falling. The pirogues dancing on the waves next to the large ships were empty, apart from their exhausted oarsmen. Commander Le Bris muttered to Senator Knight: "It looks as if they are going to ask us to take them as well." They did nothing of the kind. When the rescue ships set off, they stood up in their pirogues, and respectfully raised their hats. One of the men called out: "See you tomorrow, Senator, if we are not all dead."

It was about 9.00 p.m. when the three vessels arrived in Fort-de-France. According to Emile Berté, the *Pouyer Quertier* disembarked its 526 passengers "and put them in the care of the authorities". The postmaster gave Emile Berté his brother's last letter. For an instant, Emile hoped that he could still be alive. Alas, no. Eugène had written on 6 May.

Commander Le Bris had to keep his complement of refugees on board the *Suchet* for the night "because nothing had been prepared to receive them".

The evacuation of Le Prêcheur on 11 May

On the morning of Sunday 11 May, nearly 2500 people were still waiting to be evacuated from Le Prêcheur. Commander Le Bris disembarked the

The beach stretching southwards from Le Prêcheur, from which the inhabitants were rescued in 1902.

Events in Le Prêcheur during the climax of the eruption

It was only when the inhabitants of Le Prêcheur reached the haven of Fort-de-France that the story of events in the village became known. By the morning of 8 May, the villagers of Le Prêcheur and Les Abymes had been thirsty for two days because the persistent falls of ash had clogged up the river that was their main source of drinking water. Although not yet starving, they were craving for help.

At 5.00 a.m. on 8 May, a raging torrent descended the Rivière du Prêcheur, carrying tree trunks and boulders as if they were wisps of straw and grains of rice. It severely damaged the church, broke the bridge joining Le Prêcheur and Les Abymes, widened the river mouth, and swept 400 people to their deaths.

It seemed especially ominous when the waters had half destroyed the church. Some of the terrified inhabitants resolved to seek safety in the hills at the sema-phore post on Morne Folie, which seemed an obvious place to shelter because it stood 100 m above sea-level. But it turned out to be a folly indeed. A young girl from Le Prêcheur told Emile Berté that, about 6.30 a.m., her brother had wanted to take her with him. "No", she replied, "I'll come and join you when I've tidied everything up". And she stayed at home.

At 8.02 a.m., the nuée ardente swept down the volcano and incinerated every one of the 400 villagers who had taken refuge at the semaphore post. The mayor, Monsieur Grelet, had become seriously alarmed by the terrible flood and the loud rumblings from the volcano throughout the night of 7–8 May. The sea provided the only remaining means of communication between the village and Saint-Pierre. Thus, on the morning of 8 May, he sent 20-year-old Chavigny de la Chevrotière in a pirogue canoe, manned by 12 young men, to take a telegram to Saint-Pierre. When the canoe was just opposite the semaphore at Morne Folie, Chavigny heard a deafening noise coming from the mountain. He looked up and saw the nuée falling upon them. He just had time to shout to his comrades before it hit them. The pirogue capsized and flung them all into the sea. Only five of the twelve managed to swim through the huge waves that swept them to the shore north of the village. The bodies of the other seven young men were never recovered.

Emile Berté attended to the five survivors when they were brought aboard the *Pouyer Quertier*. They all had burns on their upper bodies. The nuée ardente had hit Chavigny full in the face. The others had fallen into the sea and had been burned where the water had not protected them. They did not have the deep burns that a solid blazing mass would have produced. Their injuries reminded Dr Berté of the bad scalds that he had sometimes had to treat, caused by jets of steam from a ship's boiler.

The nuée ardente spread only as far north as the outskirts of Le Prêcheur and missed the village by 100 m. Thus, the nuée spared the settlement that had suffered falling ash for two weeks, and had been the prime concern of Governor Mouttet, although floods had killed 400 of the inhabitants and the nuée had killed another 400 villagers at Morne Folie.

refugees who had spent the night on the *Suchet*, but he was then obliged to do some bargaining in Fort-de-France. He asked the acting governor, Georges Lhuerre, to requisition the *Pouyer Quertier* once again to help him complete the evacuation from Le Prêcheur. Monsieur Lhuerre acquiesced to this perfectly normal request only when the commander agreed to call at Saint-Pierre to collect ten large powder kegs full of money and valuables from the bank, which had been left on the shore the previous evening. Clearly, Monsieur Lhuerre preferred kegs of cash to refugees. At all events, the commander obtained the help of the *Pouyer Quertier*, which was soon making post haste for Le Prêcheur.

The *Suchet* left the capital at 7.15 a.m. and called to collect the precious kegs from Saint-Pierre. About an hour later, as the *Suchet* was moored in the Bay of Saint-Pierre, the Danish cruiser, *Valkyrien*, arrived with supplies from the Danish colony of Saint Thomas. Kommandør H. P. Holm offered to help with the evacuation, put himself at the commander's disposal, and was immediately pressed into service. The *Pouyer Quertier* joined the pair, and the three vessels hurried to Le Prêcheur.

The volcano rumbled loudly and threw out enormous clouds of ash throughout the day. As the vessels reached Le Prêcheur at about 9.45 a.m., one such cloud enveloped them, so that they could see neither each other nor the rocky shore. It looked as if the operation might have to be abandoned and there seemed to be a fair chance that an eruption would kill them all. However, Commander Le Bris pressed on:

I said to myself that we must try absolutely every available means to snatch these wretched and destitute people from the jaws of death. I

The Danish cruiser Valkyrien, *which played a leading role in the rescue of the inhabitants of Le Prêcheur on 11 May 1902.*

177

slowly approached the spot where I supposed the village to be. I sounded the steam siren, as much through fear of a collision as to signal our presence. The other two vessels, which we saw vaguely from time to time, were doing the same.

Luckily the wind soon changed direction and blew the ash farther north. The village appeared out of the gloom, with the pirogues already at sea, full of the men, their luggage and "all that was most precious to each family".

The commander instructed the small landing craft from the rescue ships to go as near as possible to the coast, where the pirogues could bring the people to meet them. This was safer than trying to embark the refugees directly from the pirogues, which had proved dangerous on the previous day. In fact, the *Valkyrien* used a steam lifeboat with four landing craft, which improved the efficiency of the operation even more.

The new method saved much time. The evacuation started just after 10.15 a.m. and the task was finished at 2.30 p.m. In spite of all the swirling ash and the ever-present threat of much worse, "the population of Le Prêcheur displayed admirable calm and sang-froid . . . Everything was done in a surprisingly good order."

At length, only two old men were left standing in front of a pirogue on the shore. Just as captains are the last to leave their ships, the Mayor of Le Prêcheur, Monsieur Grelet, and the priest, Abbé Desprez, were the last two to leave the ruined ash-covered village.

"Go ahead, sir." proposed the priest.

"No, Father", insisted the mayor, "it is my duty to be the last person to leave this place". And so they shared the last pirogue. Commander Le Bris invited them aboard the *Suchet*. "I was glad", he reported, "to welcome them and shake them by the hand."

The vessels made full speed for Fort-de-France. "We were pleased", the commander confessed, "to have entirely accomplished our mission and to leave that place, where we felt we were all in perpetual danger." It had been a very hazardous mission and no-one was sure whether another nuée ardente would erupt before it ended. It was a game of Russian roulette that the rescue ships won by only nine days.

The role of the Valkyrien *at Le Prêcheur*

The part played by the *Valkyrien* in the evacuation of Le Prêcheur was described by second engineer, C. C. Jensen, whose grandson gave the manuscript to one of the Danish state archivists, Erik Gøbel. However, the Danish description of the behaviour of the people of Le Prêcheur differs so markedly from that recounted in the French version that it hardly seems to belong to the same event. There is no means of assessing which story is closer to the truth; there would seem to be no reason for C. C. Jensen to have exaggerated his own private memoire; on the other hand, Commander Le Bris always gave measured accounts in what were also essentially private reports to the French Navy Ministry.

The cruiser, *Valkyrien*, had been in the West Indies since October 1901, probably in relation to Danish attempts to sell their island of Saint Thomas to the USA. Various garbled messages had come through to Saint Thomas that first Mount Pelée and then the Soufrière of Saint Vincent were erupting.

On Friday 9 May, the *Valkyrien* received the sensational news of the annihilation of Saint-Pierre. Captain Holm decided to go and help the hapless city at once. Governor Hedemann made arrangements for the *Valkyrien* to take 10 000 francs-worth of provisions for the victims, and the vessel set sail before 3.00 p.m. En route, the crewmen showed their ingenuity by taking several practical safety measures. They made roofs of corrugated iron for their landing craft, so that any falling hot ash could burn neither the rescued nor their rescuers. They removed virtually everything inflammable from the deck, pumps were made ready, tubs and buckets were prepared, and stretchers were fashioned out of bunks.

The *Valkyrien* reached Martinique after nightfall on 10 May and tried to make for Fort-de-France. However, the air was so thick with ash that they did not know where they were. A blazing city loomed before them. "The heat and smell were intolerable." They lit flares and shone their searchlights onto the shore. No reply. They feared that the blazing city was Fort-de-France, and gloomily went out to sea for the night. Next morning, of course, they found that they were off Saint-Pierre.

The *Valkyrien* made its way gingerly towards the city, through wreckage and innumerable corpses, all burnt, scorched, scalded, twisted and mutilated. No-one could credit that an eruption could have caused such devastation. The *Valkyrien* joined the *Suchet* and the *Pouyer Quertier*, and they went together to Le Prêcheur.

179

The village of Le Prêcheur smothered in ash and dust after the evacuation.

According to C.C. Jensen, when the ash cleared at about 11.00 a.m., the villagers rowed out in their pirogues to be picked up, but they were in such a state of fear and agitation that they were almost out of their minds. They could barely manoeuvre their own boats and they wanted to set them adrift as soon as they had come aboard. The crew made them understand that they had to row back and rescue more people, especially since the rocks and breakers were preventing the Danish craft from reaching the shore. They brought about 600 people on board within 4 hours. Some families were unwilling to come aboard, but the men from the *Valkyrien* were so keen to save them that they wanted to rescue them by force. When it was pointed out that the villagers were free agents, Danish democratic ideals prevailed and the crew abandoned their thoughts of coercion. Towards the close of the evacuation, a drunken man swam out to board the last landing craft; and another man demanded his little daughter back when he discovered that she was also in that boat. She was allowed to stay with the rest of her family in the village. Second Engineer Jensen dryly added, "those who stayed behind probably believed that they would be able to loot the village in peace, now that it was almost deserted".

At last, the people of Le Prêcheur could relax after a week of torment. They were all hungry and thirsty. The crew prepared urns of tea and fed them preserved meat, biscuits and margarine, and "they were not slow to help themselves. A little black boy with lovely black eyes, and wearing only a short shirt, was sitting in his mother's arms, devouring a large biscuit held

Madame Lacroix and one of her husband's scientific assistants inspecting the destruction caused by the great river flood near the church in Le Prêcheur.

in both hands, with another tucked under his arm in reserve."

The evacuees were far from rich, and all were more or less dressed in rags. They had turned up with an amazing collection of things that they had wanted to save. Their treasures ranged from bundles of old rags, to hens, coal, firewood, kittens and puppies. One old man was carrying an antiquated lantern. The crew improvised hen-runs to house the poultry, and the cocks immediately fought each other to prove their prowess in their new territory.

The *Suchet* moored again at Fort-de-France at 4.20 p.m., and the other two vessels arrived at 4.45 p.m. Commander Le Bris at once sent barges and tugs to the *Valkyrien* to offload its passengers first. The three vessels had brought back some 2500 people: the *Valkyrien* had 500–600, the *Pouyer Quertier* about 750, and the *Suchet* nearly 1200. On Monday morning, 12 May, the *Valkyrien* unloaded its cargo of supplies from Saint Thomas. And the acting governor, Monsieur Lhuerre, actually came aboard to thank everyone on board for their help.

Commander Le Bris recommended Captain H. P. Holm for the Légion d'Honneur, "for he had given much more valuable service to France than those foreign representatives who get the award merely by attending festivities in French ports".

Monsieur Lhuerre still did not seem to realize how dangerous it was in Saint-Pierre. At a meeting in the evening of 11 May, he asked Commander Le Bris to return the next day to collect the remaining valuables from the bank; perhaps he was worried about his savings. The commander asserted that it was scarcely prudent to expose the *Suchet* to such danger for mere money. "I was ready to expose my vessel and its personnel to save lives, but I thought that there was no need to do so for a few thousand francs."

Nevertheless, the *Suchet* went back to Saint-Pierre on Monday 12 May. Supervised by one of the few surviving bank officials, a squad went to blow open the safes and recover all the remaining bank notes, jewellery, pawned valuables and securities. They loaded everything into sacks as quickly as they could because the volcano was sounding, and looking, very threatening. And the many corpses in and around the bank were giving off a ghastly smell. At 1.00 p.m., the details came back on board the *Suchet* and placed everything in the safe custody of the treasurer of the colony.

Foreign help

At last, on 13 May, the *Pouyer Quertier* could resume its search for the broken cable off Saint-Pierre and the crew of the *Suchet* could help unload the vessels that had come from all parts of the world with supplies and medicines for the victims. The disaster in Martinique had been reported in the world's press with the usual smattering of fantasies and misconceptions about how volcanoes operate. Few of the fantasies actually approached the gravity of what had happened.

As Pierre Le Bris reported, "No-one had been able to imagine that the disaster could possibly have been so complete. It was thus with stupefaction that those who arrived on the scene learned that their medicines were useless, given that very few were wounded, and there was nothing but the dead." Help arrived speedily from American, Danish, British and Dutch vessels, and the aid brought by the German cruiser, *Falke*, was particularly appreciated after the rancours of the Franco–Prussian war. One American steamer, the *Starling*, came with not only supplies and medicines but also "mules and waggons for overland transport should the need arise".

President Theodore Roosevelt also sent the American warship *Cincinnati*, which arrived in Fort-de-France on 14 May. Acting Governor Lhuerre starred once again. The American captain went to see him, was kept waiting half an hour, and was then told that he could not be seen. The somewhat ruffled American complained to Commander Le Bris, who told Monsieur Lhuerre, who at least had the tact to present his apologies the following day.

16

Louis-Auguste Sylbaris
Sunday 11 May 1902

In the city of Saint-Pierre itself, the nuée ardente killed everyone save for two exceptionally strong men who happened to have been in particularly sheltered positions on the edge of the city in the lee of the Morne Abel hill.

All those who had visited Saint-Pierre in the days immediately after the catastrophe were convinced that no-one could possibly have survived the onslaught of the nuée ardente. Their conviction was based on the horror before their eyes, and not on any thorough search of the ruins. Indeed, if such eminent and able persons as Commander Le Bris and the head of the gendarmerie believed that there were no survivors, then, clearly, there could be no survivors. In fact, horror had clouded their judgment. Their opinion even flew in the face of the facts. Compère-Léandre had escaped from Saint-Pierre. Gunner Vaillant had even produced a dying woman from the ruins on 10 May. But, in any case, as the days slipped by, the chances of finding another survivor were fading with every passing hour.

On Sunday 11 May, the second round of the general election took place in the constituency of South Martinique, which was centred on Fort-de-France. The election in North Martinique, centred on Saint-Pierre, had of course been abandoned.

It was on Sunday afternoon that the man came from the grave. Three men from Le Morne-Rouge – Léon Danglis, Georges Hilaire and Maurice Nirdé – were wandering around the ruins of Saint-Pierre. Maybe they were just taking a walk in town, for the good of their health, or to satisfy their curiosity, or maybe they were looking for valuables that undoubtedly lay buried beneath the ruins. But they were certainly not looking for prisoners when they wandered behind the theatre and made their way up towards the jail. Suddenly they heard muffled shouts. They crept behind the remnants of the

The cell, in a sheltered hollow behind the prison walls, in which Louis-Auguste Sylbaris survived for three days after the nuée ardente struck Saint-Pierre on 8 May 1902.

prison walls. The shouts were coming from the solitary confinement cell, which stood like a bomb shelter, and was still intact, in the low courtyard behind the prison. An iron grill covered a small opening above the thick padlocked wooden doors. They crept forward cautiously, not too sure whether there was a ghost or a man inside the cell. They hesitated, and then called out. The response in Créole suggested that it was not a ghost: "Messiés! Messiés! Sou plaît, t'en prie, sauvez-moi pour l'amou Bon Dié! Vini sauvé un pauv prisonnier!" ("Gentlemen! Gentlemen! Please, I beg you. Save me for the love of God. Come an' save a poor prisoner.). The men went up to the door and asked how they could possibly manage to break down the two doors with their huge padlocks. "Prends roche, Missié, zot ké voué, zot va metté moin derho, je t'en prie, prends courage!" ("Get a stone, Sir, you'll see, you'll get me out. I beg you! Take heart!")

They smashed the door open and brought the man out into the fresh air. "Messié moin pas save ca qui rivé, oti toute moune la geôle?". ("I don't know what's happened, Sir. Where are the people from the prison?") "Pa ni la geôle, tout Saint-Pierre brûlé." ("There is no prison. All Saint-Pierre is burnt.") "Alors, Messié, conduis-moun s'ou plaît, au Prêcheur, dans famille moin". ("Then, Sir, please take me to Le Prêcheur to my family".)

"Pa ni Prêcheur, pa ni Carbet, pa ni enien, mais nou va conduit o dans la main Pè Mary, curé Morne-Rouge, il va béni ou il va préparé ou bien comme il faut, I ké prend ou dans on chambre pit être même I va guéri ou". ("There is no Le Prêcheur; there is no Le Carbet; there's nothing left. We'll put you into the hands of Father Mary, the priest in Le Morne-Rouge. He'll bless you, and prepare you really well. He'll put you up in a room. He might even cure you.")

Soon, the most famous — and notorious — person ever to survive and escape from a nuée ardente was on his way to Le Morne-Rouge. He was black and badly burned. Everyone knew him, and no-one was sure how to spell his name. He was Louis-Auguste Sylbaris, or Cylbaris, Ciparis, perhaps even Cylparis. It mattered little when half the population could neither read nor write. Anyway, most people called him "Sanson" ("Samson") because of his great strength, rather than from any liaisons with local Delilahs. He was about 25 years old.

Sanson and his rescuers arrived in Le Morne-Rouge after nightfall and they went straight to the church. In spite of his ordeal, Sanson sat in the porch, artlessly telling his story to the incredulous crowd, until Father Mary had finished the service at Notre Dame de la Délivrande at 6.30 p.m.

That evening Sanson told his tale to Father Mary, who recounted it in a report to the acting governor on 30 June 1902. It was a story for which any of today's sensation-seeking newspapers would have given Sanson a fortune.

Sanson was from Le Prêcheur, and he worked as either a seaman or farm-hand. Since he was very strong and could work hard, he would often change jobs whenever the spirit moved him, or as soon as he got bored. He had a reputation as "a bit of a lad" who was too easily tempted. One day, probably between 5 and 10 April, he went out on a spree with some of his friends. He quarrelled with one of them and wounded him with a cutlass, as they were wont to do in those parts. He was arrested and sentenced to a month in jail in Saint-Pierre. On 30 April or 1 May, when he had almost finished his time, he was taken into the city to do some fatigue duty or other. Someone told him that there was a fiesta at Le Prêcheur. He couldn't resist. He escaped and went dancing all night. But on the following morning, he felt duty bound to give himself up again to complete his sentence. Such behaviour did not impress the magistrates. To teach him, and his like, a lesson, he was sentenced to eight days in solitary confinement in the small cell behind the prison. It was during this period that the nuée ardente fell upon Saint-Pierre. As Sanson told Father Mary:

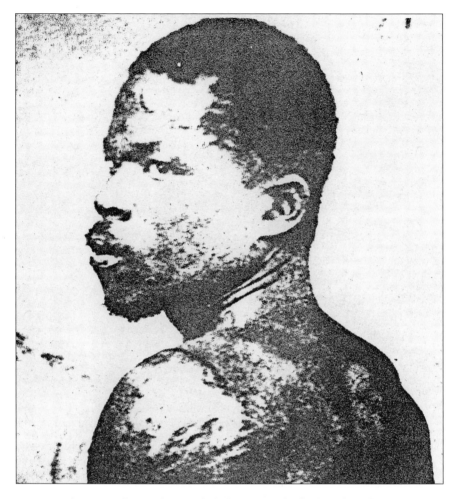

Louis-Auguste Sylbaris, photographed about a month after his release from prison.

It was eight o'clock, and they hadn't yet brought my rations for the day, when all of a sudden there was a terrifying noise. Everyone was shouting "Help, I'm burning! I'm dying!" Five minutes later, no-one was shouting any more, except me. Then a cloud of smoke gushed through the little opening above my door. For the next quarter of an hour, this smoke was burning me so much that I had to jump left and right, up and down, anywhere and everywhere, to get out of its way. An awful silence fell when it was over. I kept listening and shouting for someone to come and save me. No-one answered. So, I decided that all Saint-Pierre must have been crushed under an earthquake, in the fire.

186

Father J. Mary, priest at Le Morne-Rouge, in June 1902. He was one of the leading figures in the colony, who moved easily in all classes of society. The underprivileged members of the community revered him for his frank and open manner, his jovial good humour, and for his untiring work for their material and spiritual welfare.

Sanson spent the next four days and three nights alone, burnt, with nothing to eat, and with nothing to drink but the rainwater that trickled through the bars of the window. He was almost delirious by the time he heard the three men from Le Morne-Rouge on Sunday afternoon.

Father Mary sent for "soup and punch (water-based, of course) to strengthen the sick man". He found an old lady to dress Sanson's wounds and arranged for the sisters at the Convent of the Délivrande to provide him with lodgings. He had deep burns on his chest, thighs, back and knees, and especially on his hands and feet, and they widened when they were exposed to the open air. He was treated by amateurs, and he wore out four nurses in as many weeks, although he quickly recovered his hearty appetite. On 21 May, Father Mary himself had "to act as his nurse, changing his linen and undertaking many other humbler tasks. Cleanliness restored, the linen, vaseline, glycerine and phenic acid helped to rejuvenate him".

Sanson soon became an object of intense curiosity. People flocked to Le Morne-Rouge. Everyone wanted to inspect the man that the eruption had spared, and many also wanted to see the charismatic figure of Father Mary, whose reputation as the pillar of Le Morne-Rouge was renowned through-out the island. At the end of May, several American scientists paid homage to both. They commented on the "priest's buoyant cordiality", his "cheerful Christianity", his "unimpeachable integrity", and his "worn and shabby cassock". He was described as "impressive", "heroic", "incapable of shirking his duty", "venerable", and, at least once, as "aged". He was 51.

The sight of Sanson inspired different sentiments in his American visitors. George Kennan, who sometimes gave the impression that he was viewing some kind of Martian zoo, was genuinely appalled by Sanson's state. Medical standards were apparently different in the USA. On 25 May, he found Sanson, "an uneducated man of average intelligence", in a fly-infested room in an abandoned wooden cabin:

> The unfortunate prisoner had had no treatment, and the air of the small, hot room was so heavy and foul with the offensive odor of his neglected burns that I could hardly bring myself to breathe it. He was sitting stark naked on the dirty striped mattress of a small wooden cot, with a bloody sheet thrown over his head . . . and gathered about his loins. He had been more frightfully burned, I think, than any man I had ever seen. His face, strangely enough, had escaped injury, and his hair had not been even scorched, but there were terrible burns to his back and legs, and his badly swollen feet and hands were covered with yellow offen-sive matter that had no resemblance to human skin or flesh. The burns were apparently very deep – so deep that blood oozed from them – and to my unprofessional eye looked as if they might have been made by hot steam". [This was a diagnosis similar to that of the more professional eye of Dr Emile Berté at Le Prêcheur.]
>
> . . . Mr Jaccaci [one of George Kennan's companions], sent to the military hospital in Fort-de-France for linseed oil, limewater, phenic acid and aseptic bandages . . . The prisoner's burns . . . were [then] properly cared for and dressed, and there seemed every probability that he would live.

Sanson's will to live can never have been in doubt. His great strength did the rest. He recovered. In gratitude for Father Mary's kindness, he took to studying the scriptures and became a practising Christian. He even wanted to become the priest's manservant, but unexpected circumstances on 30 August prevented him from doing so.

Sanson's fame spread well beyond the French West Indies. For a time he became an exhibit in a famous American circus. He was given the abridged name of Ludger, because Louis-Auguste was too complicated for English-speaking tongues. Posters described him as "Ludger Sylbaris. The only living object [sic] that survived in the Silent City of Death". As his fame increased, so also did the crimes reputed to have caused his imprisonment, and even some respectable academic textbooks have described him as a murderer.

He had already been taken for a liar. The Parisian journalist, Jean Hess, echoed the view commonly held in the colony that Sanson just could not be telling the truth. His survival did not fit into a pattern that much of society found acceptable. The white inhabitants of Martinique were mortified that, of all those gathered in Saint-Pierre at the fatal hour, a prisoner in jail, and black to boot, could possibly have escaped with his life. Why should such a man have been saved when so many more worthy persons had been slaughtered? They were so stunned that they refused to believe it. An altogether more acceptable rumour went around that Sanson had not been in prison at all, but had been burned later when he had been looting in Saint-Pierre.

However, this calumny flew in the face of convincing evidence. Monsieur Lacourné, the attorney general, declared that Sanson had indeed been in solitary confinement in the prison on the night of 7–8 May. Father Mary, and no less a person than Fernand Clerc vouched that the men from Le Morne-Rouge were telling the truth when they said that they had broken down the door of Sanson's cell on 11 May. Moreover, a vital but neglected fact was even more telling. If Sanson had indeed been looting in Saint-Pierre, a nuée ardente could not have burned him, because no such nuées reached the city between the morning of Ascension Day and the Sunday afternoon when he was rescued. Sanson survived for two reasons. First, he was imprisoned in a cell, built like a bomb shelter, in a highly protected position, which was virtually the only building in Saint-Pierre that survived the nuée ardente intact and did not collapse upon him. Indeed, it is still there today. Secondly, his sheer physical strength and extraordinary resilience did the rest.

His American circus abandoned him when the novelty of his appeal wore thin, and poor Sanson died, probably in 1955, poverty-stricken in Panama.

17

The second great eruption
Tuesday 20 May 1902

There was an upsurge of sympathy for the victims as soon as the appalling extent of the catastrophe became known. Charity organizations, and public institutions such as banks and other businesses, sent money and goods for the survivors. Leaders throughout the world, such as Kaiser Wilhelm II of Germany, King Edward VII of England, Pope Leo XIII and President Theodore Roosevelt of the USA, gained much prestige by sending large and well publicized donations to the ravaged island. But, unfortunately, the gifts stopped when several articles and books propagated lies, about both victims and survivors, which have held currency practically ever since.

Lies about Louis Mouttet

One of the most serious lies was that Governor Mouttet had forced the citizens to stay in Saint-Pierre so that they would vote in the second round of the general elections on Sunday 11 May. For instance, the French geologist, De Lapparent, voiced the story in the Paris newspaper, *La Croix*, as early as 18 May. However, the source of this calumny can be traced to an interview that the election candidate of the whites, Fernand Clerc, gave to the French journalist, Jean Hess, who first recounted it in his newspaper, *Le Journal*, and then repeated it in his book about the catastrophe. The couple crystallized the psychological need to explain the disaster and, if possible, to blame someone for it.

As a scapegoat, Louis Mouttet had two tremendous advantages. First, discrediting Louis Mouttet could win votes for Clerc whenever the election took place, because the governor was reputed to have shared the reforming liberal views of the other candidate, Louis Percin. Second, Louis Mouttet was dead. If there was not a plot between the Clerc and Hess, there was certainly a communion of souls, because Jean Hess was deeply hostile to the colonial administration and strongly disliked Albert Decrais, the outgoing Minister for the Colonies, who was a radical like Louis Percin.

Clerc affirmed that:

Those who say that the danger remained unknown until the very last moment are telling lies. I saw [Gaston Landes] on the evening of 7 May and I recall exactly what he said: "I have sent a telegram to the governor to inform him that the violence of the eruption is going to make Morne Lacroix collapse, and that it constitutes a grave danger for Saint-Pierre. The governor replied: "Thank you for your message, but be careful not to warn the public." I'll never forget the sadness, worry and anxiety that poor Landes had on his face on that last evening of his life . . . The administration was guilty . . . They had received warnings about the danger, but they kept quiet about them. People asked for reassurance, and it was given to them. I am sure that if they had not wanted to re-assure the people at any price, and if they had let the people follow the dictates of their own fears and panic, then thousands would not have perished . . . Human science could not affirm that there was no danger, and thus [could not swear] that Saint-Pierre was absolutely safe. But they literally forced the people to stay in the city and put real pressure on them by making affirmations that they knew to be inane. That was the error that cost the governor his life . . .

[Clerc claimed that Albert Decrais had dictated this policy]. Mouttet was only the instrument . . . he obeyed. You could say that he died a hero's death. He was the victim of his professional duty – if the pro-fessional duty of a governor of Martinique meant absolute obedience to the Minister for the Colonies . . . and bowing down to [the radical] Senator Knight . . . That's how corpses are made . . . many corpses . . . Those who knew the personal feelings of [Gaston Landes] knew that Saint-Pierre was in grave danger. That's why most of the married civil servants in the city sent their wives and children to the capital. But they had to die at their jobs, because they had the imperative and precise order to stay in Saint-Pierre . . . I know a magistrate and a high-ranking customs official who were threatened with dismissal if they did not return to their posts at once on 7 May. They refused, and they owed their lives to the fact that they resisted . . .

There is talk of the article published in the newspaper, *Les Colonies*, which ended with the words: "To summarize, Saint-Pierre at the foot of Mount Pelée, is no more in danger than Naples is at the foot of Vesuvius." It is said that Landes' hand was forced when he wrote that report, and that the sentence just quoted did not represent the true expression of his views. Apparently, Landes was suddenly forced to change his conclusion at the last minute".

Fernand Clerc's assertions and innuendoes were incorrect. There had been no strong earthquakes. The report of the scientific commission was not a deliberate attempt to reduce anxiety but a rather woolly statement of the broad views of the few local people who knew anything about eruptions. There is no independent evidence that the governor told Gaston Landes to hide from the general public his fears (which, in any case, were unjustified fears) about the collapse of the Morne Lacroix. The conclusion to Landes' article in the newspaper was most probably added by the editor, Marius Hurard, who was undoubtedly trying to keep the population calm by claiming that there was no safer place to be than Saint-Pierre. The editor was allied to Fernand Clerc, and was no friend of Governor Mouttet, so there is no reason to suspect the governor and Marius Hurard of collusion.

If Gaston Landes believed that the city was in grave danger, it is odd that he decided to spend Ascension Day at his new house. The schools had been closed and he had no family in Martinique. He could therefore have easily moved to safety. No telegram from the ministry for the colonies has ever come to light instructing Governor Mouttet to keep the citizens in Saint-Pierre to vote. On the other hand, in *L'Opinion* on 4 October 1902, Albert Decrais vigorously denied sending any such instructions. In any case, the outgoing government certainly did not need to win the seat to ensure its parliamentary majority. Moreover, only 2141 men had voted in Saint-Pierre in the first round of the election, which was about the usual small proportion. When so few were likely to vote anyway, it would have been a considerable over-reaction to expose all the citizens to danger and stop them from leaving Saint-Pierre. And, there was no need to keep the women and children in the city, because they could not vote. If, indeed, the governor had believed that Saint-Pierre was in grave danger, it was odd that he should have asked his own wife and a cavalcade of higher civil servants to stay the night of 7–8 May in the city. No letter written by any civil servant based in Saint-Pierre makes the slightest mention of coercion. Thus, Fernand Clerc's assertion that two unnamed civil servants saved their lives by resisting the governor's orders seems to be pure invention. If they existed at all, they remained inexplicably mute after the disaster, when they would have had a wonderful opportunity to come forward and demonstrate their perspicacity and courage in the face of intolerable administrative pressure.

Finally, Fernand Clerc's own behaviour does not stand scrutiny. He, himself, took no steps to save lives. He had ample opportunity to publish his misgivings in *Les Colonies*, the editor of which, Marius Hurard, was one of his strongest political allies. Fernand Clerc made no comment whatsoever in print about his supposed fears before the eruption. He did not even try and save his own life. He stayed the night of 7–8 May in Saint-Pierre, and next morning went up to his plantation, at Le Parnasse, which was nearer the volcano. He survived only by chance when the nuée ardente passed within 500 m of the house.

Fernand Clerc's assertions were the affirmations of a rather despicable politician out for short-term gain. Such an individual would probably not greatly worry that he had done much to destroy the reputation of an honourable man, but it is sad that his claims were given completely unjustified credence for so many years.

The rumours about the governor's role spread faster and more widely than the truth. Whenever the lies were denied, more and more people became convinced that they must indeed be true. One denial was published on 18/19 May in the Parisian Catholic newspaper, *La Croix*, which was no supporter of the late governor.

LE ROLE DE M. MOUTTET

Les journaux publient la dépêche suivante de Saint-Thomas, 15 mai :

Le consul de France qui vient de revenir de la Martinique, où il s'était rendu dès la première nouvelle de la catastrophe, dément que le gouverneur de la colonie ait empêché la population de Saint-Pierre de quitter la ville.

"The newspapers are publishing the following cable from Saint Thomas, dated 15 May. 'The French consul [in Saint Thomas], who has just returned from Martinique, where he had gone on the first news of the catastrophe, denies that the governor of the colony had prevented the population of Saint-Pierre from leaving the city.'" (La Croix, 18/19 May 1902)

However, the calumny took wings. It was said that the governor had sent troops to Saint-Pierre to stop the citizens from leaving the city. The story runs counter to all that is known about Louis Mouttet's character. He had spent several days and two nights in the stricken area seeing for himself what had to be done to help and feed the victims of the eruption. He was a mild man with a social conscience, not a fool with a dictatorial streak. Moreover, French law made mayors responsible for the security of their citizens. In Saint-Pierre, this duty fell upon Rodolphe Fouché, not Governor Mouttet.

The story about the troops was apparently first reported to the USA by Monsieur Aymé, the American consul in Guadeloupe, and had also reached the French press, in Bordeaux for instance, by 17 May. The basis of this story was a fact that was inflated out of all proportion. On 7 May, Rodolphe Fouché, the mayor of Saint-Pierre, telephoned to ask the governor to send about 30 troops from Fort-de-France to help distribute food to the refugees and keep order, if necessary, although there was no immediate danger. There was no garrison in Saint-Pierre. The mayor had himself seen the disturbances that such food distributions had already caused in Le Prêcheur, and naturally wanted to prevent a repetition in Saint-Pierre. The governor acquiesced, and immediately decided to go and give his moral support to the city. The troops were scheduled to leave on the morning of 8 May, but the eruption forced their boat to return to Fort-de-France.

If Governor Mouttet had indeed "surrounded the city and blocked the roads with troops", as some claimed, then these soldiers would have died in the catastrophe. Troops did not die because they were not there. Only two soldiers, Lieutenant Hermary and Lieutenant Fouque, lost their lives, and at least one of them came to Saint-Pierre on 7 May with the governor's party. Louis Ernoult, then chief deputy mayor of Saint-Pierre, affirmed that the citizens had not been forbidden to leave the city. He could prove it: he himself had left Saint-Pierre to take his family to safety in the south. The tale of the governor's military initiative is thus pure myth. Unfortunately, less critical commentators still give it some currency, not only in Britain and the USA, but even in France, where they should have known better.

A restless volcanic interlude

The cataclysm on 8 May pacified Mount Pelée for several days. The volcano limited its efforts to producing menacing rumbles, clouds of fumes and light

Dimanche 18, lundi 19 Mai 1902

La catastrophe de la Martinique

SCÈNES DE DÉSOLATION

On télégraphie de Fort-de-France, 16 mai :

La Montagne Pelée continue à être en éruption ; mais le vent pousse maintenant vers le Nord la fumée et la plus grande partie des matières rejetées, rendant ainsi le travail plus facile pour ceux qui font des recherches à Saint-Pierre.

La scène au Carbet, est encore plus terrible qu'à Saint-Pierre. On peut voir plus de cinq cents cadavres amoncelés et dans un état avancé de décomposition. Une maison a eu ses volets et ses fenêtres enlevés, mais l'intérieur n'a presque pas été atteint. Un bœuf solitaire était le seul animal vivant rencontré. Je me suis rendu à pied du Carbet à Saint-Pierre. Le spectacle tout le long du chemin était lamentable à voir.

Au pied d'une statue de la Vierge, j'ai trouvé le corps d'un homme qui était certainement mort en priant. Les corps de nombreux habitants qui avaient essayé de s'enfuir gisaient épars dans toutes les directions. Tout indique qu'une vague de feu a dû balayer le pays avec la violence d'un cyclone.

La tour de la cathédrale est encore debout. La grosse cloche est tombée au milieu des ruines. La plus grande partie de l'autel est détruite. On a retrouvé cependant les calices en or, quoique très abîmés par la chute des décombres. Un grand calice contenait les cendres d'une hostie ; un petit était plein d'hosties intactes. Les cadavres de ceux qui s'étaient réfugiés dans la cathédrale étaient ensevelis sous les ruines.

J'ai visité l'emplacement du Club, de la Banque, de la Bourse et du bureau télégraphique. Partout la même scène de désolation et la mort s'offre à la vue. Au poste de police, il y avait un monceau de cadavres, le visage tourné contre la terre, comme si ces malheureux étaient tombés en se précipitant vers la station. On a trouvé des barriques de rhum intactes à la distillerie.

LE RÉCIT D'UN TÉMOIN

M. Albert, filateur, dont la propriété est située à un mille au nord-est de la Montagne Pelée, vient d'arriver à Port d'Espagne avec sa ...couler, et tout danger n'est pas encore écarté. On a retrouvé et enlevé 1 300 cadavres ; 180 victimes sont à l'hôpital.

3 000 personnes sont sustentées par l'Assistance publique. On étudie les moyens de leur fournir un abri.

2 000 bêtes de somme ont péri.

Neuf grandes plantations ont gravement souffert. L'une d'elles est complètement enfouie. La végétation a disparu. La culture est arrêtée pour longtemps.

LES DISPARUS

M. Chomereau-Lamotte, sous-gouverneur de la Banque de France, reçoit ce matin 17 mai un télégramme, daté du 9 mai, de son frère, directeur de l'usine du Lamentin, lui disant que deux de ses neveux, MM. Georges et Jules Pinel de Golleville, sont parmi les disparus. Aucune nouvelle des autres membres de la famille Pinel de Golleville, au nombre de onze.

LES RELIGIEUX A LA MARTINIQUE

Nos lecteurs savent déjà que le P. Malleret, originaire de Menat, de la Congrégation du Saint-Esprit, supérieur du séminaire-collège Saint-Louis de Gonzague, à la Martinique, était heureusement à Servant le jour du désastre. Trois autres Pères, le P. Guyot, de Cellule ; le P. Chassagnol, de Saint-Martin-des-Olmes, et le P. Desnier, de Servant, originaires aussi de cette région, ont dû succomber le 8 mai.

Voici le reste des noms des autres ecclésiastiques originaires du diocèse de Clermont qui sont à la Martinique, d'après la *Semaine* du diocèse :

M. l'abbé Fournioux, de Tours-sous-Meymont, curé de Gros-Morne, à 12 kilomètres au sud-est de Saint-Pierre ;

M. l'abbé Fargette, d'Issoire, curé de Sainte-Luce, au sud de l'île. Il devait s'embarquer le 10 mai pour la France ;

M. l'abbé Domas, de Volvic, vicaire du Vauclin, sud de l'île ;

M. l'abbé Beyssérias, du Monestier, vicaire au Lamentin.

En outre, au collège de Saint-Pierre, en dehors des PP. Chassagnol, Guyot et Desnier, déjà signalés, il faut citer : Le P. Schott, ancien élève et professeur à Cellule ; le P. Frivault, ancien professeur ; les PP. Garin et Gallo, anciens élèves de Cellule ; le P. Lanore, d'Ennezat. Signalons aussi le frère du Père Supérieur de Cellule, P. Wœtgli, au sujet duquel on est sans nouvelles jusqu'ici.

Enfin, il y a actuellement à Cellule deux élèves originaires de la Martinique.

Part of the newspaper La Croix, *published on 18/19 May 1902.*

ash, and to spewing small nuées ardentes into the valley of the Rivière Blanche. At night, it often put on spectacularly beautiful displays that belied the threat behind them. On the evening of 16 May, the *Pouyer Quertier* was resting off Saint-Pierre after a fruitless day's grappling for the broken cable. Emile Berté and Captain Thirion, watched the "magical sight", spellbound, from the bridge in the moonlight. The city seemed to be lit up almost like the old days, but now the lights were coming only from the cremation pyres set up by the soldiers. Every now and again, Mount Pelée sent up brilliant flares that splayed out like the distress signals sent from a stricken vessel. Suddenly, Emile Berté saw "the most frightening thing" that he had ever seen. It was a small nuée ardente. "A cascade of liquid fire, the colour of molten metal, started bouncing from a crater below the crest and careered down the Rivière Blanche". As Mount Pelée had done on 7 May, it was warning that worse was to come. "We are not safe here", murmured the captain, as he ordered the *Pouyer Quertier* out to sea. Emile Berté could but agree.

Closer at hand, in Saint-Pierre itself, the threat loomed perpetually on the northern skyline for those who were taking part in the daily expeditions to cremate the pathetic remains of the dead, and, indeed, for those who were criss-crossing the city in search of loot as soon as the authorities turned their backs. Abbé Parel had been sending a couple of priests to Saint-Pierre every day to bless the corpses that the squads of soldiers were cremating in the ruins. But from 16 May, the swirling ash and dust stopped the expeditions from landing. The volcano was becoming more restless with every passing day. On 17, 18 and 19 May, loud explosions from the volcano showered thick dust at intervals all over northern Martinique and as far as Fort-de-France. The rivers draining the northern flanks of Mount Pelée had once again become vigorous muddy torrents. There could be no question of anyone making the joyful annual Whit Sunday excursion to the summit of the volcano on 18 May. And few of those who had ever eaten their picnics beside the Lac des Palmistes were now still alive.

A reconnaissance to the northern villages

Now that the main evacuations had been completed, and many refugees had been given shelter, Commander Le Bris wanted to find out exactly what had happened to the villages on the northern flanks of Mount Pelée. Once more the commander acted on his own initiative, but the idea appealed to Monsieur Lhuerre, who asked to come along. Thus, supplies were loaded and the *Suchet* sailed at 7.15 a.m. on Friday 16 May. Several dignitaries were also on board, including Senator Knight and Homère Clément, the newly elected member of parliament for South Martinique, the Colonel commanding the troops, and a medical commission. The *Suchet* had no sooner moored at

Saint-Pierre than Mount Pelée launched a great salvo of ash and fumes, and erupted a nuée ardente that swirled down the valley of the Rivière Blanche. Most of the passengers had never seen anything so fearsome in their lives, and came, trembling, to Commander Le Bris to ask if they were in danger. "I replied that I could give them no assurance to the contrary. Whereupon, it was decided to abandon the disembarkation for Saint-Pierre."

As the officials recovered their composure, the vessel continued northwards to Grande Rivière, Macouba and Basse-Pointe, where the acting governor and Senator Knight landed and discussed the needs of the villagers with their respective mayors. The eruption had largely spared this part of the island and the animals could find their food because the ash falls had mostly been light. The main damage in these villages had come from the streams flooding down from Mount Pelée, which had destroyed plantations and carried houses away. Luckily, there had been no casualties, because those living near the torrents had been warned of the danger and had already left their homes.

When the *Suchet* returned to Saint-Pierre, Mount Pelée had calmed down. The dignitaries therefore felt able to visit the ruins of the city. However, they did not linger long enough to tempt the volcano into another aggressive spasm, and the party returned to Fort-de-France at 7.30 p.m.

Problems and a lesson for the French navy

The main problem in Fort-de-France was that it was taking too much time to unload all the vessels that had docked with supplies. The organizing powers of the acting governor, in particular, did not meet with the unalloyed approval of Commander Le Bris.

It seemed to me that the organization of the different services on land left much to be desired . . . because of the lack of any energetic direction. Thus, for example, no plans had been made for unloading the vessels that were bringing supplies. This placed me in a most unpleasant position, because I received the complaints from the commanders, who were annoyed to see that [the authorities] seemed to be unaware of their very presence. I therefore proposed to the [acting] governor that the navy should be put in charge of unloading the supplies, and he readily agreed to my request. Lieutenant Allemand took charge of this service and I seconded an officer to help him. It was clearly stipulated that we should bring the barges to the quaysides, but that we would not unload the packets onto the land, because the municipality was responsible for this. My men were very tired by all the hard service that they had put in since the beginning of these events, and I did not want to make them work on land in the full heat of the Sun.

However, the problem was not resolved overnight. On 18 May, for instance, the British cruiser, *Indefatigable*, arrived laden with 120 tonnes of supplies from Barbados. Commander Le Bris had them unloaded onto the quays, and then went to see how the work was progressing. "I saw that [the work] was going on with disheartening slowness, and that the means provided by the civil authorities were totally insufficient, especially since the few workers recruited brought the utmost sluggishness to their task." Yet again, the commander protested to Monsieur Lhuerre.

Lieutenant Allemand himself had voiced his own protests to the naval authorities. He declared that:

> Fort-de-France had only 12 barges, which could take only 400 barrels all told . . . only 3 or 4 are covered, and several leak. Thus, merchandise has been lost because it was soaked either by sea water or the rain . . . I believe it is my duty, minister, to inform you how painful it was for me when I could not prevent foreign naval vessels . . . from observing the true dilapidated and useless state of the equipment that the navy has here. Fortunately, the tireless energy of the sailors had upheld the good reputation of the French navy and masked the inertia and unwillingness of the population . . . I would therefore urgently request all the barges, tugs and cisterns we need if we are to avoid the humiliating inferiority in the future, which even the good will of all concerned could not hide from the foreign officers . . . Before the destruction of Saint-Pierre, we could always count on the marine equipment of the merchant houses in the city in an emergency. This is no longer the case since all that equipment has vanished. In every eventuality in the future, the navy will have to rely only on itself to supply its vessels.

soit prévu d'urgence pour Fort-de-France
les chalands, remorqueurs et citernes nécessaires
pour éviter à l'avenir l'infériorité humiliante
que le bon vouloir de chacun n'a pu cacher
aux yeux des officiers étrangers.

-On pouvait, avant la destruction
de Saint-Pierre, compter en cas d'urgence
sur le matériel flottant des maisons de
commerce de cette ville.

Il n'en est plus de même aujourd'hui
tout ce matériel ayant disparu et ce n'est
plus que sur ses propres moyens que la
Marine doit compter pour le ravitaillement
des navires en toutes circonstances.

The last few lines and signature of Lieutenant Allemand's protest to the Navy. The English translation begins "I would therefore" at the end of the ninth line of the extract on p. 198.

Another great nuée ardente

Between 2.00 p.m. and 3.00 p.m. on 19 May, the ash was thick enough to bring darkness to the Bay of Saint-Pierre, and two hours later a huge columnar cloud, like balls of white cotton, rose skywards from the crater. But the night was calm. Just as on Ascension Day, Mount Pelée was giving off a magnificent column of steam when dawn broke on 20 May. Off Saint-Pierre, the first mate of the *Pouyer Quertier* was on watch when he saw "a thick sooty-black cloud escape from the crater and fall towards the ship in no time at all". The captain started to make for the open sea, but no ship could have won a race against a nuée ardente. Luckily for them, it did not reach the ship and the crew was saved.

Soon there seemed to be as much wreckage in the bay as on 8 May. Gigantic tree trunks floated past the vessel on the current. Emile Berté observed that "some were cut as if they had been sawn down, but the ends of many others were twisted, ripped up and frayed like enormous paint brushes". But there were no corpses now. There had been few people left to kill. Soon, amid all the desolation, Captain Thirion's crew started grappling again.

At the same time, Abbé Altéroche at Le Morne-Vert had seen a series of huge puffs of fumes leave the crater. Then he heard a large explosion, and a great nuée ardente surged forth. It was almost as powerful as that which had destroyed Saint-Pierre, and it covered just about the same area. Within minutes, ash and stones were lashing down on Le Morne-Vert, then mud, and yet more ash fell. The showers lasted for about an hour all told. The nuée ardente also sent a sea wave crashing onto the shore at Le Carbet. It swept into Saint-Pierre, but there was now so little left to destroy in the city. The nuée threw down most of the remaining tottering walls in the city, including the cathedral tower and the facade of the military hospital. The fountains stopped flowing at last. A few corpses were exposed: a few others were buried. The human drama was minimal, although perhaps some early-morning looters were surprised and killed.

The drama of the second great nuée ardente took place in Fort-de-France. At 5.20 a.m., two enormous explosions reverberated from Mount Pelée. A few moments later, a huge cloud of steam, ash and fumes soared up from a black point above the northern horizon and spread high over the city. The rising Sun tinged the billowing mass a rich golden orange. On another day, on another island, such a sumptuous cloud would have sent any artist reaching for his canvas. Now, it unleashed an electric charge of sheer terror throughout the length and breadth of Fort-de-France. Abbé Parel was one of thousands who "fell to their knees, waiting for the Lord's hour to come".

An immense clamour rose from the streets and almost drowned the thunderous explosions from the volcano. People rushed for safety, panic-stricken and half clothed. As Commander Le Bris noted, such was the terror that "all classes of society were mingled together in their fear. Women and half-naked children (having tumbled half awake from their beds) ran about aimlessly, and many men did the same." Some people lay down on the ground and waited to die. Dozens of citizens sought refuge aboard the *Suchet* and other vessels on the quay. Some dashed to Fort Saint-Louis out at the southern end of the harbour. Many hurried, terrified, into the church, where the curate begged them to pray with their arms crossed over their breasts. The end of the world seemed nigh. But no masonry fell upon those who were staring death in the face. It must have been so very much worse during that awful moment in the cathedral in Saint-Pierre on 8 May. As it was, the state of extreme anguish lasted only for an interminable quarter of an hour in Fort-de-France. Dust, then ash, then mud splattered down. Then people began to realize that "only a miracle had saved them once again from the terrible fire".

Until the second nuée ardente erupted, the people of Martinique had just been starting to regain a little of their usual confidence. As Commander Le Bris remarked, the people had eventually come to accept that the great nuée ardente on 8 May had been an event that surpassed anything that the imagination could conceive. It was as if it had been some kind of "mystery". No-one could believe that it would ever happen again. This second nuée ardente therefore dealt them a severe blow. They became totally disheartened. How many more of these scourges would follow? How could they expect to escape a third or fourth time? It would be safer to leave. At once. Anywhere. People packed their trunks and embarked in their hundreds, if not their thousands, for Saint Lucia, Guadeloupe, Trinidad, or even for France itself. That very day, 500 people embarked on a liner for Guadeloupe, and a British ship took a similar number to Saint Lucia.

The people who had stayed on in upland villages in the north, such as Fonds-Saint-Denis and Le Morne-Rouge left for the new safe haven of Fort-de-France. Father Mary at last abandoned his post, mounted his horse and started to lead his flock towards the capital. They spent the first night at La Grand' Anse. Next morning, however, Father Mary decided to return to the church and collect the holy vessels that he had left there, and many in his flock took it upon themselves to follow him and to go back to their homes. Thus, Father Mary felt obliged to stay with between 200 and 400 villagers who were determined to see out the crisis, or die, in the familiar surroundings of their own homes.

The acting governor was afraid that this second great eruption might have brought catastrophe to the far north of the island. On 21 May, he actually took an initiative and asked Commander Le Bris to take him on another reconnaissance to assess the situation. The commander, of course complied, but he might have preferred to spend his 46th birthday in more congenial company. In fact, alarming rumours of great damage in Le Carbet had reached the authorities. The acting governor sent the *Jouffroy* to inspect the village, and the ship returned to Fort-de-France with 240 refugees that after-noon. The *Suchet* set off at 11.15 a.m., as soon as the vessel could get up steam, but there was little new damage in the northern coastal villages. The rivers had merely brought down yet more mud and destroyed yet more houses that the inhabitants had already abandoned. Those who had stayed at home just asked for more food, for they were beginning to starve. The *Suchet* was back in Fort-de-France by 8.00 p.m. That same day, the American cruiser, *Dixie*, had arrived with many supplies, but had found it hard to get its valuable cargo unloaded.

Mount Pelée calmed down for only a few days after its second great out-burst on 20 May. Then, the seemingly incessant parade of nuées ardentes resumed down the valley of the Rivière Blanche. Most lost their impetus en route, but some were powerful enough to reach the sea. The nuées ardentes expelled on 26 May, 6 June and 9 July, for instance, were particularly mem-orable. People who had witnessed the greatest outbursts were beginning to become accustomed to this majestic display, but those who were seeing the nuées ardentes for the first time thought that they were the most terrifying spectacle they had ever set eyes upon. The infernal triangle between Mount Pelée, Le Prêcheur and Saint-Pierre was still one of the most dangerous places on Earth in which to linger. And yet, linger people did – some out of greed, some out of duty, and some out of the demands of science.

Within hours of the catastrophe on 8 May, rumours of the legendary wealth buried in the ruins of Saint-Pierre had spread like wildfire throughout the West Indies. The city became a magnet for every looter who could carry a sack and a pick-axe onto a boat. The eruptions had wreaked immense destruction, but it soon became known that all manner of valuable objects could have escaped damage. There were jewels to be wrenched from unpro-testing hands, antiques to be dislodged from the rubble, and tills, safes and strong boxes galore to be prised open – all for the taking, apart from the threat of a few guards, and a volcano that menaced everything and everyone with masterly indifference. But for the poor in particular, the chances of gain far outweighed those of being arrested or killed. The pillage began early and went on for months; and every available mattress and table were soon spirited away in the darkness. The ruins could not be effectively protected, although on 14 May, for instance, 45 looters were arrested and the guilty were sentenced to five years in jail.

Duty obliged others to come to the ruins. Every day, a couple of priests and squads of soldiers came to give the dead as decent a cremation as they could. It was a ghastly job, which had to be done as quickly as possible because the heat was hastening the putrefaction of the corpses. They were gathered on wooden pyres set up at intervals throughout the city, and were left to burn for a day before their remains were interred or otherwise disposed of. Nevertheless, most of the corpses lay hidden and made their own unmistakable and indescribable contribution to the atmosphere from beneath the rubble.

Survivors applied to the acting governor for permission to search the remains of their homes to try and recover some of their property. Few, if any, families could have been insured against such a cataclysm. The survivors had every prospect of being destitute, unless some stroke of fortune had preserved, for example, their safes or their jewellery. They landed at the remnant of the old jetty and wandered in a daze through the melancholy desolation to find their old homes. Consequently, as soon as the *Pouyer Quertier* had repaired the submarine cable on 27 May, Emile Berté hurried to Saint-Pierre.

> I had permission from Monsieur Porry, the director of excavations, to go to Saint-Pierre on 30 May to see what was left of my house. Monsieur Cappa, who was in charge of the cremation of the bodies, gave me a passage on the *Pholade,* which took him and his men to Saint-Pierre every day . . . I wanted to go to my old home in the Centre district as soon as possible, but the streets were obstructed by piles of stones, mud, and beams that were still smoking [from the cremations] . . . The Centre district had completely disappeared . . . It is a plain of mud, with nothing sticking out. I reckoned there would be about 1.5 m of mud covering everything. I could see two round objects, two cannonballs, on the ground . . . all that remained of the marines' barracks . . . It was only then that I was able to orientate myself and reach home. All that remained of my house was a section of wall, rising 25 cm above the ground. I sat down on this wall. I was trampling on the very ground where all my family was buried.

The following day, Emile Berté and a colleague returned on foot to the ruins. They left Fort-de-France at 4.00 p.m., spent the night in the home of the only villager still living in Le Carbet, and began walking the 4 km to

The ruins of the Centre district of Saint-Pierre, with the Morne Abel hill on the right and Mount Pelée erupting in the background. Emile Berté could no longer find his family home here amid the devastation. Note that the houses sheltered by the Morne Abel, on the right, retained some of their walls. Compare with the photograph on p. 25.

Saint-Pierre before dawn. It proved easier than usual to walk on the road because the rains had turned the volcanic ash into mortar, which had dried in the sunshine. At dawn, they saw that all the plantations had been abandoned and the houses were open. All the horses, oxen, pigs and goats were running wild in the sugar-cane fields, where they seemed to have plenty to eat but were desperately thirsty.

> The crater . . . was an immense lighted furnace on the slope facing Saint-Pierre . . . [We] sat on a milestone until sunrise, contemplating the grandiose and terrifying spectacle . . . The splays of ash and fumes escaping from the monster's throat were surging vertically to a prodigious height. We could also see another smaller crater that was also giving off smoke . . . We went into the old Trédos plantation. There used to be a great allée, 100 m long, leading to the house and its outbuildings, which was planted with age-old trees. All the trees had been thrown down in the same direction: towards the south . . . What prodigious power could have produced such effects?
> We started to notice the smell of putrefying organic matter near the

houses. In the first house, we found 25 or 30 dead bodies, or their remains. Their flesh was no longer attached to their bones. Some of the bones had been burnt [by the second nuée ardente]. We went into the outbuildings and we found skeletons lying on the ground in every one. We came upon a kitchen. The remains of a woman were lying on the floor. The coffee pot was still on the stove, and nothing else had moved: only the roof had gone . . . We were now only a quarter of an hour from Saint-Pierre. The remains of stinking bodies lined the road . . . The latest rains had washed the earth away, and several putrefying bodies were now exposed beneath the rubble . . . [In Saint-Pierre] I took some more photographs. I tried to collect a souvenir of any sort from the remains of my old home. Even a pebble would have pleased me, but I couldn't find a thing. The volcanic mud was covering everything.

In late June, a team of scientific investigators from Paris joined the other groups searching the ruins. Professor Alfred Lacroix, the most eminent French geologist of his day, was appointed to conduct a thorough scientific investigation into the causes and effects of the eruption. His account has

Alfred Lacroix (centre) and an assistant at work in the ruins of Saint-Pierre. A remnant of a building in the Rue Victor-Hugo rises behind them. The notch from which the nuée ardente issued can clearly be seen in the rim of the crater on the crest of the volcano to the right of the professor's pith helmet.

remained one of the foundations of volcanology ever since and it is absolutely essential to any study of the destruction of Saint-Pierre and the deaths of its inhabitants. Other scientists, notably George Kennan and Angelo Heilprin, came from the USA, and "Tempest" Anderson and John Flett came from the UK, but none of their works approached the depth of the monograph of Alfred Lacroix.

Alfred Lacroix.

Alfred Lacroix

Alfred Lacroix was born in Macon, in Burgundy, in 1863. He was the son of a pharmacist, but he soon chose to embark upon an academic career. At university in Paris, he quickly developed the passionate interest in geology, which was to become his life's work. By 1902, Alfred Lacroix had been a professor at the Museum d'Histoire Naturelle in Paris since he was 30. As soon as the impact of the eruption was realized in Paris, he was appointed to investigate the events that had destroyed Saint-Pierre. He was assisted by Monsieur Rollet de l'Isle and by Dr Jean Giraud.

The commission and Madame Catherine Lacroix arrived at Fort-de-France on 23 June. The naval escort vessel, the *Jouffroy*, was placed at their disposal. They studied, photographed and examined every whim of the volcano, and interviewed the survivors. They became a familiar sight as they strode fearlessly up and down the ash-clad flanks of Mount Pelée, often at great risk to their own safety: Lacroix with his great beard, pith helmet and large boots, his wife with her bobbing parasol, their servants and two junior partners following in their wake.

Towards the end of July. Professor Lacroix indicated to the authorities that he believed that the worst was over, and took the liner home again on 1 August. But even a great savant can err. He bargained without Mount Pelée, which resumed serious activity two weeks afterwards and culminated in another major eruption on 30 August. Thus, Lacroix had to return to Martinique earlier than planned on 1 October for another stint of research, which lasted until 13 March 1903. He aimed to appraise the risks of future eruptions and to establish a permanent observatory to keep the volcano under constant surveillance. Thus, Lacroix became one of the pioneers of volcanic risk assessment, as well as one of the first geologists to make a full study of a volcanic eruption. He published the results of his considerable investigations in *La montagne Pelée et ses eruptions*. It made a worthy companion to Rogier Verbeek's great study of the eruption of Krakatau, published in 1885, and surpassed the study of Santoríni published by his own father-in-law, Ferdinand Fouqué, in 1879. Lacroix gave the first epoch-making descriptions and analyses of nuées ardentes, with which his name and that of Mount Pelée will always be associated. Elected a member of the Académie des Sciences à Paris in 1904, he became permanent secretary of that illustrious body.

He was a man of immense industry, for whom the term "workaholic" would have been too feeble had it been used during his lifetime. Alfred Lacroix wrote no fewer than 665 learned articles and books. Phénoménal! He died in 1948 and left his valuable archives to the Muséum d'Histoire Naturelle in Paris.

18

Aftermath

During the weeks that followed Mount Pelée's second great nuée ardente on 20 May, the administrators and people of Martinique had to assess their situation and alleviate their dreadful plight. Response to the catastrophe did not always proceed smoothly.

Victims of the nuée ardente on 8 May

At the census in 1901, Saint-Pierre had a population of 26 011, the figure that provides the basis for all calculations of the number of victims killed by the nuée ardente on Ascension Day. But, of course, refugees had flocked to Saint-Pierre, and some citizens had fled from it as the eruption developed. In order to estimate the number of people who might have left Saint-Pierre as the crisis reached its climax, Commander Le Bris arranged for a study to be made of the passengers carried by the Girard company's steamers between Saint-Pierre and Fort-de-France. Some 1640 people had left Saint-Pierre between 1 and 7 May and about 290 had made the return journey from Fort-de-France. Thus, approximately 1350 people could have abandoned Saint-Pierre. But this figure makes no allowance for the relatively small number of residents of Fort-de-France who might have gone to Saint-Pierre and then returned home. Moreover, since the eruption had started, perhaps over a thousand people had left their villages on the flanks of Mount Pelée and had taken refuge in Saint-Pierre. No-one knew the exact number, but it was believed that the influx into Saint Pierre had probably more or less counterbalanced the number who had left the city. A broad estimate of some 26 000 deaths in Saint-Pierre itself would therefore seem to be reasonable.

In addition, several hundred people must have lost their lives in the vessels in the bay, and about 400 people died when the fringe of the nuée ardente struck the semaphore at Le Morne-Folie, just south of Le Prêcheur. Consequently, the nuée ardente probably killed about 27 000 people on 8 May, and it is hard to justify the figures in excess of 30 000 or even 40 000 that were bandied about just after the catastrophe.

These figures included many black people and far fewer whites. This seems obvious now, but it was not always obvious then. For most of the surviving white population, non-whites not only did not count, they were scarcely ever mentioned in their accounts of the catastrophe. It was almost as if they had not been there. The grandmother of the French poet, Saint-Jean Perse, revealed perhaps one of the most outrageous instances of this attitude when she was reputed to have bemoaned the death of 7000 people at Saint-Pierre. Asked if the number of deaths had not been much higher, she conceded "Oh yes, if you include the coloured people".

Survivors of the nuée ardente on 8 May

A survivor of the nuée ardente should be defined as someone who lived after being touched, burned or buffeted by the eruption. Thus, for instance, Simon Taudilas, who was thrown down by the blast, was a survivor of the nuée ardente, whereas Abbé Altéroche, who watched it untouched from Le Morne-Vert, was not. Only two men withstood the nuée ardente within the confines of Saint-Pierre itself. A kind of semantic slip has led many to assert that only two people survived the whole nuée. It also made for a more dramatic story, which added to the human interest of the eruption. In fact, at least 64 people lived through the onslaught of the nuée ardente, because they happened to be where its effects were attenuated at the critical moment. On land, they were on its outermost edges. On board ship, some people survived in well sealed rooms; others were protected by the bodies of comrades who fell on top of them; and one or two lived because they managed to stay under water until the nuée passed over. Some of the victims lived on only for a few hours, or a few days, and should not be considered as survivors. Gaston Landes endured four hours of agony. Monsieur Monferrier lasted for five days. Joseph Plissonneau struggled for life in Saint Lucia for ten days. But, even within these controls, it is still impossible to make a really accurate estimate of the number of survivors.

On the land 13 people lived after the nuée ardente burned them. Sylbaris and Compère-Léandre survived in Saint-Pierre itself. On the inland edges of the nuée ardente, Edouard Lasserre, his farm manager and his coachman; Madame Montferrier; Simon Taudilas and the three women with him; and Passioniste Lesage, who went to Le Carbet; as well as the two ladies barricaded in the Laugier shop, all lived through their ordeal, although people within a few metres of them died. The remaining cases are much more doubtful. The insane lady who arrived alone in Fort-de-France was most probably not covered by the nuée ardente; and Monsieur Raybaud took 20 victims to hospital from his plantation, but it is not known whether any recovered, and thus none can be counted among the definite survivors.

When the *Roddam* reached Saint Lucia, 20 victims were still alive, but some, like Joseph Plissonneau, might have died soon afterwards. The *Suchet* rescued at least 12, and possibly as many as 20 people from the *Roraïma*, three from the *Nord America*, five from the *Gabrielle*, and 13 from the *Teresa Lo Vico*, and one from the *Diamant* (as well as Lesage, who had gone down to the shore at Le Carbet). Commander Le Bris said that 9 of these died on the *Suchet* leaving "about 30" victims who reached hospital at Fort-de-France. Five lived after the nuée ardente overturned Chavigny's pirogue canoe near Le Prêcheur. In addition, Raphaël Pons, stoker on the *Roraïma* was apparently rescued from Saint-Pierre by Vaillant and Tribut.

On this basis, if the smallest numbers are taken into account in each case, then a minimum of 64 people survived the nuée ardente. If the largest figures in each case are taken into account, then 72 survived. Unfortunately, there is a further complication. In fact, a total of 151 people were admitted to hospital, although they included an unknown number of victims of respiratory problems, falling ash and flood damage. Of these 151 people, 111 recovered. Thus, an absolute maximum of 111 people withstood the nuée ardente, whereas the absolute minimum number of survivors amounted to 64.

Displaced persons

As the weeks passed, the number of refugees from the northern parts of the island rose to about 25 000. Some 15 000 of these were crowded into every public building and many private homes in Fort-de-France, where their plight was a constantly increasing worry for the mayor, Victor Sévère. A fear of disease became almost as great as the fear of another eruption, especially after typhoid fever broke out in the capital. The mayor arranged for the

The poorer refugees jostling each other for their government allowance outside the city hall in Fort-de-France in June 1902.

refugees to be given a daily ration of bread, salted pork, cod and dried vegetables. Naturally, the system was abused. Refugees with large appetites or mercenary instincts collected food from more than one relief centre; and many people flocked from undamaged areas to take up the windfall. The very notion that the administration might be giving out free food also caused more than one set of hackles to rise. One Breton officer, for example, declared that it was disgraceful to distribute white bread of quality to "these negroes", whereas thousands of Bretons and soldiers would never be in a position to receive such a bounty in their lives.

At first, the refugees received quite a generous grant by the colonial standards of the day: 1.25 francs per person per day in cash, food and clothing. This was more than most had earned in their lives, the average daily wage of a farm worker being often less than 1.50 francs. And, of course, this apparent generosity fermented the jealousy of all those who had lost nothing, and therefore still had to work. Thus, the administration tried to counter such feelings by setting some refugees to build and repair roads around Fort-de-France.

211

The colonial authorities were afraid that the refugees would get used to a life of idleness. In fact, senior officials had already complained about the continual lethargy of the black population, notably when it came to unloading supply ships, or building new settlements. However, this unwillingness to work was related more to the aftermath of past civil disturbances rather than to any desire to live on the proceeds of charity forever. Nevertheless, the administration began to fear that idleness would force the refugees into becoming a ready prey to movements of anarchy and unrest like those that had caused the strife in 1900. This fear quickly transformed itself into the view that the refugees were, indeed, idle. Before long, the rumour spread well beyond Martinique that the indolent refugees were dancing and partying on the profits from the international donations that they had received. In fact, there is no evidence that they spent the months after the eruption in riotous excesses. Most of the refugees had nothing whatever to dance about. They were homesick and poverty stricken, often bereaved, almost invariably terrified and helpless, and with little prospect of finding a job. They were entirely at the mercy of public charity and the food supplies brought by the vessels reaching Fort-de-France. They had virtually no means of helping themselves. And they had nowhere to go.

The eruption of 30 August at Le Morne-Rouge

Mount Pelée stayed almost completely calm from mid-July until mid-August. It was beginning to seem as if the ordeal of Martinique had come to an end. Alfred Lacroix believed that the eruption was waning by the time he had completed the first part of his assignment and had taken the transatlantic liner back to France on 1 August. Indeed, by the beginning of August, the refugees were causing more administrative problems than the volcano. Overcrowding was spreading diseases. The acting governor, Georges Lhuerre, convinced himself that it would be much more convenient if the refugees were to return to their own villages, where he thought that they would be better able to fend for themselves. They would also, of course, be farther from his own doorstep. Not surprisingly, he found it hard to persuade the villagers to comply with his instructions. They had virtually no crops; their animals had probably wandered all over the place, if they had survived at all; and many homes had been damaged, and probably robbed. On 2 August, the acting governor therefore callously offered the carrot of assistance to those who returned to their own villages. The corresponding stick was that they must do so before 15 August. He himself organized the help of the *Suchet* to take the refugees to their homes and undertook to provide them with food until they could resume their work. On the other hand, those who refused go back home would get no further help from the administration. They were therefore, in effect, at liberty to starve. Thus, for instance, some 1200 people who had fled from Le Morne-Rouge had virtually no option but to return.

Le Morne-Rouge became the focus of attention because it was one of the still-inhabited villages lying closest to the volcano. The villagers had no sooner returned to their homes than the volcano had a change of heart. On 13 August, Mount Pelée expelled a nuée ardente into the valley of the Rivière Blanche. On the Feast of the Assumption on 15 August, glowing viscous lava, with the consistency of stiff molten glass, oozed up from the volcanic chimney and started to form another huge red-hot dome in the crater. On the following day, its crest had risen above the rim of the crater and was exposed to the terrified gaze of the villagers of Le Morne-Rouge.

On 21 August, Jean-Baptiste Lemaire took up his post as the new governor of Martinique. Mount Pelée celebrated his arrival with great gusto and sent a whole series of nuées ardentes rushing down the Rivière Blanche and into the sea. White ash blanketed all the northern flanks of the volcano. On 24 August, an ominous earthquake shook the whole island. At 10.00 a.m. the next day, Mount Pelée began to expel an enormous column of ash and fumes, and at 10.00 p.m. it threw out a great spray of glowing fragments like a firework display. The people of Le Morne-Rouge were terrified. Many ran off as fast as they could towards the nearest villages to the south. Some of those who opted to stay in Le Morne-Rouge rushed into the sanctuary of the church. During the night of 25–26 August, the intensity of the eruption increased, and the volcano rumbled and roared incessantly. Dawn revealed that the dome had expanded well above the rim of the crater. The threat from Mount Pelée was there for all in Le Morne-Rouge to see.

Father Mary's admirers claimed that he had become a kind of general factotum, playing pharmacist, food supplier and doctor to body and soul. He organized the daily distribution of food aid and the orderly killing of the farm animals to maintain regular supplies of meat. The animals themselves were starving and had to be sacrificed because the constant falls of ash had all but destroyed their pastures. However, since the volcano was becoming increasingly threatening, the villagers sent a delegation to Fort-de-France on 26 August to plead with Governor Lemaire to arrange for them to be evacuated

Mount Pelée approaching the climax of its eruption, seen from Le Morne-Rouge in the after-noon of 30 August 1902. This is one of the rare photographs, taken from relatively close range, of Mount Pelée in eruption in 1902.

to safety. Unlike his predecessor, Louis Mouttet, the new governor had no great sympathy with the problems of colonial peoples. He showed it at once. He gave them short shrift. Governor Lemaire was satisfied to implement the inglorious policy recently devised by the acting governor. He ordered the hapless delegation to go back home forthwith, and tell the people of Le Morne-Rouge to stay in their village – otherwise their food allowance would be cut off altogether. They had no alternative but to do as they were told, and await the fury of the volcano towering above them. Not for long.

If Mount Pelée were ever to direct a nuée ardente towards Le Morne-Rouge, then Governor Lemaire had effectively signed the death warrant of the villagers. On 27 and 28 August, more and more columns of fumes rose skywards, ash and stones rained down all around the summit of the volcano, and nuées ardentes raced down the valley of the Rivière Blanche. On 29 August, the eruption became even more powerful, and the whole volcano seemed to be shuddering continuously. Crockery rattled on the shelves. Houses, and the people within them, trembled. At 1.30 a.m. on 30 August, muddy rain began to patter down onto the village. The volcano glowed and glowered on the northern skyline. By now, many people were too terrified to move, and they barricaded themselves in their homes to keep the dreadful marauder at bay as best they could. Mount Pelée had given plenty of warning. Indeed, this was the only great outburst that displayed a regular increase in activity until the volcano reached its climactic crescendo.

Mount Pelée unleashed its third great nuée ardente of the year at 8.45 p.m. on 30 August. The first two nuées on 8 and 20 May had blasted directly down towards Saint-Pierre and had covered a relatively small area. The third nuée ardente was rather less powerful, but it still extended, with hurricane force, over twice the area of its predecessors.

There was a fearsome noise. A huge cloud of red-hot ash and fumes rose 5 km into the night sky, followed at once by an even denser, even brighter mass. It not only spewed down over Saint-Pierre and stopped once again at Le Carbet, but it spread, this time, over the southeastern flanks of the volcano as well. Lightning riddled the huge cloud as it fell upon Le Morne-Rouge.

Several gendarmes in the barracks in Le Morne-Rouge saw the nuée ardente leave the crater. They jumped onto their horses and rode off in a frantic posse towards Fort-de-France. The fastest racehorses in the world at the time could not have saved them. Two were burned to death before they could escape from the barracks. The third man died in the church porch, 45 m away, where he had leaped for shelter, and the nuée caught his horse a farther 40 m along the road. The fourth gendarme galloped 225 m from the barracks before he fell. He was so badly burned that he was trying to take off his trousers to ease his pain when he died. The fifth gendarme was leading their desperate race when the nuée caught him, burned him and his horse to death, and flung them into the ditch.

Three gigantic hot whirlwinds surged successively over Le Morne-Rouge.

During the first blast, police inspector Arnuel had sealed himself firmly in the police station. But he had to dash for the shelter of the cells when the building caught fire. As he ran, his legs felt scalded, as if he was running through boiling water. The cells protected him from the second blast, but the third blast set them on fire. Monsieur Arnuel rushed outside again, only to be burned by the final gusts of the nuée. He died soon afterwards, probably from his burns.

Some villagers had narrow escapes, while their companions died around them. Four people, for example, were together in a house facing the volcano when the nuée erupted. One man died on his bed. Another went outside at the crucial moment and died on the doorstep. Pauline Daubat threw herself to the ground and was burned on her exposed limbs, but she survived. In the same room, the nuée had thrust open the door and trapped Paul Lucile behind it when he tried frantically to shut it. He was not burned at all and was able to run for help to Fonds-Saint-Denis.

Father Mary was in his presbytery at 8.45 p.m. when the first blast of the nuée hit Le Morne-Rouge. As the roof of the building caught fire, the priest went to open the church so that his parishioners could shelter and seek solace with him inside it. He was crossing the courtyard when the second blast arrived, burned him and threw him down, gasping for breath. He managed to drag himself into the church as the final blast swirled through the courtyard.

The ruins of Le Morne-Rouge after the eruption on 30 August 1902. The damage was less severe than that caused in Saint-Pierre on 8 May 1902.

216

The agony of this legendary figure generated its own legends (or truths – who knows?): of how Father Mary had struggled to the feet of the Madonna; how he had absolved sinners as badly burnt as he; how parishioners had held up his arm so that he could give the last rites to the poor black villagers who were dying alongside him . . . A certain Mademoiselle Cara and her friends carried him to their lodgings through the streets littered with corpses. They cut his cassock to bandage his burns. Like all those who had "swallowed the fire", Father Mary was desperately thirsty. Edith Duchâteau-Roger averred that Mademoiselle Cara then ran over 5 km to Fonds-Saint-Denis to get him water. She had been so preoccupied with her errand that she had forgotten to put on her shoes. It is hard to judge whether this aberration was a result of excessive eagerness, stupidity or shock.

At 9.00 a.m. on 31 August, Father Mary was placed on a hammock to be taken to the capital. As he left Le Morne-Rouge, he insisted on blessing and absolving those parishioners who still had some sign of life left in them. At Fonds-Saint-Denis, a vehicle sent by Abbé Parel took him to Fort-de-France, where he arrived at the hospital at 2.00 a.m. on 1 September. There, Father Mary took the last sacraments and died at 11.00 a.m. that morning.

Abbé Parel himself took the funeral service in Fort-de-France, which was attended by a vast crowd, the event taking place "without distinction of race or opinion". It is said that grief-stricken black members of his congregation insisted on carrying his coffin to the grave. Father Mary had worked for 19 years in Le Morne-Rouge and had always been renowned for giving special attention to his underprivileged parishioners.

The victims of the eruption on 30 August 1902

All that remained of Le Morne-Rouge was the church, the jail and hundreds of wrecked houses. However, the houses where the doors and windows had been closely sealed had resisted the nuée ardente more effectively because the eddying effects had been reduced. On the other hand, the Convent of the Délivrande was also badly damaged, in spite of the religious protection it was reputed to have enjoyed. Hot ash blanketed the whole village. Corpses were strewn in the streets. Nevertheless, the troops and the gendarmes from Fonds-Saint-Denis rescued over 250 injured casualties. The eruption killed at least 800 people in Le Morne-Rouge, a further 250 in Ajoupa-Bouillon, 25 in Basse-Pointe, and 10 in Le Morne-Capot, making a grand total of not less than 1085 victims. Some 2000 refugees from the area crowded into Fort-de-France and strained the resources of the capital to the very limit once again. The survivors abandoned Le Morne-Rouge for over a year. The outburst of 30 August was the last lethal nuée ardente that Mount Pelée expelled in 1902, although many others rolled down the now sterile valley of the Rivière Blanche for over a year.

The acting governor, Georges Lhuerre, and the new governor, Jean-Baptiste Lemaire, were largely to blame for this additional disaster. However, they had the full support of Gaston Doumergue, the new Minister for the Colonies, and a future president of France. All three escaped censure because they proved to be skilfully economical with the truth. It is surprising, though, that their ignominious behaviour has escaped criticism until quite recently.

Parsimony and planning

As a former finance officer in Martinique, Governor Lemaire was shocked by what he perceived as the parlous state of the colony's finances. He was appalled, for instance, that some two million francs had been spent on the refugees during the past three months, although the identities of the recipients had never been firmly controlled. Of course, he could have had no idea of the trauma and chaos that the eruptions had produced on the island. He brought a new language to the crisis. Economies, he believed, had to be made immediately if the financial situation was to be brought under control. As he reported to the Minister for the Colonies, he "decreased the food allowance to a level more in keeping with that in our African possessions and in Madagascar". On 29 August, he therefore reduced the grant to 70 centimes per day for men, to 50 centimes per day for women, to 30 centimes for children between six and sixteen, and to 20 centimes for those under six. But the maximum allowance for each family was to be limited to 1.60 francs. He was proud to emphasize that this reduction had stopped the abuse of these grants "among the refugees who had been too well fed". But, he now sensibly gave the grant in cash, which enabled the refugees to buy locally produced goods and thereby stimulate the agriculture of the island, rather than relying on imported goods from relief ships. Encouraged by his success, one month later, on 27 September, the governor reduced the grants further: to 50 centimes a day per adult and 20 centimes per child. With such sums there was not much danger that the refugees would be "too well fed".

The governor was also distressed that richer refugees had not been given special treatment. They could not be expected to stay as impoverished as the poor for very long. He thus "gave different treatment to those of a different social class, and reserved goods of higher quality for them".

Notwithstanding the governor's financial stringency, he also initiated plans for the economic and agricultural revival of the island. He took steps to persuade the plantation and factory owners in the untouched areas of the south and east of the island to accept new workers and, in many cases, to give them a small plot of land where they could start to produce their own food and build their lives again. At the same time, Monsieur Lemaire started planning entirely new settlements to house the refugees in more salubrious surroundings, where homes, schools, roads, bridges, a church and other necessary amenities could be built, which would offer the added advantage of providing jobs for a variety of workers. The government purchased or rented land to build refugee cabins, and provided seeds, stock, tools, boats and other necessities that would form the basis of the new society.

Such projects presented major difficulties in an age when town and regional planning was in its infancy. Attitude problems, born of the troubles that culminated in the strike in 1900, delayed progress considerably. The refugees also believed that the administration wanted to confiscate the land that they had been forced to abandon, so that they could make them slaves again. Thus, they continually frustrated the soldiers in charge of construction "by wasting as much time as possible and slowing down the work on any trivial pretext". The soldiers were not used to the ways and attitudes of the refugees, and the refugees themselves found the military discipline in the new villages irksome, when they understood it at all. Thus, by 1905, out of some 22 000 refugees in total, about 10 000 were living in the new settlements, but 11 300 had gone back to what remained of their homes in the northern zone.

The dome and the Needle of Pelée

Little by little, the centre of attraction on the volcano changed from the nuées ardentes to the dome of fuming hot lava that was pushing out of the volcanic chimney rather like molten glass. The first dome had probably oozed up the volcanic chimney just before Ascension Day, and had been smashed to smithereens by the great eruption at 8.02 a.m. on 8 May. The eruption on 20 May probably shattered a second dome, and that on 30

Mount Pelée, seen from the remains of the Place Bertin in Saint-Pierre, with the Needle of Pelée rising on the skyline from the crest of the dome.

August a third. But by then, most of the explosive gases had escaped from the molten rock rising up the volcanic chimney. The eruptions thus became less powerful and yet another dome could then rise up the volcanic chimney and remain intact, without being destroyed by huge explosions. It grew up at a rate of about 2 m per day within the old crater of the Etang Sec, and formed a great stopper like a champagne cork, or the dome of Saint Peter's in Rome, over the volcanic chimney. Its surface more or less solidified, but it cracked open from time to time as more lava pushed up from the depths. Then a most extraordinary thing happened. At the beginning of October, an incandescent spine of hot viscous lava started to surge from the top of the eastern side of the dome, like toothpaste squeezed from its tube. On some days the spine rose by as much as 20 m, but at other times it stopped altogether, so that its crest cooled and crumbled. By 31 May 1903, it reached its maximum height of 1617 m, some 272 m above the summit of the dome, and more than 600 m above the old floor of the Etang Sec. They called this enormous spine "the Needle of Pelée". From the ruins of Saint-Pierre, it looked like a huge spell-binding finger. It was an obvious symbol, but observers were not sure whether Mount Pelée was accusing the ruins of Saint-Pierre, or the heavens, or even the administration of the colony.

Nuées ardentes continued to issue from the volcano. No less than 58 were counted between 3 November 1902 and 10 August 1903, although they became weaker and weaker as time went on. Gradually, however, explosions

The Needle of Pelée rising sheer above the surface of the dome at the crest of Mount Pelée in 1903. No trace of this needle now remains on the dome.

and weathering got the upper hand, the spine disintegrated, and by 1904 the dome stopped growing. One small nuée ardente swept half way down the Rivière Blanche on 4 July 1905 and brought the eruptions of magma to an end. Thereafter, Mount Pelée took a rest, and gave off no more than steam and fumes until 1929.

Tourists

From January 1903, the ruins of Saint-Pierre suffered the supreme indignity of becoming an attraction for boatloads of tourists. The governor insisted that they should ask for official permission to visit the site; in return, he granted them the protection of the gendarmes. He also arranged that any bones exposed by erosion, or by the looters, would be reburied so that the sightseers would not be too upset. Not surprisingly, the Americans, Britons and Germans were in the forefront of the spectators. On 25 January 1903, the RMS *Esk*, for instance, landed 300 tourists at Saint-Pierre. They had enjoyed a thrilling day out and were returning to the vessel at 5.00 p.m. when Mount Pelée suddenly disgorged a nuée ardente, which seemed to be coming straight for the ruins, before it turned, as usual, down the valley of the Rivière Blanche and swept into the sea. The eruption scared the wits out of the tourists, and about 50 passengers jumped into the sea and started swimming frantically towards Le Carbet in the vain hope that they could outpace the nuée. They returned, wet, chastened and exhausted, to the *Esk* some time later. In his report to the Minister for the Colonies, the governor uncharitably suspected that this was just the sort of thrill that they had paid for, and he wondered whether he should not ban "this new little game" before an accident happened. However, he did point out that the ships' captains always took all the necessary precautions. They never anchored their vessels, and kept up the steam pressure throughout the visit so that they could make a quick exit from the bay, if the need arose. If Mount Pelée had unleashed a fourth great nuée ardente, of course, they would have been annihilated as quickly as the city that they were inspecting.

19

Conclusion

During the weeks that followed Mount Pelée's second nuée ardente on 20 May, the administrators and the people of Martinique had to reassess their situation and alleviate their dreadful plight. Not since Vesuvius had buried Pompeii and Herculaneum in AD 79 had a volcano so completely destroyed a city. But the loss of Saint-Pierre was much more disastrous to Martinique than the loss of the Pompeii and Herculaneum had been to Campania, where Naples had been the most important centre. Saint-Pierre had been the hub of practically every aspect of society, trade and industry in the island. Fort-de-France had merely been the administrative capital and the naval base. When the nuée ardente removed Saint-Pierre almost completely from the face of the Earth, Fort-de-France had to assume the functions of the devastated city, and it became the sole centre of importance in the colony, and most of the economic power concentrated within it. When the nuée ardente destroyed Saint-Pierre, Fort-de-France was the second largest city in Martinique with some 22 000 people. A century later, Fort-de-France has over 100 000 inhabitants, three times the size of any other settlement on the island, and 20 times larger than the present population of Saint-Pierre.

In the wake of such an unexpected catastrophe, many asked why Saint-Pierre had not been evacuated, or why the citizens had not taken it upon themselves to leave the city as soon as the threat became clear. The questions themselves reveal a complete misunderstanding of the whole nature of the difficulties that Mount Pelée presented to Saint-Pierre. Evacuation posed three interrelated problems: volcanic, administrative and psychological.

The eruption itself came to a rapid climax, although the threat never, in fact, became as crystal clear as might have been imagined afterwards. The first modest falls of ash rained down on Saint-Pierre on 3 May and the nuée

223

Modern Saint-Pierre is no longer the "pearl of the West Indies".

ardente annihilated the city on 8 May. At that time, the geological history of the volcano and its many violent explosions was unknown, and few volcanic eruptions anywhere in the world had been studied in enough detail to enable useful predictions to be made about what might happen in Martinique. Even after the eruption began in April, the significance of the volcanic warnings was not understood. All the *available* evidence suggested that Saint-Pierre was safe. As Professor Lacroix pointed out, "none of the events that might logically have been forecast in fact occurred". Instead, Mount Pelée produced a nuée ardente, the most devastating and murderous instrument in the volcanic repertoire, which had never been studied before. Moreover, if Mount Pelée had blasted the nuée ardente in any other direction, then Saint-Pierre would have been spared. Thus, in terms of what Mount Pelée might have been expected to produce in 1902, the nuée ardente caused the same effect as a nuclear bomb would have produced at the Battle of Waterloo.

The colonial administration could not possibly have taken such an extraordinary eventuality into account. Indeed, *before the event*, they would have been considered idiotic to do so. Forecasting volcanic eruptions is easy when they have happened. Only hindsight poses the question of an evacuation of Saint-Pierre. Although the volcano had made much noise, relatively little ash had fallen on Saint-Pierre, and the administration had no logical reason to consider removing any citizens until 7 May at the earliest. And on that very date, the scientific commission had declared that Saint-Pierre was in little danger. Moreover, the authorities had no guidelines for the task. At the time, there was no precedent known in the Western world for an evacuation of a city threatened by an eruption. (In 1730–1736, a few thousand people had been taken from the Canary Island of Lanzarote after the authorities had dithered and considered the matter for six months, but, in 1902, that event had not yet even come to light). The administrators in Martinique would also have been obliged to direct the people to clearly designated places of refuge where they could live for some months with all the necessary facilities. No such places existed on the island. It is in the nature and duties of the authorities to keep public order. What administrator could ever tell people just to run away? Eruptions later in the twentieth century also demonstrated that it is a nearly impossible task to choose the exact date of an evacuation, especially after false alarms have occurred. Since the administrators in Martinique had no idea what was in store for them, they had absolutely no means of guessing when they would have to remove the citizens. Thus, criticism would have been inevitable and, no doubt, vociferous. If a departure is delayed too long, people run the grave risk of becoming casualties. On the other hand, refugees become most ungrateful if they are kept in uncomfortable camps for weeks before an eruption reaches its climax – and they blame the authorities, not the volcano.

The rapid removal of some 27 000 people from Saint-Pierre would have presented major problems, even if the operation could have been planned well in advance. It was impossible within a few days. The scenes on 8 May, when fewer than a thousand people were taken from the beach at Le Carbet, showed only too eloquently the chaos that would have developed if many more had been involved. The evacuation from the city could have taken place by road or by boat. The single road to Fort-de-France and the south was poor. The refugees would thus have been forced to walk. The most popular form of transport had long been by sea. Lieutenant Allemand's report to the Navy Ministry revealed that many naval vessels were in such a parlous state that they would have been practically useless. The steamers of the Girard company could have been used only in an auxiliary capacity, because they were far too small, and each one could probably have crowded no more than 200 people on board. It would, no doubt, have been possible to make use of naval and commercial vessels, but they too were relatively small and ill adapted for large numbers of passengers. Of course, transatlantic liners could have been requisitioned, but it would have taxed the ingenuity of even the most resourceful administrators in the West Indies to find and requisition the dozen or so liners needed to accomplish the task in the few days available. The evacuation would also have been painfully slow. Small craft would have had to transfer the refugees to the larger vessels moored off store. And, whether the refugees had gone by road or by sea, they would have been forced to leave most of their possessions behind in Saint-Pierre, thereby offering a glittering bait to every marauding looter in the region.

Governor Mouttet and his administration were perfectly correct to behave as they did. They acted logically in response to what they knew. The governor offered the first refugees from Le Prêcheur food and temporary lodging in Saint-Pierre, which was exactly where they wanted to go. The administration remained calm, even when the population began to succumb to unreasonable panic, which is what administrators are supposed to do. They acted in good faith, and Governor Mouttet and some of his colleagues gave their lives to prove it. They could not possibly have known that Mount Pelée would trick them so tragically. That a craven politician should then have succeeded in making capital out of the catastrophe reveals much about him and the ignoble local environment in which he operated . . .

The psychological problems facing the citizens of Saint-Pierre are the hardest to assess. Fears and reactions obviously varied according to the intelligence, common sense, temperament and knowledge of every individual and those who formed opinion around them. The extraordinary and inexplicable behaviour of nature had bewildered and terrified almost everyone in the city. They did not understand the workings of the environment very well and they were thus quite incapable of forming a clear and logical view of events. But, then, perhaps even Descartes himself might have had difficulties in this situation. In quick succession, they had suffered earthquakes, a continual eruption, a mudflow and a tidal wave. Rivers had dried up and flooded when it had not rained. A neighbouring volcano had erupted too, and it was said that there had even been an odd sort of eclipse on the morning of Ascension Day. Whenever the eruption seemed to have shot its bolt, another weird disaster supervened and increased the tension. The fears of the citizens were related to the disasters that they knew had already happened in the area. They knew less about eruptions, and so, paradoxically, many of those who had still kept their wits about them believed that the eruptions of Mount Pelée were merely portents of worse to come – a large sea wave, a powerful earthquake, a disastrous mudflow, a hurricane, or something else?

Unfortunately, they had no means of telling what kind of disaster was likely to afflict them. They could not identify their enemy. That was their tragedy.

Although many people were afraid, only a small proportion of the citizens actually left Saint-Pierre. The city remained the protecting fold, safe on solid rock: shelter, the haven. Faced with the choice between staying at home and the prospect of an existence in distant tents, even those living in abject poverty would probably have chosen Saint-Pierre, not least because they had never been anywhere else. Fort-de-France was the only settlement with remotely enough facilities to receive refugees, but everyone in Saint-Pierre knew that the capital was unhealthy and dangerously prone to natural calamities. It had two advantages only: it was farther from the volcano, and it had an energetic and efficient mayor in Victor Sévère.

The wealthier, mainly white, section of the community had a wider choice, but rarely took advantage of it. Wives and children were sent, or, better still, taken to safe accommodation with relatives or friends in southern Martinique or to neighbouring islands. The men had to keep a stiff upper lip, do their duty, and return to look after the business, the safe and the house. This self-imposed need to keep up appearances thus trapped most of them in the city until the nuée ardente struck.

The vital lesson that the catastrophe teaches then is that violent volcanoes are never wholly predictable. When danger threatens, it is better to play safe and run away as a coward, rather than die as a hero. The second lesson from the events of the eruption of Mount Pelée is that the volcano may be following its own logic, which is not apparent to the humans on its flanks. Thus, at Saint-Pierre, the rational people, with common sense and intelligence, saw less danger from the volcano, and died, whereas those who followed their gut reactions and panicked survived because Mount Pelée produced a weapon that defied all expectations and all the logic that they knew.

After the catastrophe, the first general election in North Martinique was held in May 1906, when Victor Sévère, the mayor of Fort-de-France, was returned. Saint-Pierre was still empty, but, eventually some of the braver people began to return to the ruins and collected the rubble to build themselves small homes on the shattered foundations. It was a slow process: only 500 people had settled there by 1910. In 1923, Saint-Pierre had a population of about 3000 and became a municipality again. Louis Ernoult, who had been deputy mayor at the moment of the catastrophe, was elected mayor. Mount Pelée erupted again between 1929 and 1932. The inhabitants fled at once, although the nuées ardentes were less furious than those of 1902, and

The new Rue Victor-Hugo rises from the old, with an old bollard in the foreground and a fragment of the walls of old Saint-Pierre forming the base of a new wall across the road.

Saint-Pierre was not damaged. Nowadays Saint-Pierre is a hot and sleepy village of about 5000 people. Along the almost silent streets, an old bollard, or a stretch of rough wall, recall every now and again the greatest volcanic catastrophe of the age.

Granted all the errors, misinterpretations, anguish, panic, fear, accusations, justifications, lies, legends and myths, the catastrophe created a great human tragedy. The loss of Saint-Pierre was a body blow to all the survivors. Many working people from the north had to seek jobs in the south during an economic crisis when rum distilling and the area planted with sugar cane had both been cut by one third. They were displaced and they then settled in new villages where soldiers enforced an almost military style of discipline, which they neither understood nor appreciated. They did not recover for decades.

The destruction of Saint-Pierre was the terrible climax of a series of social political and economic disasters that had beset the white elite for more than half a century. It was by far the worst, because it removed the physical and human presence of the city. Things would never be the same again. The balance of power passed irrevocably to Fort-de-France. Old Saint-Pierre had gone forever. The Almighty had blasted a terrible and unprecedented punishment upon the city, and the survivors sought in vain for an explanation. The whites were mortified to see that Mount Pelée had awarded them no special privileges befitting their station. The volcano had annihilated everyone with masterly impartiality. The deserving had died with the un-deserving, and no-one could tell their corpses apart. The catastrophe became a kind of divine mystery that had martyred a whole society, which could never be recreated; and the city could never be rebuilt. The memory of Saint-Pierre had to be born again, romanticized, in the imagination of the survivors. The past became a legend, and the legend became a myth. The dead citizens of Saint-Pierre thus became larger than life, full of *joie de vivre*, noble, virtuous and industrious. And the city itself became a shining bastion of French traditional values, a glory of French colonization, the pearl of the West Indies.

Nothing could ever equal that awesome moment when the people in Saint-Pierre heard that deafening explosion, and saw the gigantic violet cloud swirling down upon them like a raging monster rampaging out of hell, tearing the city apart, and flinging its pitiful relics to the ground. Doom crashed along the streets. They turned in horror to each other and saw indescribable terror stamped onto every face. Death was certain. They clung together in the supreme moment, not to perish alone. The scorching blast seared their faces and burned down their throats and into their lungs. They had to breathe to live, and when they breathed they died. And the rubble of old Saint-Pierre battered and buried the last frantic spasms of their bodies.

Bibliography

Adélaïde-Merlande, J. & J. P. Hervieu 1996. *Les volcans dans l'histoire des Antilles*. Paris: Karthala.

Allemand, J. E. 1902. *Eruption volcan de la montagne Pelée. Rapport du Lieutenant de Vaisseau J. E. Allemand à Monsieur le Ministre de la Marine, le 11 mai 1902*. Archives, Service Historique de la Marine, Château de Vincennes, France.

Allemand, J. E. 1902. *Rapport au sujet du déchargement des vivres apportés à Fort-de-France par les navires étrangers du Lieutenant de Vaisseau J. E. Allemand à Monsieur le Ministre de la Marine, le 24 mai 1902*. Archives, Service historique de la marine, Château de Vincennes, France.

Anderson, T. & J. S. Flett 1903. Report on the eruption of the Soufrière in St Vincent, in 1902, and on a visit to montagne Pelée in Martinique. *Royal Society of London, Philosophical Transactions A* (part I) **200**, 353–553.

Antilles (Les) 1902. Newspaper edited by Léon Sully and published daily, except on Sundays and holidays, in Saint-Pierre. (Numbers published in April and 1–7 May 1902.) [The editions published on 26 April 1902 and on 30 April 1902 are reproduced in L. Domergue et al. 1972].

Ariès, P., C. Daney, E. Berté 1981. *Catastrophe à la Martinique*. Paris: Herscher.

Arnoux, R. 1902. Le cataclysme de la Martinique. *Société Astronomique de France, Bulletin* (août 1902) 361–5. (See also Heilprin (1903: 321–6).)

Baxter, P. J. 1990. Medical effects of volcanic eruptions. *Bulletin of Volcanology* **52**, 532–44.

Berté, E. 1902. Les éruptions de la montagne Pelée. Récit et observations d'un témoin. *La Géographie* (September 1902), 133–41.

Boudon, G. 1993. La montagne Pelée, Martinique: évolution volcanologique. *Société Géologique de France, Mémoires* **163**, 231–8.

Boudon, G. & A. Gourgaud (eds) 1989. Mount Pelée. *Journal of Volcanology and Geothermal Research* **38**, special issue.

Boudon, G., J. L. Bourdier, A. Gourgaud, J. Lajoie 1990. The May 1902 eruptions of Mount Pelée: high velocity directed blasts or column collapse nuées ardentes? Reply to Fisher and Heiken. *Journal of Volcanology and Geothermal Research* **43**, 359–64.

Bourdier, J. L., G. Boudon, A. Gourgaud 1989. Stratigraphy of the 1902 and 1929 nuée ardente deposits, Mt Pelée, Martinique. *Journal of Volcanology and Geothermal Research* **38**, 77–96.

Cambon, J. 1902. *Destruction de Saint-Pierre. Trois dépêches relatives à la situation à la Martinique, de Monsieur Jules Cambon, Ambassadeur de le République Française à Washington à Monsieur Delcassé, Ministre des Affaires Etrangères à Paris. 13 mai 1902*. Archives, Service Historique de la

Marine, Château de Vincennes, France.

Charpentier, H. 1981. *Saint-Pierre, 8 mai 1902*. Le Carbet (Martinique): Editions du Centre d'Art, Musée Paul Gaugin.

Chrétien, S. & R. Brousse 1988. *La montagne Pelée se réveille*. Paris: Société Nouvelle des Editions Boubée.

Colonies (Les) 1902. Newspaper edited by Marius Hurard and published daily, except on Sundays and holidays, in Saint-Pierre. (Numbers published in April and 1–7 May 1902). [The editions published on 6 May 1902 and 7 May 1902 are reproduced in L. Domergue et al, 1972]

Contour, S. 1989. *Saint-Pierre (Martinique) tome II: la catastrophe et ses suites*. Paris: Editions Caribéennes.

Coeur Créole (Canon L. Lambolez) 1905. *Saint-Pierre Martinique, 1635–1902, Annales des Antilles Françaises – Journal et Album de la Martinique. Livre d'or de la Charité*. Paris: Berger-Levrault.

Corzani, J. 1999. La fortune littéraire de la "catastrophe de Saint-Pierre". See Yacou (1999: 75–97).

La Croix 1902. Newspaper published daily in Paris (notably issues published in May and June 1902).

Dauphite, M. 1983. *Saint-Pierre avant et après*. Le Carbet (Martinique): Editions du Centre d'Art, Musée Paul Gaugin.

De Raynal, A. & L. Hayot 1992 *Saint-Pierre. Trois siècles d'histoire*. Fort-de-France.

Domergue, L., R. Cucchi, L. Hayot 1972. *Plaquette commémorative de l'éruption de la montagne Pelée*. Fort-de-France: Société de distribution et de culture, Imprimerie Berger-Bellepage.

Drosne, Monsieur 1902. *Note au sujet de quelques observations recueillis sur l'aspect de la montagne Pelée, 31 mai 1902*. Archives, Service Historique de la Marine, Château de Vincennes, France.

Duchâteau-Roger, E. 1903. *Une histoire vécue des cataclysmes de la Martinique*. Paris: Desclée de Brouwer.

Dujon, E. 1905. *Récit d'une survivante de la catastrophe de la montagne Pelée*. (Published originally without name of author, publisher or town of publication in Trinidad in 1902; reproduced in entirety in Coeur Créole (1905: 366–77).)

Dumas, J. 1902. *Lettre à sa femme et ses enfants, le 8 mai 1902*. In *La Croix* [newspaper], 17 June 1902. (Reproduced in entirety in Coeur Créole (1905: 366–77).)

Dupuget, Citoyen 1796 (Ventôse An IV). Coup d'oeil rapide sur la physique générale et la minéralogie des Antilles. Annotations sur la Soufrière de la Martinique. *Journal des Mines* ,43–60.

Du Tertre, Père 1654. *Histoire générale des isles de Saint-Christophe, de la Guadeloupe, de la Martinique et autres dans l'Amérique* [4 vols]. Paris.

Fine, J. C. 1982. When a volcano destroyed a fleet. *Surveyor* . February 1982, 28–31. (Published by the American Bureau of Shipping).

Fisher, R. V. & G. Heiken 1982. Mount Pelée: May 8 and 20, 1902, pyroclastic flows and surges. *Journal of Volcanology and Geothermal Research* **13**, 339–71.

Fisher, R. V. & G. Heiken 1990. Discussion of four papers in the Mt Pelée special issue. *Journal of Volcanology and Geothermal Research* **43b**, 353–64

Flammarion, C. 1902. *Les éruptions volcaniques et les tremblements de terre*. Paris: Flammarion.

Freeman, E. W. 1902. The awful doom of St Pierre. *Pearson's Magazine* **14**, 313–25.

Gøbel, E. 1993. Med krydseren *Valkyrien* til Martinique under vulkanudbruddet i 1902 ("With the *Valkyrien* to Martinique during the volcanic eruption of 1902", in Danish). *Siden Saxo* **10**(2), 2–8.

Heilprin, A. 1903. *Mount Pelée and the tragedy of Martinique*. Philadelphia: Lippincott.

Heilprin, A. 1904. *The Tower of Pelée: new studies of the great volcano of Martinique*. Philadelphia: Lippincott.

Heilprin, A. 1908. *The eruption of Pelée: a summary and discussion of the phenomena and their sequels*. Philadelphia: Lippincott (on behalf of the Geographical Society, Philadelphia).

Hearn, L. 1890. *Two years in the French West Indies*. New York: Harper.

Hess, J. 1902. *La catastrophe à la Martinique: notes d'un reporteur*. Paris: Charpentier & Fasquelle.

Hill, R. T. 1902. A study of Pelée: impressions and conclusions of a trip to Martinique. *Century Magazine* **64**, 764–85.

Hovey, E. O. 1904. The 1902–1903 eruptions of Mount Pelée, Martinique and the Soufrière, St Vincent. IX *Congrès International de Géologie (Vienna) 1903–4, comptes rendus* **1**, 707–738.

Jérémine, E. & A. Michel-Lévy. 1950. Alfred Lacroix. *Bulletin Volcanologique* **10**, 173–89.

Jourdain, E. undated. *Le sablier renversé* [unpublished memoirs]. (The chapter entitled: *L'éruption de la montagne Pelée en Martinique (en 1902)* has been extracted and published on internet at http://www.dormoy.com/Famille/Histoire/2016.htm.

Jussier, Madame. 1978. L'eruption de la montagne Pelée de 1902 vécue par un Icaunais originaire d'Irancy. *Société des Sciences Historiques et Naturelles de l'Yonne, Bulletin* **110**, 143–56.

Kennan, G. 1902. *The tragedy of Pelée*. New York: Outlook.

Labat, Père 1722. *Nouveau voyage aux isles de l'Amérique, contenant l'histoire naturelle de ces pays* [6 vols]. Paris.

Lacroix, A. 1904. *La montagne Pelée et ses éruptions*. Paris: Masson.

Lacroix, A. 1904. *L'éruption de la Martinique*. Paris: Gauthier-Villars.

Lacroix, A. 1908. *La montagne Pelée après ses éruptions*. Paris: Masson.

Lambolez, C. 1905. See Coeur Créole.

Landes, G. 1900. *Notice sur la Martinique, publiée à l'occasion de l'exposition de 1900*. Paris: Livret Guide de l'Exposition de 1900.

Lapparent, A. de 1905. La montagne Pelée et ses éruptions. *Annales de Géographie* **14**, 97–110.

Leblond, J-B. 2000. *Voyage aux Antilles (1767–1773)*. Paris: Karthala.

Le Bris, P. 1902. *Rapport du 12 mai 1902 du capitaine de frégate Le Bris à Monsieur le Ministre de la Marine. Mouvements du Suchet, éruption du Mont Pelée*. Archives, Service Historique de la Marine, Château de Vincennes, France.

Le Bris, P. 1902. *Rapport du 22 mai 1902 du capitaine de frégate Le Bris à Monsieur le Ministre de la Marine. L'éruption du volcan de la montagne Pelée*. Archives, Service historique de la marine, Château de Vincennes, France.

Le Bris, P. 1902. *Rapport du 31 mai 1902 du capitaine de frégate Le Bris à Monsieur le Ministre de la Marine. Rapport sur les évènements qui se sont produits à la Martinique à la suite de l'éruption volcanique de la montagne Pelée*. Archives, Service historique de la marine, Château de Vincennes, France.

Le Prieur, Monsieur 1854. Rapport sur les bouches de la montagne Pelée à la Martinique. *Revue Coloniale* (2nd series) **12**, 66–77.

Le Prieur, Monsieur, E. Rufz and P. Peyraud 1852. Eruption du volcan de la montagne Pelée.

Bulletin Officiel de la Martinique **40**, 3–32 (and Fort-de-France: Ruelle et Arnaud).
Lloyd's 1902–1903. *Register of shipping*. London: Lloyd's Register of Shipping.
Lloyd's 1902–1903. *Wreck returns, second quarter 1902*. London: Lloyd's Register of Shipping.
Lloyd's 1894. *War ships of the world* . London: Lloyd's Register of Shipping.

Nicolas, A. 1996. *Histoire de la Martinique*, vol. 2: *De 1848 à 1939*. Paris: L'Harmattan.

L'Opinion. Newspaper published in Fort-de-France on Tuesdays, Thursdays and Saturdays. Notably the issue of 22 May 1902.

Parel, Abbé G. 1902. *Rapport à Monsignor de Cormont, evèque de la Martinique*. (See Coeur Créole (1902: 395–405) and *La Croix* (1902: 11 and 13 June).
Parel, Abbé G. 1902. The last days of Saint-Pierre. *Century Magazine* **64**, 610–17. [English translation of the above report to Monsignor de Cormont].
Perret, F. A. 1935. *The eruption of Mt Pelée 1929–1932*. Publication 458, Carnegie Institution, Washington DC.
Petitjean Roget, J. 1972. A propos de livre: *Le volcan arrive. Bulletin de la Société d'Histoire de la Martinique, Annales des Antilles* **17**, 3–87.
Philémon, C. 1930. *La montagne Pelée et l'effroyable destruction de Saint-Pierre, Martinique*. Paris: Courville.
Politiken. Newspaper published daily except on Sundays in Copenhagen. Notably the issues of 13–18 May 1902.

Revert, E. 1931. La montagne Pelée et ses dernières éruptions. *Annales de Géographie* **40**, 275–91.
Roobol, M. J. & A. L. Smith 1976. Mount Pelée, Martinique: a pattern of alternating eruptive cycles. *Geology* **4**, 521–4.
Russel, I. C. 1902. Volcanic eruptions on Martinique and St Vincent. *National Geographic Magazine* **13**(July), 267–285.

Scarth, A. 1999. *Vulcan's fury: man against the volcano*. London: Yale University Press.
Scott, E. S. 1902. The eruption of Mount Pelée. *Cosmopolitan Magazine* (July), 243–52.
Servan, Contre-Amiral 1902. *Rapport sur les mouvements du Suchet et l'éruption du Mont Pelée du Contre-Amiral Servan à Monsieur le Ministre de la Marine 26 mai 1902*. Archives, Service Historique de la Marine, Château de Vincennes, France.
Servan, Contre-Amiral 1902. *Rapport sur les causes et la nature de l'éruption du 8 mai du Contre-Amiral Servan à Monsieur le Ministre de la Marine 1 juin 1902*. Archives, Service Historique de la Marine, Château de Vincennes, France.
Smith, A. L. & M. J. Roobol 1990. *Mt Pelée, Martinique: a study of an active island-arc volcano*. Memoir 175, Geological Society of America, Washington DC.
Sparks, R. S. J. 1983. Mont Pelée, Martinique: May 8 and 20 1902, pyroclastic flows and surges (discussion). *Journal of Volcanology and Geothermal Research* **19**, 175–84.

Tanguy, J-C. 1994. The 1902–1905 eruptions of Montagne Pelée, Martinique: anatomy and retrospection, *Journal of Volcanology and Geothermal Research* **60**, 87–107.
Tanguy, J-C., C. Ribière, A. Scarth, W. S. Tjetjep 1998. Victims from volcanic eruptions: a revised database. *Bulletin of Volcanology* **60**, 137–44.

Tauriac, M. 1996. *Martinique: les années créoles.* Paris: Omnibus.

Thibault de Chanvallon 1763. *Voyage à la Martinique, contenant diverses observations sur la physique, l'histoire naturelle, l'agriculture, les moeurs et les usages de cette isle, faites en 1751 et dans les années suivantes.* Paris.

Thierry, Monsieur. 1902. Sur l'éruption volcanique du 8 mai à la Martinique. *Académie des Sciences à Paris, comptes rendus* **135**, 71–2. (See also text with alterations and additions in Lacroix 1904: 235–7).)

Traineau, H., D. Westercamp, J. M. Bardintzeff, J. C. Miskovsky 1989. The recent pumice eruptions of Mt Pelée volcano, Martinique, part I: depositional sequences, descriptions of pumiceous deposits. *Journal of Volcanology and Geothermal Research* **38**, 17–33.

Ursulet, L. 1997. *Le désastre de 1902 à la Martinique.* Paris: L'Harmattan.

Vincent, P. M., J. L. Bourdier, G. Boudon 1989. The primitive volcano of Mount Pelée: its construction and partial destruction by flank collapse. *Journal of Volcanology and Geothermal Research* **38**, 1–15.

Westercamp, D. & H. Tazieff 1980. *Martinique, Guadeloupe, Saint-Martin, La Désirade* [Guides Géologiques Régionaux]. Paris: Masson.

Westercamp, D. & H. Traineau 1983. The past 5,000 years of volcanic activity at Mt Pelée, Martinique (FWI): implications for assessment of volcanic hazards. *Journal of Volcanology and Geothermal Research* **17**, 159–85.

Westercamp, D. 1987. L'éruption de la montagne Pelée. *La Recherche* **190**, 914–923.

Yacou, A. (ed.) 1999. *Les catastrophes naturelles aux Antilles.* Paris: Karthala.

Index

Gérard, Brother   74, 95, 132
Germonté, Paulémie   130
Gerbault, Lieutenant-Colonel   92, 98, 109
Girard company   8, 54, 71, 73, 77, 93, 98, 101, 138, 148, 157, 162, 174, 208, 225
Giraud, Dr Jean   207
Gøbel, Erik   179
God   11, 55, 60, 62, 85, 105, 106, 125, 132, 153, 184
gossip   94, 112
    See also rumours
Gouyé, Louis   86
government coalition   42, 43
governors
    acting   See Lhuerre, Georges; Merlin
    of Guyana (brother of Paul Merwart)   44
    Hedemann   179
    Lemaire   213–15, 218, 219
    Merlin   163–4
    Mouttet   7, 41, 54, 56, 76, 77, 79, 84, 92, 97, 98, 100, 109, 120, 164, 169, 176, 190, 191, 192, 194, 214, 226
        career of   56
    secretary general   See Lhuerre, Georges
Grand' Case   30, 32, 36, 48, 55
Grandmaison, Monsieur de   58, 61
Grelet, Monsieur, Mayor of Le Prêcheur
    See mayors
Guadeloupe   16, 32, 33, 56, 59, 64, 71, 76, 111, 149, 154, 163, 165, 174, 194, 201
Guérin
    Auguste   66, 68, 69, 104, 159
    Eugène   34, 66, 67, 69, 71
    Madame   61
Guyana, French   See French Guyana

Havana   76, 88, 100, 150, 152, 164
Hébert, Georges, Lieutenant   94, 154, 155, 157, 159
Hedemann, Governor   See governors
Heilprin, Angelo   206
hen-runs, temporary   181
Herculaneum   49, 93, 115, 223
Hermary, Lieutenant   194
Hess, Jean   189, 190, 191
Hilaire, Georges   183
Holm, Kommandør H. P.   177, 179, 181
Holy Spirit, Fathers of   39, 73, 95
hospitals   9, 22, 92, 117, 130, 132, 144, 188, 200, 210, 217
    See also Saint-Pierre (military hospital)
household objects   20, 68, 182, 202, 203, 205, 207

Hugore, Georges   71
Humboldt, Alexander von   22
Hurard, Marius   42, 75, 93, 169, 192, 193
hurricanes   See atmospheric phenomena
Husson, Monsieur, private adviser to
    governor   98
hydrogen sulphide   20, 23, 24, 31, 32, 44
    See also smells

illiteracy   8, 41, 185
informed opinion   62, 92, 94, 99, 104
injuries   124, 145, 153, 155
Innocent, Jean-Baptiste   117, 140
innuendoes, invention   58, 192–3
interview, with G. Landes in Les Colonies   92, 93, 190
Isnard, Monsieur   66, 67, 68, 69, 83
Italian sailors on Roraïma   146–7, 155

Jaccaci, Mr   188
Jallabert, Monsieur, director of cable
    company   98
Jensen, C. C., Second Engineer   179, 180
jewellery   135, 158, 159, 182, 203
Josse, Duno-Emile   30, 35–6
Jourdain, Elodie (née Dujon)   12, 58, 74, 86, 87, 101, 104, 158, 159, 160
Journal Officiel de la Martinique   24

Kennan, George   188, 206

La Croix (French newspaper)   190, 193, 195
La montagne Pelée et ses éruptions   12, 115
La montagne Pelée se réveille   12
La Roche family   135
Labat, Monsieur   150, 151, 163
labourers, workmen   7, 30, 39, 67, 69, 87, 129, 147, 158
    foremen   68
    visited summit on 26 April   39
Lacroix
    Madame Catherine   115, 207
    Professeur Alfred   12, 29, 39, 62, 90, 97, 103, 115, 133, 181, 191, 192, 205–207, 212, 224
Lagrosillière, Joseph   42, 43, 84
Landes, Gaston   31, 32, 33, 35, 37, 44, 46, 61, 65, 69, 70, 84, 88, 92–3, 97, 100, 124–6, 169, 191, 192, 209
Lanzarote   75, 225
Lasserre
    Edouard   131–2, 210
    Hélène   131
Laugier shop   130, 210